AMERICAN FOREIGN SERVICE OFFICER

Eve P. Steinberg
Arva C. Floyd

MACMILLAN
U.S.A.

With special thanks to Phil,
whose research papers are liberally represented in these pages.

Second Edition

Macmillan General Reference
A Prentice Hall/Macmillan Company
15 Columbus Circle
New York, NY 10023

An Arco Book

MACMILLAN is a registered trademark of Macmillan, Inc.
ARCO is a registered trademark of Prentice-Hall, Inc.

Library of Congress Cataloging-in-Publication Data

Steinberg, Eve P.
  American foreign service officer / Eve P. Steinberg, Arva C. Floyd.—2nd ed.
  p. cm.
  At head of title: Arco.
  ISBN 0-13-037250-1
    1. United States—Diplomats and consular services—Examinations, questions, etc.
2. Civil service—United States—Examinations. I. Floyd, Arva C. II. Arco Publishing.
III. Title.
JX1706.Z6S74   1992   92-3265
341.3'5'076—dc20   CIP

Manufactured in the United States of America

10 9 8 7 6 5 4

CONTENTS

Part Four: Review of English Grammar and Usage

FOREIGN SERVICE CAREERS

What Are the Advantages of a Foreign Service Career? The Foreign Service offers challenging, important work, variety, the chance to grow, and the pride and satisfaction of representing America abroad.

If you are looking for this very special type of career satisfaction and you think you can shoulder some of the responsibilities that come with the rewards, you may be a candidate for the Foreign Service of the United States of America.

What is the Foreign Service? The Foreign Service of the United States is America's diplomatic, consular, commercial and overseas cultural and information service. It assists the President and the Secretary of State in planning, conducting, and implementing our foreign policy at home and abroad. Some 4,000 Foreign Service Officers (FSO's) of the Department of State serve as administrative, consular, economic, and political officers in more than 230 U.S. embassies and consulates in over 140 nations, in Washington, D.C., and with other government agencies. Some 850 Foreign Service Officers of the United States Information Agency (USIA) serve abroad as public affairs, information, and cultural affairs officers, at USIA's headquarters in Washington, and elsewhere in government. The Foreign Commercial Service has some 165 officers serving abroad and in Washington, D.C. Some 3,500 Foreign Service Specialists serve as secretaries, communications technicians, financial and personnel managers, physicians and nurses, and in other fields of expertise needed to meet Foreign Service responsibilities around the world.

Is the Foreign Service for You? A Foreign Service career is more than a job. It involves uncommon commitments and occasional hardships, as well as unique rewards and opportunities. A decision to enter this career must involve unusual motivation and a firm dedication to public service. Foreign Service personnel are committed to support U.S. policy publicly, whatever their private views. The Foreign Service is a mobile profession. Personnel must agree to serve at any U.S. diplomatic or consular post abroad, or in any domestic position, according to the needs of the Foreign Service. Personnel spend an average of 60 percent of their careers abroad, moving at 2- to 4-year intervals. This imposed mobility presents challenges to family life and raising children not found in more settled careers. Many overseas posts are in small or remote countries where harsh climates, health hazards, and other discomforts exist, and where American-style amenities frequently are unavailable. Overseas service may also involve security risks to personnel and their families.

However, careers in the Foreign Service offer special rewards too: the pride and satisfaction of representing the United States and protecting American interests abroad; the challenge of working in a demanding, competitive, action-oriented profession; opportunities for change and growth; contact with stimulating American and foreign colleagues in government, business, the press, and other professions; frequent travel; and the enriching cultural and social experience of living abroad.

Part One

WHAT FOREIGN SERVICE OFFICERS DO AND HOW THEY ARE SELECTED

FOREIGN SERVICE OFFICERS

PROFILE OF ENTRY LEVEL OFFICERS

Entry level Officer Career Candidates typically enter the Foreign Service in Class 6 or 5.* Recent candidates have ranged in age from the early twenties to the middle fifties, with a median age around 31. Of those officers recently appointed, some 54 percent had masters degrees, 11 percent had law degrees, and 6 percent had Ph.D.s. Many have some years of professional work experience as well. All have keen awareness of the significance of current events and trends, breadth of knowledge

of domestic and international affairs, and a wide range of interests. Some 45 percent of the recently appointed Officer Career Candidates possessed acceptable skills in at least one foreign language; 7 percent qualified in two or more foreign languages. The principal areas of study of these officers included international relations, political science, history, economics, foreign languages, English/American literature, and law.

WORKING FOR THE DEPARTMENT OF STATE

What do Foreign Service Officers do? For centuries, maintaining relationships between nations through the exchange of representatives has been the first task of diplomacy. Foreign Service work is on the frontline of the process by which nations establish and maintain official contact with one another in pursuing their respective goals, objectives, interests, and policies. It embraces the making, implementation, and support of foreign policy at all levels, in Washington and abroad. It involves the functions of representation; administering our overseas establishments; caring for the interests of Americans abroad; and reporting, communicating, and negotiating on political, economic, consular, and administrative affairs.

Today's Foreign Service Officer must continue to excel in carrying out these nation-to-nation responsibilities but also is called upon to do much more. The growth in the number and importance of international organizations brings new demands for competence in multilateral diplomacy. Hand-in-hand with this development is the growing importance of a range of increasingly technical issues which are global rather than primarily bilateral in nature and which require new skills and better insights into the foreign policy implications

of such areas as science and technology, narcotics, and refugee affairs.

And today a significant portion of a Foreign Service Officer's career will be served in Washington, D.C., participating in the complex process by which national policy is made and supported.

At home and abroad, Foreign Service Officers of the Department of State carry out responsibilities in these main career areas: administrative, consular, economic, and political.

Administrative Affairs

One administrative officer puts it this way: "If you are a doer or manager, this is the place to be. . . . We need innovators. In the administrative field, if you come up with an imaginative approach, you stand an excellent chance of selling it."

Overseas, administrative officers are responsible for the support operations of U.S. embassies and consulates, where a misunderstanding or a missed deadline can have serious consequences and where skillful, sympathetic management is vital to efficiency and morale. On Washington

*Expression of pay grades in the Foreign Service is precisely the reverse of that in the more familiar GS scale. While the GS scale begins at an entry level of GS-1, GS-2 or GS-3 and has a top of GS-18, the FS scale begins with FS-9 and rises to the top level of FS-1.

assignments they hold administrative jobs in the geographic or functional bureaus of the department and provide support and guidance for overseas operations.

Administrative officers abroad are usually given more responsibility earlier in their careers than those in other fields. Junior officers often run their own sections in smaller posts. A senior officer might be responsible for hundreds of employees, a large embassy complex, and the needs of many different U.S. government agencies.

Administrative officers perform six main categories of work:

—**Budget and Fiscal.** Financial and budget planning, determining priorities with limited resources and competing demands.

—**General Services.** Responsibility for maintenance of property, procurement of supplies, negotiating leases and contracts for housing and buildings, and making travel, transportation, and shipping arrangements.

—**Personnel.** Processing assignments, providing counseling, taking part in labor-management negotiations, and administering the foreign national personnel program.

—**Security.** Maintaining the physical security of embassies and consulates.

—**Communications.** Operating telecommunications and pouch/mail facilities.

—**Information Systems.** Operating and maintaining word processing and computer systems.

One of the attractions of administrative work is its variety. Administration might involve coordinating an overseas trip by the president, vice-president, or secretary of state; escorting and making arrangements for a congressional delegation; developing computer techniques for information and communications systems or financial and management services; preparing a budget submission to Congress; negotiating with foreign customs officials; or preparing an emergency evacuation plan.

Consular Affairs

Consular officers work closely with the public and make decisions affecting the lives of many people. They must combine the skills of the diplomat, social worker, manager, lawyer, and judge. They must be sensitive to people and foreign cultures, service oriented, tactful, and humane. They also must be wise and decisive in making dozens of tough decisions daily, some of which may have major foreign policy and legal implications. Many

consular matters are governed by U.S. laws and regulations which can be analyzed and interpreted, but consular officers frequently are called on to solve knotty problems without much guidance or precedent. They often work without direct supervision and must have the flexibility to work under pressure, occasionally handling heavy loads of casework.

Consular officers abroad, who have more constant contact with foreign citizens than other American officials, also work closely with foreign government officials, and they depend heavily on their foreign language skills. At the junior level, Foreign Service consular officers abroad often gain management experience by supervising foreign national employees. At more senior levels, especially in big consular sections, consular officers have broad management responsibilities. In policy terms, consular officers are concerned with the movements of people. In service terms, the daily work focuses on visas for foreigners and assistance to fellow Americans overseas.

Issuing visas in accordance with the U.S. Immigration and Nationality Act is a principal consular duty. Owing to the tremendous pressure for access to the United States that exists in many foreign countries, visa issuance often is also a major bilateral political issue. Granting or denying a visa, which is a preliminary finding of eligibility to enter the United States as a visitor or immigrant, is a very important decision—for the applicant, for the United States, and for U.S. foreign policy.

For American travelers and residents abroad, the U.S. consulate represents America away from home in time of need. Consular officers help Americans in serious accidents or emergencies, assist those in foreign jails to assure them equal treatment with nationals of the country, help locate lost relatives, and arrange for the sick or destitute to get home.

Consular officers also provide documentation services such as issuing birth certificates to U.S. citizens, registering absentee voters, performing notarials, and taking testimony for U.S. courts. They assist American shipping and sailors, and they help Americans abroad who receive federal benefits such as social security and veterans' payments. Consular officers also issue passports and handle questions relating to citizenship.

In Washington, D.C., consular officers serve throughout the department, including the Bureau of Consular Affairs, where they backstop consular officers abroad, help resolve complex cases of consular policy, and deal with Congress, interest groups, and the public on problems of common concern.

As one consular officer said: "Being a consul has met my criteria for joining the Foreign Service—challenging, responsible work in a fascinating environment with the opportunity to grow as a person and to serve others. I wouldn't trade it—at least not on most days."

Economic Affairs

Today, the economic dimensions of foreign policy are immense and often of controlling importance. The growing indivisibility of domestic and international economics and the complexity of America's stake in international trade, finance, business, and development, have brought new challenges to the Foreign Service.

In Washington, D.C., economic officers are concerned with issues involving trade, investment and monetary matters, and energy. They also deal with economic development, aviation, transportation, food, and maritime matters. In all these areas they work in conjunction with other U.S. government agencies concerned with national and international economic policies and with foreign embassies.

Abroad, economic officers analyze and report on key economic trends and events which affect U.S. interests. They gather and interpret data, present U.S. economic positions to foreign officials, and negotiate agreements, both bilaterally and multilaterally. They keep in close touch with foreign business representatives, bankers, economists, and politicians. They also maintain close ties with American investors and exporters to represent their interests on economic policy issues. In addition to knowing economics, they must be politically and culturally perceptive, skillful in drafting, and flexible.

Economic work is enormously varied. For example, officers might monitor oil and gas production and prices, seek foreign government support for a U.S. economic initiative at the United Nations, or report on a foreign nation's balance of payments. They might analyze the local or international steel or textile industry or steer a key U.S. policy through the Washington bureaucracy. An officer might also serve as a science attaché at an embassy, advising the ambassador on key issues which have a high scientific or technological component, such as nuclear nonproliferation, population growth, or environmental cooperation.

Commenting on her work, one economic officer said: "It combines theoretical economics, political analysis, and getting things done. You are involved in both theory and action, and that is what I like." Another officer put it this way: "I know of no other work where a young economist can be exposed to such a wide range of problems, have access to so much information, and deal with so many different situations."

Political Affairs

Political officers analyze and report on political matters that affect U.S. interests. They convey U.S. government views on political issues to foreign officials, negotiate agreements, and maintain close contact with political and labor leaders, third-country diplomats, and others of influence.

In Washington, D.C., political officers often work in offices specializing in the affairs of particular countries or regions. They analyze reports from overseas staff, prepare guidance for U.S. embassies, and brief senior Department of State officials. They work closely with other U.S. government agencies and with foreign embassies in Washington.

Political work requires an ability to report and interpret events and trends in a variety of cultures and political systems. Officers must persevere in a field in which visible results are not always immediately apparent. They must also be able to communicate rapidly and concisely, and be flexible in handling diverse responsibilities, especially at smaller posts. Some political officers have more specialized duties. Those who qualify may become area specialists, knowledgeable about the language, history, culture, and politics of a nation or region, such as the Soviet Union or Latin America. Many political officers also serve in the labor attaché program abroad and in Washington as international labor experts. Political officers, as well as economic officers, may also serve as science attachés abroad or in science and technology-related positions in the department.

A typical week for a political officer overseas might include reporting on a foreign election or change of government, seeking support for a U.S. foreign policy initiative, analyzing a border dispute, briefing and suggesting remarks for a visiting senior U.S. official, and perhaps escorting the official, while handling the daily flow of cables and correspondence relating to the visit.

WORKING FOR THE UNITED STATES INFORMATION AGENCY

The development of mass communications networks and rapid transportation systems has accelerated and expanded the flow of information among nations and stimulated public interest in foreign relations. The corresponding increase in the importance of public opinion in shaping official attitudes and policies has made public diplomacy, which is the mandate of the U.S. Information Agency, a significant adjunct to the traditional government-to-government diplomacy conducted by the Department of State.

The U.S. Information Agency is an independent organization within the executive branch responsible for the U.S. government's overseas information and cultural programs. USIA's principal tasks are to strengthen foreign understanding and support for U.S. policies and actions; to counter attempts to distort the objectives and policies of the United States; to advise the president, the secretary of state, and other key officials of the implications of foreign opinion for present and contemplated U.S. policies; and to promote and administer educational and cultural exchange programs in the national interest to bring about greater understanding between the people of the United States and the peoples of the world.

USIA officers are on-the-scene practitioners of public diplomacy. Many have come from academia and the arts; others are from journalism, radio, motion pictures, and television; some have been drawn from the business world. Officers abroad are expected to move into the local social and cultural environment and to cultivate personal contact with key persons in government, education, the media, the arts, and the professions. In the course of dealing with the general public, USIA officers define and explain U.S. policies and society, correct misconceptions, and analyze and report on public perceptions of the United States.

USIA's overseas posts range in size from one American officer to those with a dozen or more, supported by a staff of foreign national employees. The typical post, located within the American embassy, is composed of a public affairs officer, an information officer, and a cultural affairs officer.

The public affairs officer (PAO) has overall responsibility for the management and supervision of public diplomacy activities of the embassy, and acts as the ambassador's principal advisor on trends in local media and public opinion and their implication for U.S. foreign policy. At some posts, the PAO may also be the embassy's primary spokesperson.

The information officer, or press attaché, is responsible for activities which directly concern the mass media—press, publications, radio, and television—and normally serves as the embassy press spokesperson on U.S. government policies, provides background information, and publicizes embassy activities. The information officer holds briefings and makes appointments for American journalists and plays a major role in handling public relations arrangements, including press conferences and interviews, whenever congressional or other senior U.S. officials visit the country.

The cultural affairs officer, or cultural attaché, administers educational and cultural exchange programs, arranges lectures and seminars with American speakers, manages American libraries, organizes exhibits, assists local publishers with reprints and translations of American books, and works closely with bilateral educational-exchange entities, such as the Fulbright Commission. The cultural affairs officer may manage the programming of a Broadway play or organize an exhibit by an American gymnastics team, followed by the coordination of a seminar featuring a prominent American university professor or the presentation of an American dance troupe. USIA posts cooperate with local organizations dedicated to the development of mutual understanding with the United States. In many countries, Binational Cultural Centers, autonomous associations supervised by boards of directors composed of prominent local citizens and resident Americans, cooperate with USIA in providing English teaching, libraries, and cultural and social events aimed at fostering closer ties with the United States. In some cases, the executive directors of these centers are USIA officers.

Officers normally serve a minimum of 5 years overseas before returning to Washington for domestic assignments of about 3 years. Officers in Washington support USIA's overseas activities: coordination of programs for a particular geographic area, publication of periodicals, production of television and film programs, recruitment of academic and professional specialists for overseas presentations, preparation of policy guidance and analysis, and direction of Voice of America (VOA) broadcast services.

In addition to a permanent Washington-based staff, the VOA has several FSOs assigned to its headquarters. VOA is the global radio network of USIA, broadcasting more than 1,000 hours a week in 42 languages via short- and medium-wave to an estimated 120 million listeners. VOA strives to be a credible and authoritative source of news, bal-anced and comprehensive in its portrayal of American society and thought. The bulk of the pro-graming is news and news analysis, supplemented by music and the arts.

Every year USIA selects several officers for uni-versity training, for assignments to units of state and local government, public institutions, or for work with the U.S. Congress as Congressional Fellows.

WORKING FOR THE DEPARTMENT OF COMMERCE

The Foreign Commercial Service (FCS), the over-seas element of the U.S. and Foreign Commercial Service of the Department of Commerce, is the government's international trade agency with a global field organization and delivery system giv-ing American business direct access to more than 95 percent of the world market for U.S. exports of goods and services.

Abroad, the FCS Officer works at some 65 em-bassies and posts with governments, business re-presentatives, and individuals concerned with in-ternational trade. FCS Officers facilitate U.S. exports by identifying agents and distributors for U.S. and foreign companies, helping to locate sources of financing for businesses, and conduct-ing market research for American firms. They in-troduce local business representatives who wish to import or represent American products to U.S. firms, and they help resolve trade and investment disputes. They also organize trade promotion pro-grams and events and operate export development offices. The work requires a strong entrepreneurial orientation, knowledge of local business condi-tions, and an ability to win the confidence of American and foreign business. One officer de-scribed commercial work as "fast-paced, opera-tional, and always different. There is a great ac-cess to the local community because you have a service to offer, and local commercial activities give rare insight into the country where you work. And maybe best of all, you can be satisfied with the results of your work."

The FCS Officer works closely with other For-eign Service Officers in the economic and political sections of the embassy, as well as with foreign nationals employed by the U.S. government.

A management expert from the private sector who studied the multifaceted role played by com-mercial officers overseas described the job as re-quiring "a highly activist broker who represents the U.S. government to foreign governments and American businesses to foreign businesses and governments." He concluded that a commercial officer needs to analyze and evaluate financial, marketing, and government policy in a large num-ber of different international environments in order to assist American business.

In order to accomplish this, the commercial of-ficer must acquire highly developed skills in inter-personal and intercultural dealings, in program and personnel management, in communication with a wide variety of audiences, in analysis for differing clients, and an intensive knowledge of the international operations of American business and U.S. government programs designed to assist them. Each FCS Officer is counseled in career development through the FCS Office of Foreign Service Personnel and is provided with the how-to skills for a successful career. In addition, FCS Officers will spend a portion of their careers fur-ther improving their skills through advanced edu-cation and training.

THE SELECTION PROCESS

The Foreign Service needs qualified men and wo-men who reflect the breadth and variety of Ameri-can society. To be truly representative of the United States, the Foreign Service must reflect the diversity of the American people. The Foreign Ser-vice needs men and women from all backgrounds—Americans of all racial and ethnic origins and from all regions of the country. The Foreign Service also seeks officers from diverse educational backgrounds. Some 750 American colleges and universities are represented by today's FSOs. They come from every state in the union. Most officers have entered the Foreign Service after undergraduate or graduate school, with degrees in a variety of subjects. A few do not have university degrees. Others have worked in teaching, business, law, science, journalism, the military, government, or other fields, bringing valuable skills and experience to the Foreign Service. Most officer candidates have backgrounds in history, political science, economics, or management, but needs are increasing in foreign affairs for scientists, systems analysts, language and area experts, business managers, industrial development specialists, and others. Today the Foreign Service needs such diversity of education, talents, and experience to handle the complex and many-sided tasks of foreign affairs.

Importance of English-Language Skills

Success in the Foreign Service requires a strong command of the English language. All Foreign Service Officers must be able to speak and write clearly, concisely, and correctly. The success of much of their work depends on their ability to speak and write persuasively and to analyze and defend policies and proposals. The Departments of State and Commerce and USIA give high priority to English-language skills in selecting officers and evaluating their performance.

Foreign Languages

Knowledge of foreign languages is not required for appointment, but once hired, all new officers must demonstrate professional competency in at least one foreign language prior to the end of their initial probationary period. If necessary, an officer will attend classes at the Foreign Service Institute, which offers training in over 40 languages. Those who enter with language abilities are tested within 30 days of appointment and, if found proficient in certain designated languages, may receive a higher salary. The Department of State and USIA particularly seek persons with knowledge of "hard" or "exotic" languages (e.g., Arabic, Chinese, Russian). Candidates without prior foreign

language ability will be appointed as language probationers, and they must acquire acceptable language competency before tenure can be granted.

The Foreign Service Written Examination

About once each year, the Foreign Service written examination, for the Department of State, the U.S. Information Agency, and the Department of Commerce, is given throughout the United States and at Foreign Service posts abroad. More than 15,000 persons take the examination each year, of whom some 250 eventually may be appointed as Foreign Service Officer (FSO) Career Candidates of Classes 6, 5, or 4, depending on their qualifications and experience. Regardless of age and experience, appointments under this program cannot be made at a higher level than Class 4 (FS-4).

Eligibility Requirements To be eligible for the written examination, applicants must be:

- At least 20 years old and not more than 59 years of age on the date of the examination;
- U.S. citizens; and
- Available for worldwide assignment, including Washington, D.C.

No specific educational background is required. Success in the written examination and the subsequent oral assessment requires a broad knowledge of foreign and domestic affairs and U.S. history, government, foreign policy, and culture. The best preparation is a good general education, including, for example, courses in history, government, geography, economics, literature, international relations, and business and public administration. Most, but not all, successful candidates have at least bachelor's degrees. In recent years, about 65 percent have had advanced degrees in international relations, economics, business administration, law, journalism, and other fields. We do not recommend any particular institution or academic program to candidates for the Foreign Service. Foreign Service Officers have graduated from hundreds of large and small colleges and universities, and many have had work experience in various fields before their appointments.

Procedure for Applying The written examination is given throughout the United States and at Foreign Service posts abroad. Application forms for the examination, a form SF-171, and the form on which applicants must write a "Statement of Interest" are included in a separate booklet, which applicants may obtain from college and university placement offices, from regional offices of the Office of Personnel Management, or by writing the Recruitment Division, Department of State, Box 9317, Rosslyn Station, Arlington, Virginia 22209. Candidates whose applications are accepted will be sent tickets of admission informing them of the address of their assigned examination site at least 2 weeks before the examination date.

No other examination can be substituted for the Foreign Service written examination. *"Makeup" examinations cannot be authorized,* no matter how valid an applicant's reason for missing the scheduled examination. However, applicants whose religious beliefs preclude taking examinations on Saturdays, and applicants with certain physical handicaps who might need special arrangements to take the examination, should write to the Board of Examiners for the Foreign Service, Box 9317, Rosslyn Station, Arlington, Virginia 22209, before the stated deadline date, enclosing their application form, so that appropriate arrangements can be made for them. Applicants with physical handicaps should not interpret admittance to take the examination under special arrangements to mean that the rigorous medical requirements for the Foreign Service can be relaxed. Those who believe they or members of their family might not meet the medical standards of the Foreign Service may contact the Office of Medical Services. (For more information, see "Medical Requirements," p. 15.)

Content The written examination requires one-half day and consists of the following multiple-choice tests for all candidates:

A *Knowledge* test designed to measure a candidate's breadth of understanding of the institutions and concepts that are basic to the development of the United States and of other countries, and knowledge of subjects basic to the functions of the Foreign Service. The examination also tests knowledge of geography, international relations, the literary, artistic, and philosophical heritage of the United States and other cultures, current trends and developments in the arts, and basic scientific and management principles. Many of the questions concern the United States. Additional questions in the Knowledge test measure the knowledge and skills required to perform effectively in each of the *functional areas* of work of the Departments of State and Commerce and of USIA. A specialized knowledge

of Foreign Service procedures and operations is not required, and no particular course of study or preparation is expected. Rather, the best background for the test is a good general education, political and cultural sensitivity, and the habit of reading widely.

An *English Expression* test that measures skill in written English. It contains four sections of questions which test ability to correct sentences, to express ideas clearly and accurately, to revise sentences according to instruction, and to organize information logically.

A *Biographic Information Questionnaire* that measures the candidate's experience, skills, and achievements in school, employment, and other activities. The questionnaire does not penalize candidates who have not gone to college, who have no previous work experience, who are younger or older, or who have other varied patterns of education and experience but, rather, credits candidates for what they have achieved relative to the opportunities they have had. The questionnaire is based on research on the actual characteristics of successful people in federal government professional and administrative occupations. It is designed to supplement the other portions of the examination by providing an assessment of additional job-related characteristics.

The official sample questions beginning on p. 27 are included in order to give candidates an indication of the types of questions asked in the written examination and the rationale for each. The number who pass the examination each year is determined by the number of officers needed by the Foreign Service in subsequent years. Those who do not pass may take the examination again the following year, if they wish to do so. No limit is imposed on the number of times a candidate may compete.

Three full-length simulated Foreign Service written exams are provided in Part Two of this book.

Oral Assessment

Candidates who pass the written examination at the designated level will be eligible for an all-day assessment which will include a variety of simulation techniques, examinations, and appraisals. Candidates will be judged by a panel of trained Foreign Service examiners against a uniform and consistent set of standards, not in direct competition with each other. Candidates are assessed in groups of six during this process. Relevant observations on each candidate are reported, discussed, scored, and integrated by the examiners. The assessment day concludes with a personal interview.

The assessment procedures are based on current job analyses of Foreign Service work and the knowledge, skills, abilities, and personal characteristics considered necessary to perform that work. These procedures measure characteristics such as oral and written communication skills, administrative/problem-solving skills, leadership skills, and personal characteristics such as interpersonal skills, cultural awareness and sensitivity, stability, and resourcefulness. Assessments are given in Washington, D.C. and in a number of other major cities in the United States. Travel is at the candidate's expense. The assessment measures include the following:

1. An oral examination with two examiners lasting 45 minutes, which is designed to measure awareness of current political, economic, and cultural issues, the ability to analyze problems, oral communication skills, and personal characteristics.
2. A written essay prepared within 45 minutes on an assigned topic, which is designed to test the ability to write clear and correct English.
3. A written summary exercise lasting 45 minutes, which is designed to test the ability to analyze and organize provided materials into a concise and accurate written summary.
4. A two-part group exercise lasting 1 hour and 15 minutes. The first part consists of a short oral presentation of a proposal to the group by each candidate, based on materials provided for this purpose. The second part is a leaderless group negotiating session to discuss and seek agreement among the various proposals. Candidates are given time to prepare for this exercise, which is designed to measure oral communication skills; analyzing and synthesizing ability; interpersonal awareness; the ability to lead, negotiate, represent, and mediate; and the ability to adjust to changing situations.
5. A written In-Basket test lasting 90 minutes in which the candidate deals with a series of problems and situations presented in written form. This test is designed to measure managerial skills such as the ability to manage staff, problem-solving ability, leadership, interpersonal skills, and quality of judgment.

This exposition of the oral assessment day describes the assessment process through 1991. At the time of preparation of this book, the Board of Examiners for the Foreign Service was involved in reevaluating procedures and in revising tests, questions, and exercises for the assessment. By the time that you report for your assessment, these new procedures will be in place. The exercises themselves and the timing may vary, but the skills and personal characteristics that you must exhibit will be similar.

Candidates who are not recommended by the assessment panels and who wish to compete again the following year may do so by taking and passing the next written examination.

A candidate normally must participate in the assessment process within 12 months of passing the written examination. If, however, the candidate is outside the United States for part or all of the 12-month period following the written examination, the candidacy may be extended upon authorization of the Board of Examiners. In such cases, the candidacy will be terminated if the candidate does not take the assessment within 3 months of first returning to the United States.

Additional information about the Oral Assessment and samples of assessment day activities are provided in Part Three of this book.

Selection and Appointment

Selection The background of candidates successful in the assessment is investigated thoroughly to determine suitability for appointment to the Foreign Service. To initiate this investigation, certain forms must be completed as soon as possible after notification of successful performance in the assessment.

Once these background investigation forms are received, authorization for a comprehensive medical examination is provided to candidates and their dependents. Medical clearances for full overseas duty are required for all candidates and their dependents. (For more information, see "Medical Requirements," p. 15.)

Candidates must submit the forms necessary for their background investigation and obtain all medical clearances within 6 months after notification of successful performance in the assessment. Candidates also must submit university transcripts and a 1,000-word autobiography within this same period. If these requirements are not fulfilled within 6 months, the candidacy normally will be terminated.

A Final Review Panel weighs a candidate's qualifications against those of others. It considers all relevant information available about a candidate: performance on the written examination and in the assessment center, the required autobiography, education, employment history, community and social activities, and results of the background investigation.

The names of those candidates who successfully complete the entire examination and selection process and who have obtained medical clearance for full overseas duty will be placed on rank-order registers in the functional fields in which they have been judged qualified. There will be six such registers: administrative, consular, commercial, economic, information/cultural, and political. Each register lists qualified candidates in the order of their combined scores in the various phases of the examination and assessment process. When classes of new FSO Career Candidates are scheduled, candidates are invited to join them in the order of their competitive rank in the functional fields then being filled. Candidates invited from the information/cultural register will become FSO Career Candidates with USIA. Candidates invited from the commercial register will become FSO Career Candidates with the Department of Commerce. Candidates invited from the administrative, consular, economic, and political registers will become FSO Career Candidates with the Department of State.

Generally, the functional register from which a candidate accepts an appointment into the Foreign Service will determine his or her career specialty. For this reason the candidate's choice of appointment register should be weighed carefully. Candidates may decline an invitation from a specific register, but no guarantee can be given that they will be invited later from that or another functional register. Candidates will not affect their relative register positions by declining an offer of appointment, however.

It is important to note that simply by being listed on one or more registers, a candidate is not assured an offer of employment. The overall number of FSO Career Candidates hired each year, as well as the number hired from any particular register, varies with the needs of the Foreign Service. Candidates remain eligible for appointment for 18 months from the date their names are placed on a register. Time spent in civilian government service abroad (to a maximum of 2 years of such service) including Peace Corps volunteer service, or in required active regular or reserve military service, will not be counted as part of the 18-month eligi-

bility period. Candidates who are spouses accompanying employees serving in civilian government service abroad or in required military service may also be entitled to similar extensions of their eligibility for appointment.

Some candidates who are already on the FSO registers have found it to their advantage to take the written examination and assessment process again in an effort to improve their relative standing on the registers. No limit is imposed on the number of times a candidate may compete.

This description of the FSO examination procedures is intended to give an indication of the types of challenges each candidate will face. The procedures described in this book are those in effect at the time of publication. Because of the long lead time between publication and the conduct of the various phases of the examination, some changes may be unavoidable in light of the needs of the Foreign Service and the revision of examination techniques and materials.

Appointment Candidates who succeed in the examination and selection process are given probationary appointments as Foreign Service Officer Career Candidates for a period of 4 years. Appointments are made at the FS-6 through FS-4 levels, depending on previous education and work experience. Career Candidates failing to perform satisfactorily may be terminated at any time during the 4-year probationary period. Successful Career Candidates can be expected to be commissioned as Foreign Service Officers by the 4th year of their probationary appointment, following approval by the Commissioning and Tenure Board.

Promotions during the probationary period are based on satisfactory performance. Promotions occur after 12 months at the FS-6 level and after 18 months at the FS-5 level. Language probation will not delay these first promotions; however, no Career Candidates can be commissioned as permanent officers or promoted beyond FS-4 until language probation is lifted.

All Career Candidate appointments must be made before the individual's 60th birthday. The maximum age for entry into the Foreign Service is based on such factors as eligibility for retirement benefits, assignment requirements, and the mandatory retirement age of 65.

Initial Training and Assignments

Before accepting employment with the Foreign Service, officers must agree to be available for worldwide assignment. Service needs, individual skills and specialization, and personal preference are all factors in selection of initial and subsequent assignments. The changing needs of foreign policy and departmental responsibilities make it difficult to predict individual career patterns. However, all Department of State Career Candidates should expect to spend a minimum of 1 year—more typically, 2 or more years—performing consular work during their first two tours of duty. During this period the department also will attempt to offer some working experience in other functional fields. After the first few assignments in a variety of geographical and functional fields, specialization at mid-career in one functional field and sometimes in a single geographical area is normal.

On entering the Foreign Service, all Career Candidates receive several weeks of basic orientation at the Department of State's Foreign Service Institute. An officer may expect up to 7 months of subsequent training prior to the first overseas assignment. Since most of this training involves language instruction, entering officers who already have professional competence in a foreign language may have a significantly shorter period in Washington prior to leaving on a first overseas assignment. Other training may include area studies and functional courses to prepare an officer for the first overseas assignment. In addition, USIA candidates receive basic professional training at the Agency's training facility.

Career Status and Career Development

Once tenured, officers will continue in the career functional field to which originally assigned unless they choose to apply and are accepted for a change of career function. In the middle grades— Classes 3 through 1—officers concentrate on their functional specialty, but most serve in occasional out-of-function assignments to broaden their experience and to prepare for senior management responsibility. In preparation for mid-level service, career officers will be assigned to a 5-month training course on foreign affairs operations and management and elective courses to broaden professional knowledge. In addition, officers may serve tours with other federal agencies or may be se-

lected for assignments to units of state and local government or public institutions, to work with the U.S. Congress as Congressional Fellows, to universities, to the Department of Defense's War Colleges, or to the Department of State's Executive Seminar in National and International Affairs.

Each USIA Foreign Service Officer is expected to be able to serve in all aspects of USIA activities. Those officers who develop special interests by the middle grades may be assigned accordingly by USIA.

After achieving career status, officers must compete for promotions. Each officer is rated by a supervisor at least once each year, and such performance evaluations are considered annually by specially appointed promotion boards. Any who fail to meet competitive standards are subject to termination or early retirement. All officers are subject to possible retirement or termination for exceeding established limits on time-in-class without a promotion.

Officers may advance beyond Class 1 by applying for promotion into the Senior Foreign Service. If selected, they generally are assigned to program direction and managerial responsibilities including (for a relative few) service as ambassadors. Small numbers of distinguished Senior Foreign Service Officers are promoted to Career Minister, or receive the highest rank of honor, Career Ambassador.

In all fairness to potential candidates and the Foreign Service, and with due regard for the risk of discouraging some applicants, potential candidates must be aware of the discipline and sacrifices the career demands, as well as the nature of the rewards and benefits. To begin with, it is highly unlikely that the Foreign Service ever will employ more than a small fraction of those who apply, and the competition—as keen as it is for entry—does not abate appreciably throughout the career. Promotions can be few and difficult to come by in some ranks and functional specialties and at certain times. Applicants with a sincere abiding interest in foreign affairs and public service are encouraged to apply and begin the examination process, but they are advised not to pin all of their career hopes on acceptance into the Foreign Service nor, if they are accepted, to measure their success and self-esteem by rapid advancement through the career ranks to the relatively few top positions.

MEDICAL REQUIREMENTS

Foreign Service personnel and their dependents must be able to serve at a wide variety of overseas posts, many of which are remote, unhealthful, or have limited medical support. In addition to other essential qualifications for entry into the Foreign Service, each applicant and family member must meet medical fitness standards which are, of necessity, more rigorous than for most other professions. In general, any medical condition is disqualifying if it would unduly restrict overseas assignability on a worldwide basis; constitute an unnecessary or significant risk to the life or limb of the applicant, dependents, or fellow employees; or be of such a nature as to require medical support not readily available at overseas posts. Generally, medical conditions which require frequent observation and examination or prolonged treatment, which may be aggravated by certain geographic or climatic conditions, or which may require excessive time lost from duty or premature separation from the Foreign Service, are found to be disqualifying. All dependents must pass a medical examination, whether or not they will accompany the employee abroad.

No official decision concerning medical clearance can be reached until the Office of Medical Services reviews the findings of a thorough Foreign Service medical examination. However, individuals who believe they or members of their family might not meet the medical standards may contact: Medical Director, Office of Medical Services, Department of State, Washington, D.C. 20520. For Department of State candidates an Employment Review Committee has been established to review all cases of medical disqualification. This Committee makes recommendations to the Director General of the Foreign Service as to whether or not an applicant should be appointed despite a medical disqualification.

USIA maintains a similar review procedure for candidates disqualified medically. Agency candidates affected may apply for review of their cases to the Director, Office of Personnel, USIA, 301 4th Street SW, Washington, D.C. 20547.

INFORMATION FOR FAMILY MEMBERS

A Foreign Service career deeply involves not only the employee but also the entire family. The Departments of State and Commerce and USIA recognize that members of a Foreign Service family essentially are private individuals. However, the diplomatic community and people of the country of assignment often view the entire family as representatives of the United States.

Foreign Service life affects family members in many ways. Education of children and health care are both special factors to be considered. The quality of overseas education is uneven, and providing continuity of subjects and of instructional methods is difficult. Testing and college counseling are often inadequate. In brief, parents tend to take much greater responsibility for a child's schooling than in the United States. As for medical facilities, they too are uneven. Some posts have no resident American doctor or nurse. It may be necessary to travel by air to reach an acceptable hospital. Some restrictions in lifestyle may occur in the interest of personal safety at some locations.

Married applicants whose spouses seek their own careers should weigh carefully the implications of joining a highly mobile service in which worldwide availability is required. Both in Washington and overseas, the Foreign Service spouse is at a career disadvantage. Prospective employers often are reluctant to hire a spouse for a limited period of time. It is difficult to maintain professional contacts and to keep up-to-date in a given field. Abroad, where about 60 percent of a person's career may be spent, some spouses are able to work, but local regulations and circumstances typically limit opportunities severely or salaries may be considerably reduced. However, continued efforts to improve employment prospects are underway.

On the other hand, close involvement in other societies and cultures provides unique opportunities for spouses with varied interests, transferable skills, and portable professions. Involvement in community life abroad and the opportunity to take part in representing the United States are voluntary; but many families find that such activities broaden their contact with the citizens and culture of the country of assignment. Undeniably, a Foreign Service existence can be very rewarding. However, applicants have to decide how flexible they and their families are willing to be in matters of schooling, medical care, and employment for spouses. Child care facilities vary greatly overseas.

When a husband and wife are both members of the Foreign Service, the Departments of State and Commerce and USIA make every reasonable effort to assign them to the same post without placing other employees at a disadvantage. While tandem assignments can usually be arranged, couples must be prepared to accept the possibility that they may, during their careers, have to accept separate assignments or leave without pay for one spouse.

Additional information on Foreign Service family life abroad, including schools, educational benefits, health care and medical facilities, and job opportunities for dependents can be obtained by writing for the brochure "Information for Foreign Service Applicants and Family Members," to the Recruitment Division, Department of State, Box 9317, Rosslyn Station, Arlington, Virginia 22209; or by contacting the Family Liaison Office, Department of State, Washington, D.C. 20520, telephone (202) 647-1076. The Overseas Briefing Center, Foreign Service Institute, telephone (703) 235-8784, also can answer questions about living abroad.

SALARIES AND BENEFITS

Salary Schedule

New entry-level officers are appointed at Classes 6, 5, or 4, depending on their qualifications, experience, and salary record.

Appointment at entry level FS-5 normally required a master's degree. Appointment at entry level FS-4 normally requires a master's degree and 18 months of experience in a field closely related to the Foreign Service and in a position equivalent to at least the FS-5 level.

Benefits

Annual and sick leave, group life and medical insurance, and Foreign Service retirement benefits are provided.

The government bears the expense of the travel of employees and their families to Washington, D.C. for appointment; for any subsequent temporary duty assignments to Washington; and to and from posts of assignment abroad.

Basic salaries of Foreign Service personnel serving *overseas* may be supplemented by:

- Shipment of automobile and personal effects to and from posts abroad (automobiles cannot be shipped within the United States at government expense);
- Government-provided quarters or housing allowances;
- Government-provided furniture and storage of personal furniture, or shipment of personal furniture;
- Home leave, including travel expenses; and
- Hospitalization benefits.

The following benefits are provided *when appropriate*:

- Education allowance;
- Education travel for dependent children;
- Temporary lodging allowance;
- Separate maintenance allowance;
- Cost-of-living allowance;
- Hardship post salary supplements;
- Danger pay; and
- Travel for children of separated parents.

APPLYING FOR THE FOREIGN SERVICE OFFICER PROGRAM

Application to the Foreign Service Officer Program begins with application to take the written examination. The application packet consists of three separate documents: a combined application form and personal data questionnaire; application for federal employment, also known as SF-171; and a statement of interest. The entire application packet is sent to Educational Testing Service in Princeton, NJ, the administrator of the written exam. (Note that you do not need to include a check. There is never a charge for taking an examination for a federal job.)

THE APPLICATION FORM

The application form itself is a computer-scannable form that requests much of the basic information you would expect to enter on a test-registration form: name; mailing address; date of birth; sex; social security number; and telephone numbers. Since the form is used to assign applicants to testing centers, it also provides spaces for entry of the code number of the test center you request. Codes are provided in the application information booklet.

Because the application form is also a personal data questionnaire for the use of the foreign service board of examiners, it asks many other questions about your education and background and about you as a person. Codes are provided in the information booklet so that your answers can easily be interpreted by the computer. Personal questions concern racial and national origin; handicapped status; source of your information about the exam; and whether or not you have ever taken this exam before. Experience questions concern length of military service, if any; length of full-time work experience; field of work in which currently employed; and the length and nature of overseas experience—student, dependent, Peace Corps, military, government, etc. Education questions concern current student status; highest level of education attained; names (codes) of undergraduate and graduate institutions; undergraduate and graduate majors fields of study; and undergraduate and graduate grade point averages. A detailed scheme is provided for converting various grading schemes into uniform grade point averages.

For each question, you are permitted only one response. This means that if you attended more than one graduate school but graduated from none, you must choose the institution that you consider most significant. Likewise, if your experience abroad spans more than one category, you must choose which experience to report. Aside from making these few decisions and the nuisance of accumulating scholastic records or transcripts so as to calculate the requisite grade point averages, filling out the application form is quite routine. This first step is by far the easiest in the whole application process.

SF-171

SF-171, the federal employment application form, is part of the Foreign Service Officer exam application. The SF-171 Personal Qualifications Statement serves in place of a résumé. If you have prepared a résumé to accompany your applications for jobs in the private sector, you have a ready resource at hand for filling in the blanks on the SF-171. If any agency asks you for an SF-171, you must submit one. You may not substitute your résumé. Much of the information you will need for the SF-171 can be taken from your résumé. However, the SF-171 is more detailed, goes back farther, and asks for "older" information. You probably will not be un- der great time pressure in filling out the SF-171, but it never hurts to prepare in advance.

On the pages that follow, you will find copies of parts of the official instructions for completing an SF-171 and a reproduction of the form itself. Use this reproduction as you prepare to fill out the form. Find out where you must look to gather the needed facts and figures. Fill out this dummy copy in ad- vance so that you don't find yourself with "mystery blanks" when the time arrives to file the important copy.

Standard Form 171
Application for Federal Employment

Read the following instructions carefully before you complete this application.

- **DO NOT SUBMIT A RESUME INSTEAD OF THIS APPLICATION.**
- TYPE OR PRINT CLEARLY IN DARK INK.
- *If you need more space* for an answer, use a sheet of paper the same size as this page. On *each* sheet write your name, Social Security Number, the announcement number or job title, and the item number. Attach all addi- tional forms and sheets to this application at the top of page 3.
- If you do not answer *all* questions fully and correctly, you may delay the review of your application and lose job opportunities.
- Unless you are asked for additional material in the announcement or qualification infor- mation, *do not attach* any materials, such as official position descriptions, performance evaluations, letters of recommendation, cer- tificates of training, publications, etc. Any materials you attach which were not asked for may be removed from your application and will *not* be returned to you.
- We suggest that you *keep a copy* of this ap- plication for your use. If you plan to make copies of your application, we suggest you leave items *1, 48,* and *49* blank. Complete these blank items each time you apply. *You must sign and date, in ink, each copy you submit.*

WORK EXPERIENCE *(ITEM 24)*

- Carefully complete each experience block you need to describe your work experience. Unless you qualify based on education alone, *your rating will depend on your description of previous jobs. Do not leave out any jobs you held during the last ten years.*

- Under "Description of Work," write a *clear* and *brief,* but *complete* description of your *major* duties and responsibilities for each job. Include any supervisory duties, special assignments, and your accomplishments in the job. Expect your descriptions to be veri- fied with your former employers.
- If you had a major change of duties or re- sponsibilities while you worked for the same employer, describe each major change as a separate job.

VETERAN PREFERENCE IN HIRING *(ITEM 22)*

- *Do not leave Item 22 blank.* If you do *not* claim veteran preference place an "X" in the box next to "no preference."
- You *cannot* receive veteran preference if you are retired or plan to retire at or above the rank of major or lieutenant commander, *un- less* you are disabled or retired from the ac- tive military Reserve.
- To receive veteran preference your separa- tion from active duty must have been under honorable conditions. This includes honora- ble and general discharges. A clemency dis- charge does not meet the requirements of the Veteran Preference Act.
- Active duty for training in the military Re- serve and National Guard programs is not considered active duty for purposes of vet- eran preference.
- To qualify for preference you must meet *one* of the following conditions:

1. Served on active duty anytime between De- cember 7, 1941 and July 1, 1955 (If you were a Reservist called to active duty between Feb- ruary 1, 1955 and July 1, 1955, you must meet condition 2, below);

or

2. Served on active duty any part of which was between July 2, 1955 and October 14, 1976 or a Reservist called to active duty between February 1, 1955 and October 14, 1976 *and* who served for more than 180 days;

or

3. Entered on active duty between October 15, 1976 and September 7, 1980 or a Reservist who entered on active duty between October 15, 1976 and October 13, 1982 *and* received a Campaign Badge or Expeditionary Medal *or* are a disabled veteran;

or

4. Enlisted in the Armed Forces after September 7, 1980 or entered active duty other than by enlistment on or after October 14, 1982;

and

   a. completed 24 months of continuous active duty or the full period called or ordered to active duty, or were discharged under 10 U.S.C. 1171 or for hardship under 10 U.S.C. 1173 *and* received or were entitled to receive a Campaign Badge or Expeditionary Medal;

or

   b. are a disabled veteran.

- If you meet one of the four conditions, you qualify for 5-point preference. If you want to claim 5-point preference *and* do not meet the requirements for 10-point preference, discussed below, place an "X" in the box next to "5-POINT PREFERENCE."
- If you think you qualify for 10-Point Preference, review requirements described in the Standard Form (SF) 15, Application for 10-Point Veteran Preference. The SF 15 is available from any Federal Job Information Center. The 10-point preference groups are:

   Non Compensably Disabled or Purple Heart Recipient.

   Compensably Disabled (less than 30%).
   Compensably Disabled (30% or more).
   Spouse, Widow(er) or Mother of a deceased or disabled veteran.

If you claim 10-point preference, place an "X" in the box next to the group that applies to you. *To receive 10-point preference you must attach a completed SF 15 to this appliction together with the proof requested in the SF 15.*

Even after you have filled out the entire SF-171 on these pages, you will find that filling out the actual SF-171 offers special challenges. Chief of these is fitting your information into the provided spaces neatly and legibly or by typewriter, as preferred.

The first thing to do when you receive your official SF-171 form is to make several photocopies. Then you can practice transferring the information that you handwrote into this book onto photocopies of the form. It may take a number of tries before it works.

Since filling out the SF-171 is such a chore, you want to do it only once. But, you may need to submit an SF-171 form to more than one agency, for more than one position. The SF-171 is the official application form for many federal service careers; its use is by no means limited to the Foreign Service. Therefore, when you complete the form you plan to submit for the first position, *leave spaces 1 and 2 blank. Do not sign and date* the completed first original. When you have reached this point, return to the photocopying machine and make a number of copies of the completed SF-171 with spaces 1 and 2 and the signature block blank.

Now, take one copy and fill in blocks 1 and 2 with the information for the position for which you are filing the SF-171 right now. Also, sign and date that one copy in ink. Save the original and all other copies for future use. A clear photocopy is perfectly acceptable for submission; only the signature and date must be original and in ink on each copy. You will save yourself many hours and much frustration by following this procedure.

Application for Federal Employment—SF 171

Read the instructions before you complete this application. *Type or print clearly in dark ink.*

Form Approved:
OMB No. 3206-0012

GENERAL INFORMATION

1 What kind of job are you applying for? *Give title and announcement no. (if any)*

2 Social Security Number

3 Sex
☐ Male   ☐ Female

4 Birth date *(Month, Day, Year)*

5 Birthplace *(City and State or Country)*

6 Name *(Last, First, Middle)*

Mailing address *(include apartment number, if any)*

City   State   ZIP Code

7 Other names ever used *(e.g., maiden name, nickname, etc.)*

8 Home Phone
Area Code | Number

9 Work Phone
Area Code | Number   Extension

10 Were you ever employed as a civilian by the Federal Government? If **"NO"**, go to **Item 11.** If **"YES"**, mark each type of job you held with an **"X"**.

☐ Temporary   ☐ Career-Conditional   ☐ Career   ☐ Excepted

What is your **highest** grade, classification series and job title?

Dates at **highest** grade: FROM   TO

AVAILABILITY

11 When can you start work? *(Month and Year)*

12 What is the **lowest** pay you will accept? *(You will not be considered for jobs which pay less than you indicate.)*

Pay $_____ per _____ OR Grade _____

13 In what geographic area(s) are you willing to work?

14 Are you willing to work:

	YES	NO
A. 40 hours per week *(full-time)*?		
B. 25-32 hours per week *(part-time)*?		
C. 17-24 hours per week *(part-time)*?		
D. 16 or fewer hours per week *(part-time)*?		
E. An intermittent job *(on-call/seasonal)*?		
F. Weekends, shifts, or rotating shifts?		

15 Are you willing to take a temporary job lasting:

A. 5 to 12 months *(sometimes longer)*?		
B. 1 to 4 months?		
C. Less than 1 month?		

16 Are you willing to travel away from home for:

A. 1 to 5 nights each month?		
B. 6 to 10 nights each month?		
C. 11 or more nights each month?		

MILITARY SERVICE AND VETERAN PREFERENCE

17 Have you served in the United States Military Service? *If your only active duty was training in the Reserves or National Guard, answer "NO". If* **"NO"**, *go to item 22.* . . . .

YES	NO

18 Did you or will you retire at or above the rank of major or lieutenant commander?. . . . .

THE FEDERAL GOVERNMENT IS AN EQUAL OPPORTUNITY EMPLOYER
PREVIOUS EDITION USABLE UNTIL 12-31-90

FOR USE OF EXAMINING OFFICE ONLY

Date entered register

Form reviewed:
Form approved:

Option	Grade	Earned Rating	Veteran Preference	Augmented Rating
			☐ No Preference Claimed	
			☐ 5 Points *(Tentative)*	
			☐ 10 Pts. *(30% Or More Comp. Dis.)*	
			☐ 10 Pts. *(Less Than 30% Comp. Dis.)*	
			☐ Other 10 Points	

Initials and Date

☐ Disallowed   ☐ Being Investigated

FOR USE OF APPOINTING OFFICE ONLY

Preference has been verified through proof that the separation was under honorable conditions, and other proof as required.

☐ 5-Point   ☐ 10-Point--30% or More Compensable Disability   ☐ 10-Point--Less Than 30% Compensable Disability   ☐ 10-Point--Other

Signature and Title

Agency   Date

MILITARY SERVICE AND VETERAN PREFERENCE *(Cont.)*

19 Were you discharged from the military service under honorable conditions? *(If your discharge was changed to "honorable" or "general" by a Discharge Review Board, answer "YES". If you received a clemency discharge, answer "NO".)* If **"NO"**, provide below the date and type of discharge you received.

YES	NO

Discharge Date *(Month, Day, Year)*	Type of Discharge

20 List the dates *(Month, Day, Year)*, and branch for all **active duty** military service.

From	To	Branch of Service

21 If all your active military duty was after October 14, 1976, list the full names and dates of all campaign badges or expeditionary medals you received or were entitled to receive.

22 Read the instructions that came with this form before completing this item. When you have determined your eligibility for veteran preference from the instructions, place an **"X"** in the box next to your veteran preference claim.

☐ NO PREFERENCE

☐ 5-POINT PREFERENCE -- You must show proof when you are hired.

10-POINT PREFERENCE -- If you claim 10-point preference, place an **"X"** in the box below next to the basis for your claim. **To receive 10-point preference you must also complete a Standard Form 15, Application for 10-Point Veteran Preference, which is available from any Federal Job Information Center. ATTACH THE COMPLETED SF 15 AND REQUESTED PROOF TO THIS APPLICATION.**

☐ Non-compensably disabled or Purple Heart recipient.
☐ Compensably disabled, less than 30 percent.
☐ Spouse, widow(er), or mother of a deceased or disabled veteran.
☐ Compensably disabled, 30 percent or more.

NSN 7540-00-935-7150   171-109   Standard Form 171 (Rev. 6-88)
U.S. Office of Personnel Management
FPM Chapter 295

WORK EXPERIENCE *If you have no work experience, write "NONE" in A below and go to 25 on page 3.*

23 May we ask your present employer about your character, qualifications, and work record? *A "NO" will not affect our review of your qualifications. If you answer "NO" and we need to contact your present employer before we can offer you a job, we will contact you first.* . . . .

	YES	NO

24 READ **WORK EXPERIENCE** IN THE INSTRUCTIONS BEFORE YOU BEGIN.

- Describe your current or most recent job in Block **A** and work backwards, describing each job you held **during the past 10 years.** If you were **unemployed** for longer than **3 months** within the past 10 years, list the dates and your address(es) in an experience block.

- You may sum up in one block work that you did **more than 10 years ago.** But if that work **is related** to the type of job you are applying for, describe each related job in a separate block.

- INCLUDE VOLUNTEER WORK *(non-paid work)*--**If the work** *(or a part of the work)* **is like the job you are applying for,** complete **all** parts of the experience block just as you would for a paying job. You may receive credit for work experience with religious, community, welfare, service, and other organizations.

- INCLUDE MILITARY SERVICE--You should complete **all** parts of the experience block just as you would for a non-military job, including all supervisory experience. Describe each major change of duties or responsibilities in a separate experience block.

- IF YOU NEED MORE SPACE TO DESCRIBE A JOB--Use sheets of paper the same size as this page (be sure to include **all** information we ask for in **A** and **B** below). On **each** sheet show your name, Social Security Number, and the announcement number or job title.

- IF YOU NEED MORE EXPERIENCE BLOCKS, use the SF 171-A or a sheet of paper.

- IF YOU NEED TO UPDATE (ADD MORE RECENT JOBS), use the SF 172 or a sheet of paper as described above.

A Name and address of employer's organization *(include ZIP Code, if known)*

Dates employed *(give month, day and year)*

From: To:

Average number if hours per week

Number of employees you supervise

Salary or earnings

Starting $ per

Ending $ per

Your reason for wanting to leave

Your immediate supervisor

Name   Area Code   Telephone No.

Exact title of your job

If Federal employment *(civilian or military)* list series, grade or rank, and, if promoted in this job, the date of your last promotion

Description of work: Describe your specific duties, responsibilities and accomplishments in this job, **including** the job title(s) of any employees you supervise. *If you describe more than one type of work (for example, carpentry and painting, or personnel and budget), write the approximate percentage of time you spent doing each.*

For Agency Use (skill codes. etc.)

B Name and address of employer's organization *(include ZIP Code, if known)*

Dates employed *(give month, day and year)*

From: To:

Average number of hours per week

Number of employees you supervised

Salary or earnings

Starting $ per

Ending $ per

Your reason for leaving

Your immediate supervisor

Name   Area Code   Telephone No.

Exact title of your job

If Federal employment *(civilian or military)* list series, grade or rank, and, if promoted in this job, the date of your last promotion

Description of work: Describe your specific duties, responsibilities and accomplishments in this job, **including** the job title(s) of any employees you supervised. *If you describe more than one type of work (for example, carpentry and painting, or personnel and budget), write the approximate percentage of time you spent doing each.*

For Agency Use (skill codes. etc)

— ← **ATTACH ANY ADDITIONAL FORMS AND SHEETS HERE**

EDUCATION

25 Did you graduate from high school? *If you have a GED high school equivalency or will graduate within the next nine months, answer* **"YES".**

26 Write the name and location *(city and state)* of the last high school you attended or where you obtained your GED high school equivalency.

| YES | ▶ | If **"YES"**, give month and year graduated or received GED equivalency: . . . . |
| NO | | If **NO"**, give the highest grade you completed: . |

27 Have you ever attended college or graduate school?   **YES**   **NO**   ▶ If **"YES"**, continue with **28.** If **NO"**, go to **31.**

28 NAME AND LOCATION *(city, state and ZIP Code)* OF COLLEGE OR UNIVERSITY. *If you expect to graduate within nine months, give the* **month** *and* **year** *you expect to receive your degree:*

Name	City	State	ZIP Code	MONTH AND YEAR ATTENDED From	To	NUMBER OF CREDIT HOURS COMPLETED Semester	Quarter	TYPE OF DEGREE *(e.g. B.A., M.A.)*	MONTH AND YEAR OF DEGREE
1)									
2)									
3)									

29

CHIEF UNDERGRADUATE SUBJECTS *Show major on the first line*	NUMBER OF CREDIT HOURS COMPLETED Semester	Quarter
1)		
2)		
3)		

30

CHIEF GRADUATE SUBJECTS *Show major on the first line*	NUMBER OF CREDIT HOURS COMPLETED Semester	Quarter
1)		
2)		
3)		

31 If you have completed any **other courses or training related to the kind of jobs you are applying for** *(trade, vocational, Armed Forces, business)* give information below.

NAME AND LOCATION *(city, state and ZIP Code)* OF SCHOOL	MONTH AND YEAR ATTENDED From	To	CLASS-ROOM HOURS	SUBJECT(S)	TRAINING COMPLETED YES	NO
School Name 1)						
City State ZIP Code						
School Name 2)						
City State ZIP Code						

SPECIAL SKILLS, ACCOMPLISHMENTS AND AWARDS

32 Give the title and year of any honors, awards or fellowships you have received. List your special qualifications, skills or accomplishments that may help you get a job. *Some examples are: skills with computers or other machines; most important publications (do not submit copies); public speaking and writing experience; membership in professional or scientific societies; patents or inventions; etc.*

33 How many words per minute can you:
TYPE? TAKE DICTATION?

Agencies may test your skills before hiring you.

34 List **job-related** licenses or certificates that you have, such as: *registered nurse; lawyer; radio operator; driver's; pilot's; etc.*

LICENSE OR CERTIFICATE	DATE OF LATEST LICENSE OR CERTIFICATE	STATE OR OTHER LICENSING AGENCY
1)		
2)		

35 Do you speak or read a language other than English *(include sign language)?* **Applicants for jobs that require a language other than English may be given an interview conducted solely in that language.**   **YES**   **NO**   If **"YES"**, list each language and place an **"X"** in each column that applies to you. If **"NO"**, go to **36.**

LANGUAGE(S)	CAN PREPARE AND GIVE LECTURES Fluently	With Difficulty	CAN SPEAK AND UNDERSTAND Fluently	Passably	CAN TRANSLATE ARTICLES Into English	From English	CAN READ ARTICLES FOR OWN USE Easily	With Difficulty
1)								
2)								

REFERENCES

36 List three people who are not related to you and are not supervisors you listed under **24** who know your qualifications and fitness for the kind of job for which you are applying. At least **one** should know you well on a personal basis.

FULL NAME OF REFERENCE	TELEPHONE NUMBER(S) *(Include Area Code)*	PRESENT BUSINESS OR HOME ADDRESS *(Number, street and city)*	STATE	ZIP CODE
1)				
2)				
3)				

Page 3

BACKGROUND INFORMATION-- *You must answer each question in this section before we can process your application.*

		YES	NO
37	Are you a citizen of the United States? *(In most cases you must be a U.S. citizen to be hired. You will be required to submit proof of identity and citizenship at the time you are hired.)* If **"NO"**, give the country or countries you are a citizen of: _____		

> **NOTE: It is important that you give complete and truthful answers to questions 38 through 44.** If you answer **"YES"** to any of them, provide your explanation(s) in **Item 45. Include** convictions resulting from a plea of nolo contendere *(no contest)*. **Omit:** 1) traffic fines of $100.00 or less; 2) any violation of law committed before your 16th birthday; 3) any violation of law committed before your 18th birthday, if finally decided in juvenile court or under a Youth Offender law; 4) any conviction set aside under the Federal Youth Corrections Act or similar State law; 5) any conviction whose record was expunged under Federal or State law. We will consider the date, facts, and circumstances of each event you list. In most cases you can still be considered for Federal jobs. However, **if you fail to tell the truth or fail to list all relevant** events or circumstances, this may be grounds for not hiring you, for firing you after you begin work, or for criminal prosecution (18 USC 1001).

		YES	NO
38	During the last **10 years**, were you **fired from any job** for any reason, did you **quit after being told that you would be fired**, or did you leave by mutual agreement because of specific problems?.		
39	Have you **ever** been convicted of, or forfeited collateral for **any felony violation?** *(Generally, a felony is defined as any violation of law punishable by imprisonment of longer than one year, except for violations called misdemeanors under State law which are punishable by imprisonment of two years or less.)*		
40	Have you **ever** been convicted of, or forfeited collateral for **any firearms or explosives violation?**		
41	Are you **now** under charges for **any violation of law?**		
42	During the **last 10 years** have you forfeited collateral, been convicted, been imprisoned, been on probation, or been on parole? Do **not** include violations reported in 39, 40, or 41, above.		
43	Have you **ever** been convicted by a military **court-martial?** If no military service, answer **"NO"**.		
44	Are you **delinquent** on any Federal debt? *(Include delinquencies arising from Federal taxes, loans, overpayment of benefits, and other debts to the U.S. Government **plus** defaults on Federally guaranteed or insured loans such as student and home mortgage loans.)*		

45 If **"YES"** in: 38 - Explain for each job the problem(s) and your reason(s) for leaving. Give the employer's name and address.

39 through 43 - Explain each violation. Give place of occurrence and name/address of police or court involved.

44 - Explain the type, length and amount of the delinquency or default, and steps you are taking to correct errors or repay the debt. Give any identification number associated with the debt and the address of the Federal agency involved.

NOTE: If you need more space, use a sheet of paper, and include the item number.

Item No.	Date (Mo./Yr.)	Explanation	Mailing Address
			Name of Employer, Police, Court, or Federal Agency
			City State ZIP Code
			Name of Employer, Police, Court, or Federal Agency
			City State ZIP Code

		YES	NO
46	Do you receive, or have you ever applied for retirement pay, pension, or other pay based on military, Federal civilian, or District of Columbia Government service?		
47	Do any of your relatives work for the United States Government or the United States Armed Forces? Include: *father; mother; husband; wife; son; daughter; brother; sister; uncle; aunt; first cousin; nephew; niece; father-in-law; mother-in-law; son-in-law; daughter-in-law; brother-in-law; sister-in-law; stepfather; stepmother; stepson; stepdaughter; stepbrother; stepsister; half brother; and half sister.*		

If **"YES"**, provide details below. If you need more space, use a sheet of paper.

Name	Relationship	Department, Agency or Branch of Armed Forces

SIGNATURE, CERTIFICATION, AND RELEASE OF INFORMATION

YOU MUST SIGN THIS APPLICATION. **Read the following carefully before you sign.**

- A false statement on any part of your application may be grounds for not hiring you, or for firing you after you begin work. Also, you may be punished by fine or imprisonment (U.S. Code, title 18, section 1001).
- If you are a male born after December 31, 1959 you must be registered with the Selective Service System or have a valid exemption in order to be eligible for Federal employment. You will be required to certify as to your status at the time of appointment.
- I **understand** that any information I give may be investigated as allowed by law or Presidential order.
- I **consent** to the release of information about my ability and fitness for Federal employment by *employers, schools, law enforcement agencies and other individuals and organizations, to investigators, personnel staffing specialists, and other authorized employees of the Federal Government.*
- I **certify** that, to the best of my knowledge and belief, **all** of my statements are true, correct, complete, and made in good faith.

48 SIGNATURE *(Sign each application in dark ink)*	**49** DATE SIGNED *(Month, day, year)*

*U.S. Government Printing Office: 1988-241-175/80208

Standard Form 171-A— *Continuation Sheet for SF 171*

Form Approved:
OMB No. 3206-0012

• Attach all SF 171-A's to your application at the top of page 3.

1. Name *(Last, First, Middle Initial)*	2. Social Security Number
3. Job Title or Announcement Number You Are Applying For	4. Date Completed

ADDITIONAL WORK EXPERIENCE BLOCKS

☐ Name and address of employer's organization *(include ZIP Code, if known)*

Dates employed *(give month, day and year)*

From: To:

Average number of hours per week

Number of employees you supervised

Salary or earnings

Starting $ per

Ending $ per

Your reason for leaving

Your immediate supervisor

Name   Area Code   Telephone No.

Exact title of your job

If Federal employment *(civilian or military)* list series, grade or rank, and, if promoted in this job, the date of your last promotion

Description of work: Describe your specific duties, responsibilities and accomplishments in this job, **including** the job title(s) of any employees you supervised. *If you describe more than one type of work (for example, carpentry and painting, or personnel and budget), write the approximate percentage of time you spent doing each.*

For Agency Use (skill codes, etc.)

☐ Name and address of employer's organization *(include ZIP Code, if known)*

Dates employed *(give month, day and year)*

From: To:

Average number of hours per week

Number of employees you supervised

Salary or earnings

Starting $ per

Ending $ per

Your reason for leaving

Your immediate supervisor

Name   Area Code   Telephone No.

Exact title of your job

If Federal employment *(civilian or military)* list series, grade or rank, and, if promoted in this job, the date of your last promotion

Description of work: Describe your specific duties, responsibilities and accomplishments in this job, **including** the job title(s) of any employees you supervised. *If you describe more than one type of work (for example, carpentry and painting, or personnel and budget), write the approximate percentage of time you spent doing each.*

For Agency Use (skill codes, etc.)

THE FEDERAL GOVERNMENT IS AN EQUAL OPPORTUNITY EMPLOYER
PREVIOUS EDITION USABLE

Standard Form 171-A (Rev. 6-88)
U.S. Office of Personnel Management
FPM Chapter 295

STATEMENT OF INTEREST

The Board of Examiners for the Foreign Service requires that all applicants for the Foreign Service Written Examination submit a brief (one typed page maximum) Statement of Interest in a career in the Foreign Service. The statement should be TYPED or WRITTEN NEATLY in ink, with the applicant's name in the upper right-hand corner of the page. The Statement of Interest should explain the applicant's motivation for taking the Foreign Service Written Examination and comment on the quotation reproduced at the top of the form provided. A reduced facsimile of this form appears below.

Name: _____

Address: _____

Statement of Interest

Secretary of State James A. Baker III has called for "a new generation of diplomats who understand the policy implications of science, oceanography and the environment, economics and economic statesmanship, who can and will think broadly about the impact of computers, agricultural technology and nuclear science in a changing world. At the same time, Foreign Service officers will continue to perform their traditional functions of political and economic reporting, administrative management and providing consular services to American citizens and foreign residents." In the space below, describe your interest in such a career.

ANSWER SHEET FOR SAMPLE WRITTEN EXAMINATION QUESTIONS

Tear out this answer sheet and use it to mark your answers to the official sample written examination questions that follow. Mark your answers by completely blackening the circle of the answer you choose. Mark only one answer for each question.

Knowledge Questions

1 Ⓐ Ⓑ Ⓒ Ⓓ   7 Ⓐ Ⓑ Ⓒ Ⓓ   13 Ⓐ Ⓑ Ⓒ Ⓓ   19 Ⓐ Ⓑ Ⓒ Ⓓ   25 Ⓐ Ⓑ Ⓒ Ⓓ

2 Ⓐ Ⓑ Ⓒ Ⓓ   8 Ⓐ Ⓑ Ⓒ Ⓓ   14 Ⓐ Ⓑ Ⓒ Ⓓ   20 Ⓐ Ⓑ Ⓒ Ⓓ   26 Ⓐ Ⓑ Ⓒ Ⓓ

3 Ⓐ Ⓑ Ⓒ Ⓓ   9 Ⓐ Ⓑ Ⓒ Ⓓ   15 Ⓐ Ⓑ Ⓒ Ⓓ   21 Ⓐ Ⓑ Ⓒ Ⓓ

4 Ⓐ Ⓑ Ⓒ Ⓓ   10 Ⓐ Ⓑ Ⓒ Ⓓ   16 Ⓐ Ⓑ Ⓒ Ⓓ   22 Ⓐ Ⓑ Ⓒ Ⓓ

5 Ⓐ Ⓑ Ⓒ Ⓓ   11 Ⓐ Ⓑ Ⓒ Ⓓ   17 Ⓐ Ⓑ Ⓒ Ⓓ   23 Ⓐ Ⓑ Ⓒ Ⓓ

6 Ⓐ Ⓑ Ⓒ Ⓓ   12 Ⓐ Ⓑ Ⓒ Ⓓ   18 Ⓐ Ⓑ Ⓒ Ⓓ   24 Ⓐ Ⓑ Ⓒ Ⓓ

English Expression Questions

1 Ⓐ Ⓑ Ⓒ Ⓓ Ⓔ   6 Ⓐ Ⓑ Ⓒ Ⓓ Ⓔ   11 Ⓐ Ⓑ Ⓒ Ⓓ Ⓔ   16 Ⓐ Ⓑ Ⓒ Ⓓ Ⓔ   21 Ⓐ Ⓑ Ⓒ Ⓓ Ⓔ

2 Ⓐ Ⓑ Ⓒ Ⓓ Ⓔ   7 Ⓐ Ⓑ Ⓒ Ⓓ Ⓔ   12 Ⓐ Ⓑ Ⓒ Ⓓ Ⓔ   17 Ⓐ Ⓑ Ⓒ Ⓓ Ⓔ   22 Ⓐ Ⓑ Ⓒ Ⓓ Ⓔ

3 Ⓐ Ⓑ Ⓒ Ⓓ Ⓔ   8 Ⓐ Ⓑ Ⓒ Ⓓ Ⓔ   13 Ⓐ Ⓑ Ⓒ Ⓓ Ⓔ   18 Ⓐ Ⓑ Ⓒ Ⓓ Ⓔ   23 Ⓐ Ⓑ Ⓒ Ⓓ Ⓔ

4 Ⓐ Ⓑ Ⓒ Ⓓ Ⓔ   9 Ⓐ Ⓑ Ⓒ Ⓓ Ⓔ   14 Ⓐ Ⓑ Ⓒ Ⓓ Ⓔ   19 Ⓐ Ⓑ Ⓒ Ⓓ Ⓔ

5 Ⓐ Ⓑ Ⓒ Ⓓ Ⓔ   10 Ⓐ Ⓑ Ⓒ Ⓓ Ⓔ   15 Ⓐ Ⓑ Ⓒ Ⓓ Ⓔ   20 Ⓐ Ⓑ Ⓒ Ⓓ Ⓔ

TEAR HERE

SAMPLE WRITTEN EXAMINATION QUESTIONS

To familiarize you with representative types of questions used in the Foreign Service written examination, the following sample questions are provided. An answer key can be found on page 36.

KNOWLEDGE QUESTIONS

Directions: Each of the questions or incomplete statements below is followed by four suggested answers or completions. Select the one that is best in each case and then blacken the corresponding space on the answer sheet. Some sets of questions are presented with material such as reading passages, plans, graphs, tables, etc. Answers to such questions may require interpretation of the material and/or outside knowledge relevant to its content.

Knowledge Area: **The historical antecedents of international affairs (e.g., Islam, colonialism, industrial revolution) to aid understanding of foreign governments and societies.**

1. All of the following are necessary attributes of a nation-state EXCEPT
   (A) occupying a definite territory
   (B) having an organized government
   (C) using predominantly a single language
   (D) possessing internal and external sovereignty

2. Many of the developing nations that achieved independence after 1945 have become noted for their chronic instability. Which of the following factors generally contributes LEAST to this instability?
   (A) The rise of political factionalism
   (B) The large numbers of unassimilated ethnic and/or religious minorities
   (C) The artificiality of national boundaries drawn by former colonial rulers
   (D) The continued use of administrative systems inherited from colonial powers

Knowledge Area: **World geography (e.g., location of countries, significant physical features, distribution of key natural resources, geography-based national rivalries and alliances) in order to understand the geographic context of foreign relations and U.S. foreign policy.**

Questions 3 and 4 refer to the following map.

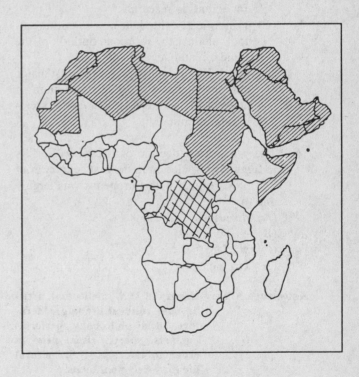

3. The cross-hatched country is a leading exporter of which of the following primary products:
   (A) Bauxite
   (B) Textile products
   (C) Copper
   (D) Diamonds

4. The shaded area on the map above identifies, as of the mid-1970s, members of which of the following?
   (A) The Organization of Petroleum Exporting Countries (OPEC)
   (B) The Arab League
   (C) The Central Treaty Organization (CENTO)
   (D) The Organization of African Unity (OAU)

Knowledge Area: Major events, institutions, and movements in the history of the United States (e.g., slavery, Constitutional Convention, Civil War, Great Depression, Civil Rights Movement) to facilitate understanding the U.S. system of government.

5. The Scopes trial of 1925 took on national significance because it
   (A) marked the first time that a U.S. court had ruled that the theory of evolution was correct
   (B) led to the first federal appropriation of aid for scientific research
   (C) symbolically pitted the new scientific outlook against the religious outlook of the Fundamentalists
   (D) was William Jennings Bryan's last major attempt to attract national attention in an attempt to capture the Democratic presidential nomination

6. The precipitous decline of the New World's indigenous population in the first century after its initial contact with Europeans was largely due to
   (A) disease
   (B) enslavement
   (C) warfare
   (D) famine

Knowledge Area: History of U.S. intellectual, artistic, and cultural life (e.g., literature, social philosophy, performing arts, sports, visual arts) in order to interpret U.S. cultural life for foreign nationals.

7. Who said, "In the future, everyone will be famous for at least 15 minutes"?
   (A) Mike Wallace
   (B) Andy Warhol
   (C) Barbara Walters
   (D) Marshall McLuhan

8. Milton Babbitt, John Harrison, Gunther Schuller, and John Cage are best known as
   (A) conductors of symphonic orchestras
   (B) ballet choreographers
   (C) playwrights
   (D) contemporary composers

Knowledge Area: Social, political, and economic trends in the United States (e.g., women and minority roles, demographic shifts, patterns of immigration, information age, biomedicine).

9. All of the following circumstances have contributed to the current emphasis on protecting the U.S. environment from toxic wastes EXCEPT:
   (A) Safe places to store toxic wastes in the United States have become scarce.
   (B) Research has increased knowledge of the toxicity of many widely used chemicals.
   (C) The amount of wastes of all kinds has grown.
   (D) Deregulation has made it easier for the public to purchase and use toxic substances.

10. In some areas of the United States, the presence of Southeast Asian refugees has produced considerable tension for which of the following reasons?
    I.   Fear of their impact on welfare rolls
    II. Anti-Asian racism
    III. Resentment of their entrepreneurial competition
    IV. Perceptions of them as clannish
    (A) I only
    (B) III only
    (C) I and II only
    (D) I, II, III, IV

Knowledge Area: Contemporary cultural trends in the United States (e.g., film, music, sports, magazines, newspapers, clothing and lifestyles).

11. Which of the following columnists is known for the conservative tone of his or her work?
    (A) Russell Baker
    (B) Carl Rowan
    (C) Meg Greenfield
    (D) George Will

12. To the argument that television gives a truer account of what happens in a courtroom than does any other news medium, all of the following objections may reasonably be advanced EXCEPT:
    (A) The television director, by choosing the image on which the camera focuses, engages in a process of selection just as a newspaper reporter or editor does.
    (B) A pictorial medium has difficulty in dealing with abstract ideas, such as points of law, which are often the most important part of a court proceeding.
    (C) Television inevitably becomes an "actor" in the courtroom proceedings and thereby changes the event as it records it.
    (D) Television reporters, because they must concentrate on the technical and theatrical aspects of electronic journalism, have little time to master the complexities of a court cast.

Knowledge Area: **U.S. political process and its impact on policy (e.g., role of special interest groups, the media, political parties).**

13. In the United States, campaigns for major public offices are increasingly being controlled by
    (A) political action committees
    (B) media consultants
    (C) candidates' press agents
    (D) local political party chairpersons

14. The major reason that it is easy to block a bill in Congress but difficult to enact one is which of the following?
    (A) Well-organized opposing political parties in Congress
    (B) The decentralized committee structure of Congress
    (C) The influence of pork-barrel politics on congressional voting
    (D) Institutional conflict between Congress and the President

Knowledge Area: **U.S. Constitution and the structure of the U.S. Government (e.g., separation of powers, functions of cabinet departments, lawmaking, federalism, appropriation process).**

15. Two key precepts of the Constitution that were not present in the Articles of Confederation were to
    (A) buffer the government from the immediate impact of popular impulse and to extend the vote to all
    (B) promote the power of individual states over that of the federal government and to keep the branches of the federal government separate but linked
    (C) keep the President closely tied to the will of the majority and to promote the power of individual states over that of the federal government
    (D) buffer the government from the immediate impact of popular impulse and to keep the branches of the federal government separate but linked

16. Which of the following statements is true about executive privilege?
    (A) It allows the President to withhold certain information from Congress and the courts.
    (B) It protects members of the executive branch from prosecution for any acts committed in the course of performing their jobs.
    (C) It is the concept that underlies the President's use of a pocket veto during a session of Congress.
    (D) It protects the members of the Cabinet when the President faces impeachment proceedings.

Knowledge Area: **U.S. economic systems, its institutions and philosophical principles, to aid in interpreting U.S. policies and actions to foreign nationals.**

17. If the Federal Reserve were to adopt an accommodative policy and then decrease the discount rate and buy government securities in the open market, it would most likely be responding to
    (A) rising interest rates by increasing the money supply
    (B) rising interest rates by decreasing the money supply
    (C) falling interest rates by increasing the money supply
    (D) falling interest rates by decreasing the money supply

18. In the United States, the last 25 years of the 19th century were characterized by several violent conflicts between capital and labor, which by 1900 resulted in
   (A) the use of federal court injunctions to jail strikers without a jury trial
   (B) the intensive participation of the American Federation of Labor (AFL) in politics
   (C) the unionization of the vast majority of factory workers
   (D) general acceptance of the closed shop by employers

Knowledge Area: U.S. educational system (e.g., public versus private institutions, scholarships).

19. All of the following were objectives of the common, or public, school movement of 1840–1860 EXCEPT:
   (A) primary school education for all white Americans regardless of sex
   (B) a professionally trained teaching force
   (C) establishment of a uniform national curriculum
   (D) introduction of a new pedagogy based on the idea that children were capable of infinite improvement

20. In the United States, at which of the following levels of education are there more privately than publicly controlled schools?
   I. Elementary
   II. Secondary
   III. Postsecondary
   (A) III only
   (B) I and II only
   (C) II and III only
   (D) I, II, and III

Knowledge Area: Foreign political systems (e.g., parliamentary, federal, dictatorship, one-party).

21. A major difference between U.S. political parties and political parties in European parliamentary systems is that
   (A) European parties are less ideologically rigid
   (B) U.S. parties have stronger local organizations
   (C) European parties exercise more discipline over their elected representatives in the legislature
   (D) U.S. parties better represent special interests

22. A distinguishing feature of the parliamentary form of government is that
   (A) parliament is the sole respository of legitimacy and may not delegate governmental authority to regional or local units
   (B) no final action may be taken on a bill until all members of parliament have had an opportunity to speak either for or against it
   (C) members of the government are not allowed to take part in parliamentary debates that involve appropriations
   (D) parliament has the power to require the prime minister to resign or call for an election

Knowledge Area: Basic principles of economics (e.g., supply and demand, money supply, international trade, comparative economic systems).

Question 23 refers to the following graph.

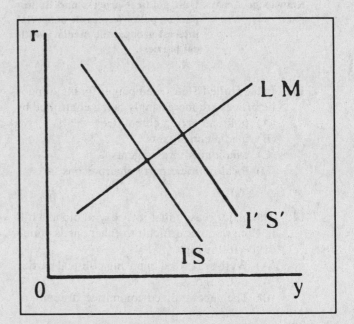

23. In the graph above, the shift of the IS curve to the new position, $I'S'$, illustrates the Keynesian proposition that increases in both gross national product (GNP) and interest rates could result from increases in
   (A) the money supply
   (B) the demand for money
   (C) government spending
   (D) taxes

24. A ''dirty float'' system is one in which
  (A) exchange rates are permitted to fluctuate freely
  (B) governments act to influence the exchange value of their own currencies
  (C) assets of foreign banks are undervalued
  (D) exchange rates are determined by an automatic gold standard

Knowledge Area: **Major contemporary international economic and commercial issues (e.g., unemployment, inflation, trade deficit, Third World debt) in order to understand the impact of economic conditions on a foreign country and on U.S. programs and policy interest.**

25. To conform with the chronological sequence most commonly followed by U.S. manufacturers that are launching international operations, the activities below should be undertaken in which of the following sequences?

  I. Establish a foreign sales branch.
  II. Initiate overseas assembly of parts manufactured in the United States.
  III. Begin full-scale manufacturing overseas.
  IV. Export U.S. goods through a foreign distributor.
  (A) I, II, III, IV
  (B) I, IV, III, II
  (C) III, IV, II, I
  (D) IV, I, II, III

26. All of the following statements concerning dumping in international trade are correct EXCEPT:
  (A) It is defined as selling at less than fair value.
  (B) It forms the basis for a claim in the World Court.
  (C) It constitutes an unfair trade practice under GATT.
  (D) It is subject to U.S. law.

ENGLISH EXPRESSION

Directions: The following sentences contain problems in grammar, usage, diction (choice of words), and idiom.

Some sentences are correct.
No sentence contains more than one error.

You will find that the error, if there is one, is underlined and lettered. Assume that all other elements of the sentence are correct and cannot be changed. In choosing answers, follow the requirements of standard written English.

If there is an error, select the one underlined part that must be changed in order to make the sentence correct, and fill in the corresponding oval on the answer sheet.

If there is no error, mark answer space E.

EXAMPLES:

  I. He spoke <u>bluntly</u> and <u>angrily</u> to <u>we</u> <u>spectators</u>.
          A   B   C   D

  <u>No error</u>
  E

  II. She <u>works</u> <u>every day</u> <u>so that she</u> would become
          A   B   C

  <u>financially</u> independent in her old age. <u>No er-</u>
     D   E

  <u>ror</u>

SAMPLE ANSWERS

I. Ⓐ Ⓑ ● Ⓓ Ⓔ
II. ● Ⓑ Ⓒ Ⓓ Ⓔ

1. Paul Klee <u>awaited</u> many long years <u>to receive</u>
                   A   B
the recognition <u>due</u> <u>him</u> as a painter. <u>No error</u>
                 C   D   E

2. Acting in skits or plays <u>have frequently proved</u>
                                  A
of great benefit to mentally ill patients, <u>per-</u>
                                             B
<u>haps because</u> <u>such activity</u> allows them to act
     B   C
out <u>their own</u> inner conflicts. <u>No error</u>
       D   E

3. <u>According to</u> the theory, some types of human
        A
behavior <u>once considered</u> the result of great
            B
psychological disturbance <u>is in reality</u> caused
                              C
by a chemical imbalance <u>within</u> the body. <u>No</u>
                            D   E
<u>error</u>

4. The author's novels <u>may seem</u> <u>somewhat</u> old
                       A   B

and musty, but <u>their</u> form <u>survives</u> in modern
                C   D

popular novels. <u>No error</u>
                E

5. No sooner <u>had</u> the Great Fire burned <u>itself out</u>
           A   B

<u>than</u> plans were <u>laid</u> for the rebuilding of the
 C   D

city. <u>No error</u>
      E

6. The candidate directed <u>her appeal</u> to the young
                         A

once <u>realizing that</u> <u>she could not win</u> <u>without</u>
      B   C   D

their votes. <u>No error</u>
          E

7. <u>Because of the increasing</u> popularity of our na-
          A

tional parks, the park service must <u>deal with</u>
                            B

the almost unsolvable problem of <u>how you can</u>
                             C

let every visitor <u>in and still keep</u> the wilderness
                  D

intact. <u>No error</u>
        E

8. Herschel's catalogs of stars, <u>first published in</u>
                      A

the <u>late</u> eighteenth century, <u>did much</u> <u>to</u> pro-
   B   C   D

gress astronomy. <u>No error</u>
            E

Directions: In each of the following sentences, some part or all of the sentence is underlined. Below each sentence you will find five ways of phrasing the underlined part. Select the answer that produces the most effective sentence, one that is clear and exact without awkwardness or ambiguity, and fill in the corresponding oval on your answer sheet. In choosing answers, follow the requirements of standard written English. Choose the answer that best expresses the meaning of the original sentence.

Answer (A) is always the same as the underlined part. Choose answer (A) if you think the original sentence needs no revision.

EXAMPLE:

Laura Ingalls Wilder published her first book <u>and she was sixty-five years old then.</u>
- (A) and she was sixty-five years old then
- (B) when she was sixty-five years old
- (C) at age sixty-five years old
- (D) upon reaching sixty-five years
- (E) at the time when she was sixty-five

SAMPLE ANSWERS

Ⓐ ● Ⓒ Ⓓ Ⓔ

9. Finally, public and legal pressures forced the auto manufacturers to abandon <u>racing, and they would thus then develop more rapidly</u> pollution controls and safety devices.
- (A) racing, and they would thus then develop more rapidly
- (B) racing and exchange it for more rapid development of
- (C) racing, and thus they would favor the more rapid development of
- (D) racing to be developing more rapidly
- (E) racing in favor of more rapid development of

10. Almost all folk singers have several ballads from the Child collection in their repertoires, <u>whether they know it or not.</u>
- (A) whether they know it or not
- (B) whether or not they know anything about it
- (C) whether knowing it or not
- (D) whether with their knowledge or without
- (E) whether knowingly or unknowingly

11. Because extremely low-frequency radio waves can penetrate deep water, <u>much research has, as a result, been devoted to their potential use in underwater communications.</u>
- (A) much research has, as a result, been devoted to their potential use in underwater communications
- (B) much research on their potential use in underwater communications has resulted
- (C) it has resulted in the devotion of much research to their potential use in underwater communications
- (D) devotion of much research to using them in underwater communications has taken place
- (E) much research has been devoted to their potential use in underwater communications

12. They have been sent to help people of developing countries, and much useful work has been done by members of the Peace Corps.

(A) They have been sent to help people of developing countries, and much useful work has been done by members of the Peace Corps.

(B) Members of the Peace Corps have been sent to help people of developing countries and much useful work has been done.

(C) They have been sent to help people of developing countries, and members of the Peace Corps have done much useful work.

(D) Sent to help people of developing countries, members of the Peace Corps have done much useful work.

(E) Having been sent to help people of developing countries, much useful work has been done by members of the Peace Corps.

13. Horseshoe crabs are not crabs at all; its nearest living relative is the spider.

(A) its nearest living relative is the spider

(B) their nearest living relatives are the spiders

(C) the nearest living relatives are the spider

(D) their nearest living relative is spiders

(E) its nearest living relatives are spiders

14. Drops of water acting like prisms refract sunlight, which process causes rainbows.

(A) sunlight, which process causes

(B) sunlight, and it causes

(C) sunlight, which is the cause of

(D) sunlight and thus cause

(E) sunlight and this, therefore, causes

Directions: In each of the following questions you are given a complete sentence to be rephrased according to the directions that follow it. You should rephrase the sentence mentally to save time, although you may make notes in your test book if you wish.

Below each sentence and its directions are listed words or phrases that may occur in your revised sentence. When you have thought out a good sentence, look in the choices A through E for the word or entire phrase that is included in your revised sentence, and fill in the corresponding oval on the answer sheet. The word or phrase you choose should be the most accurate and most nearly complete of all the choices given, and should be part of a sentence that meets the requirements of standard written English.

Of course, a number of different sentences can be obtained if the sentence is revised according to the directions, and not all of these possibilities can be included in only five choices. If you should find that you have thought

of a sentence that contains none of the words or phrases listed in the choices, you should attempt to rephrase the sentence again so that it includes a word or phrase that is listed.

Although the directions may at times require you to change the relationship between parts of the sentence or to make slight changes in meaning in other ways, make only those changes that the directions require: that is, keep the meaning the same, or as nearly the same as the directions permit. If you think that more than one good sentence can be made according to the directions, select the sentence that is most exact, effective, and natural in phrasing and construction.

EXAMPLE:

Sentence: Coming to the city as a young man, he found a job as a newspaper reporter.

Directions: Substitute He came for Coming.

(A) and so he found

(B) and found

(C) and there he found

(D) and then finding

(E) and had found

Your rephrased sentence will probably read: "He came to the city as a young man and found a job as a newspaper reporter." This sentence contains the correct answer: (B) and found. A sentence which used one of the alternate phrases would change the meaning or intention of the original sentence, would be a poorly written sentence, or would be less effective than another possible revision.

15. Root feeding is necessary for the survival of many old trees.

Begin with Many old trees need.

(A) for their surviving

(B) so they survive

(C) to survive

(D) in surviving

(E) as a survival measure

16. Only wealthy people can afford the luxury of hiring architects to design their homes.

Begin with Hiring an architect.

(A) and only

(B) therefore only

(C) luxury that only

(D) luxury; only

(E) something that only

17. The term "institutionalized racism" was coined by Stokely Carmichael and Charles V. Hamilton in their book *Black Power*.

Begin with in their book.

(A) has been coined
(B) they coined
(C) coined
(D) is coined
(E) was coined

18. The disturbance to the ecology of the area that the wastes from the new mill could create was mentioned in the article; however, greater emphasis was placed on the contributions that the mill could make to the economic development of the area.

Begin with The article placed less.

(A) rather than on the contributions
(B) than on the disturbance
(C) instead of the disturbance
(D) than on the contributions
(E) than on the ecology

19. The most extensive changes in the English language have come about through contact with different cultures, rather than through gradual changes in meaning.

Substitute about, not through for about through.

(A) but by contact
(B) but through contact
(C) rather by contact
(D) rather than by contact
(E) although through contact

20. Though, for the most part, German shepherds are intelligent and well-behaved, they often make difficult pets because of their tendency to recognize only one master.

Begin with The tendency.

(A) it is often difficult for them
(B) for difficulty in their
(C) them often have difficulty with
(D) them difficult for
(E) them difficult

Directions: In each of the following questions you are given four sentences and a question that asks for the best sequence to make a clear, sensible paragraph. Choose the correct option that reflects the ordering of the sentences that represents the best order for a clear, sensible paragraph.

21. I. Women are responsible for much of this wealth.

II. Phyllis Wheatley, the poet, was one of the earliest to write of her life.

III. Since the eighteenth century, Black women in America have been writing the stories of their lives.

IV. Although most readers have heard of the lives of Booker T. Washington, Malcolm X, and Richard Wright, they are generally ignorant of the wealth of Black autobiography.

Which of the following presents the best sequence of the sentences above to make a clear, sensible paragraph?

(A) I, III, II, IV
(B) II, III, IV, I
(C) III, I, II, IV
(D) III, II, I, IV
(E) IV, I, III, II

22. I. However, after Tito's death, the various ethnic, linguistic, and religious groups in Yugoslavia began to assert their independence.

II. Yugoslavia was formed as a federation of disparate states after the Second World War.

III. The charismatic domination of Marshal Tito was the major force binding this federation.

IV. In the last decade of the 20th century, the unity of Yugoslavia remains an open question.

Which of the following presents the best sequence of the sentences above to make a clear, sensible paragraph?

(A) I, IV, III, II
(B) II, I, III, IV
(C) II, III, I, IV
(D) IV, II, I, III
(E) IV, III, II, I

23.

I. No single group has been able to rest easy in its hegemony, however, because one or more of the other groups was always ready to dispute the first group's right to rule.

II. The Middle East's relatively dense population, its scarcity of water and arable land, and its location in a crossroads between East and West, North and South, have all contributed to this conflict.

III. Throughout recorded history, the Middle East has been an area of strife between peoples of different ethnic and religious backgrounds.

IV. Persians, Kurds, Arabs, Jews, Turks, Christians, Shi'ite and Sunni Muslims, all have struggled to gain, hold, or regain power over the territory in the Middle East.

Which of the following presents the best sequence of the sentences above to make a clear, sensible paragraph?

(A) I, II, III, IV
(B) II, III, I, IV
(C) III, I, IV, II
(D) III, II, IV, I
(E) IV, II, III, I

ANSWER KEY FOR SAMPLE TEST QUESTIONS

Knowledge Answer Key

1. C	11. D	21. C
2. D	12. D	22. D
3. C	13. B	23. C
4. B	14. B	24. B
5. C	15. D	25. D
6. A	16. A	26. B
7. B	17. A	
8. D	18. A	
9. D	19. C	
10. D	20. A	

English Expression Answer Key

1. A	11. E	21. E
2. A	12. D	22. C
3. C	13. B	23. D
4. E	14. D	
5. E	15. C	
6. B	16. C	
7. C	17. C	
8. D	18. D	
9. E	19. B	
10. A	20. E	

BIOGRAPHIC INFORMATION QUESTIONNAIRE

The Biographic Information Questionnaire, which constitutes the third part of the written exam, is set up to look like a multiple-choice test and is timed like a test, but it is not a test at all. There are no right or wrong answers. You cannot study for the biographic information questionnaire. Your preparation consists solely in gathering statistical records from your school career and in recalling what you have achieved through a lifetime of student and post-student years.

The Biographic Information Questionnaire consists of 120 questions to be answered in 30 minutes. Some questions will refer to your high school days. They ask about your best and worst grades, your favorite courses, extracurricular activities, etc. A series of questions similar to the high school questions in their scope and in the topics they cover will refer to college days. The remaining questions refer to your working life or college relationships. These questions ask for your assessment of the impression you make upon others. About half of the questions ask what you think your peers think of you; the other half ask similar questions with respect to your supervisors or teachers. You will not have much time to dwell on these questions. Just do your best to answer candidly and consistently.

The Foreign Service does not distribute official sample questions for this part of the written test. However, the model questions below are illustrative and typical.

1. My favorite subject in high school was
   (A) math
   (B) English
   (C) physical education
   (D) social studies
   (E) science

2. My GPA upon graduation from high school (on a 4.0 scale) was
   (A) lower than 2.51
   (B) 2.51 to 2.80
   (C) 2.81 to 3.25
   (D) 3.26 to 3.60
   (E) higher than 3.60

3. In my second year of high school I was absent
   (A) never
   (B) not more than 3 days
   (C) 4 to 10 days
   (D) more often than 10 days
   (E) do not recall

4. My best grades in high school were in
   (A) art
   (B) math
   (C) English
   (D) social studies
   (E) music

5. While in high school, I participated in
   (A) one sport
   (B) two sports and one other extracurricular activity
   (C) three nonathletic extracurricular activities
   (D) no extracurricular activities
   (E) other than the above

6. During my senior year in high school I held a paying job
   (A) 0 hours a week
   (B) 1 to 5 hours weekly
   (C) 6 to 10 hours a week
   (D) 11 to 16 hours a week
   (E) more than 16 hours a week

7. The number of semesters in which I failed a course in high school was
   (A) none
   (B) one
   (C) two or three
   (D) four or five
   (E) more than five

8. In high school I did volunteer work
   (A) more than 10 hours a week
   (B) 5 to 10 hours a week on a regular basis
   (C) sporadically
   (D) seldom
   (E) not at all

9. My general area of concentration in college was
   (A) performing arts
   (B) humanities
   (C) social sciences
   (D) business
   (E) none of the above

10. At graduation from college, my age was
    (A) under 20
    (B) 20
    (C) 21 to 24
    (D) 25 to 29
    (E) 30 or over

11. My standing in my graduating class was in the
    (A) bottom third
    (B) middle third
    (C) top third
    (D) top quarter
    (E) top 10 percent

12. In college, I was elected to a major office in a class or in a club or organization
    (A) more than six times
    (B) four or five times
    (C) two or three times
    (D) once
    (E) never

13. In comparison to my peers, I cut classes
    (A) much less often than most
    (B) somewhat less often than most
    (C) just about the same as most
    (D) somewhat more often than most
    (E) much more often than most

14. The campus activities in which I participated most were
    (A) social service
    (B) political
    (C) literary
    (D) did not participate in campus activities
    (E) did not participate in any of these activities

15. My name appeared on the dean's list
    (A) never
    (B) once or twice
    (C) in three or more terms
    (D) in more terms than it did not appear
    (E) do not remember

16. The volunteer work I did while in college was predominantly
    (A) health care related
    (B) religious
    (C) political
    (D) educational
    (E) did not volunteer

17. While a college student, I spent most of my summers
    (A) in summer school
    (B) earning money
    (C) traveling
    (D) in service activities
    (E) resting

18. My college education was financed
    (A) entirely by my parents
    (B) by my parents and my own earnings
    (C) by scholarships, loans, and my own earnings
    (D) by my parents and loans
    (E) by a combination of sources not listed above

19. In the college classroom I was considered
    (A) a listener
    (B) an occasional contributor
    (C) an average participant
    (D) a frequent contributor
    (E) a leader

20. The person on campus whom I most admired was
    (A) another student
    (B) an athletic coach
    (C) a teacher
    (D) an administrator
    (E) a journalist

21. Of the skills I developed at college, the one I value most is
    (A) foreign language ability
    (B) oral expression
    (C) writing skills
    (D) facility with computers
    (E) analytical skills

22. I made my greatest mark in college through my
    (A) athletic prowess
    (B) success in performing arts
    (C) academic success
    (D) partying reputation
    (E) conciliatory skill with my peers

23. My cumulative GPA (on a 4.0 scale) in courses in my major was
    (A) lower than 3.00
    (B) 3.00 to 3.25
    (C) 3.26 to 3.50
    (D) 3.51 to 3.75
    (E) higher than 3.75

24. While in college I
    (A) worked full-time and was a part-time student
    (B) worked 20 hours a week and was a full-time student
    (C) worked 20 hours a week and was a part-time student
    (D) was a full-time student working more than 10 but less than 20 hours a week
    (E) was a full-time student

25. In the past six months, I have been late to work (or school)
    (A) never
    (B) only one time
    (C) very seldom
    (D) more than five times
    (E) I don't recall

26. My supervisors (or teachers) would be most likely to describe me as
    (A) competent
    (B) gifted
    (C) intelligent
    (D) fast-working
    (E) detail oriented

27. My peers would probably describe me as
    (A) analytical
    (B) glib
    (C) organized
    (D) funny
    (E) helpful

28. According to my supervisors (or teachers), my greatest asset is my
    (A) ability to communicate orally
    (B) written expression
    (C) ability to motivate others
    (D) organization of time
    (E) friendly personality

29. In the past two years, I have applied for
    (A) no jobs other than this one
    (B) one other job
    (C) two to four other jobs
    (D) five to eight other jobs
    (E) more than eight jobs

30. In the past year, I read strictly for pleasure
    (A) no books
    (B) one book
    (C) two books
    (D) three to six books
    (E) more than six books

31. When I read for pleasure, I read mostly
    (A) history
    (B) fiction
    (C) poetry
    (D) biography
    (E) current events

32. My peers would say of me that, when they ask me a question, I am
    (A) helpful
    (B) brusque
    (C) condescending
    (D) generous
    (E) patient

33. My supervisors (or teachers) would say that my area of least competence is
    (A) analytical ability
    (B) written communication
    (C) attention to detail
    (D) public speaking
    (E) self-control

34. In the past two years, the number of full-time (35 hours or more) jobs I have held is
    (A) none
    (B) one
    (C) two or three
    (D) four
    (E) five or more

35. Compared to my peers, my supervisors (or teachers) would rank my dependability
    (A) much better than average
    (B) somewhat better than average
    (C) about average
    (D) somewhat less than average
    (E) much less than average

36. In my opinion, the most important of the following attributes in an employee is
    (A) discretion
    (B) loyalty
    (C) open-mindedness
    (D) courtesy
    (E) competence

37. My peers would say that the word that describes me least is
    (A) sociable
    (B) reserved
    (C) impatient
    (D) judgmental
    (E) independent

38. My supervisors (or teachers) would say that I react to criticism with
    (A) a defensive attitude
    (B) quick capitulation
    (C) anger
    (D) interest
    (E) shame

39. My attendance record over the past year has been
    (A) not as good as I would like it to be
    (B) not as good as my supervisors (or teachers) would like it to be
    (C) a source of embarrassment
    (D) satisfactory
    (E) a source of pride

40. My peers would say that when I feel challenged my reaction is one of
    (A) determination
    (B) energy
    (C) defiance
    (D) caution
    (E) compromise

There are no ''right'' answers to these questions, so there is no answer key.

DOING YOUR BEST ON THE EXAM

It goes without saying that you cannot learn the subject matter of the Foreign Service Officer Exam in an all-night cram session—or even a week of such sessions. Your success on the Knowledge portion of the exam will be based upon a lifetime of learning, reading, discussing, and thinking. Some brush-up on the principles of punctuation, grammar, and English usage will raise your score on the English Expression questions.

While study for the exam is of limited use, preparation for the exam is quite different. Presumably, that is why you have purchased this book.

Begin your preparation by reading Part One carefully. Understanding exactly what the work entails in each of the positions for which this exam tests will help you orient your thinking towards the knowledge and attitudes you must have.

Answer the official sample questions and check your answers against the answer key. Where your answers disagree with those given, go back to the questions. Try to understand the reasoning and logic behind the correct answer. If necessary, reconcile your personal ideology with the official ideology behind the official answers.

Then move on to Part Two. The three model exams in Part Two are not actual exams; actual exams are secure and are not released. The model exams have been prepared on the basis of official information and from the reports of persons who have taken the exam during the past two administrations. The questions have been designed to draw upon your knowledge and upon your ability to reason on the basis of essays, speeches, and graphic materials. The distribution of subject matter and difficulty level approximate the most recent actual exams.

PACE YOURSELF

Use the model exams to learn to budget your time. You want to answer every question, and you want to do justice to each question. The most important phase of your preparation is pacing.

You need not complete an entire model exam at one sitting, but you should try to complete each part in one sitting and within the allotted time. This means that you should set aside three two-hour perriods for the Knowledge questions and three one-hour periods for English Expression. You cannot learn to pace yourself if you divide a section into smaller portions.

DEVELOP YOUR EXAM STRATEGY

Another good use of the model exams is the opportunity to develop the exam strategy which works best for you. Some people prefer to work quickly through the questions that appear to be easiest for them, thus guaranteeing that they will have answered all the questions that they are certain to get right before time runs out. Then these people go back and devote the necessary time to the remaining questions. This method is good in that it guarantees a certain minimum score. The danger in skipping questions is the possibility of not skipping the corresponding answer spaces. The Foreign Officer Exam is a machine-scored exam. Every question must be answered in the right place. If you slip out of line, you must waste valuable test time finding out where you went wrong, then erasing and correcting answers. If you choose this approach, check every question against its answer space as you go along.

Another strategy is to answer every question, guessing at any answers you are not sure of, but marking all your guesses for deeper thought when all questions have been answered. This tactic prevents slipping out of line and provides for a full answer sheet at the moment that time expires. The pitfall of this method is that you may spend too much time redoing questions on which you had slight doubts at the expense of questions which really require much more thought. Be sure to mark all the guessed-at questions in the test booklet, not on the answer sheet. Any extra marks on the answer sheet must be erased or they may affect your score.

You may already know which method suits you best. If not, try the first model exam one way, the second another. Decide which one works for you; then stick with your chosen tactic on the third model exam.

On any multiple-choice test, you can raise the odds of guessing correctly by eliminating obviously wrong answers first and then making your best guess from among the remaining choices. As you eliminate wrong answers, your chances of guessing correctly increase from 1 in 5 to 1 in 4 to 1 in 3 to 1 in 2.

CHECK YOUR ANSWERS

At the end of each exam, you will find the correct answer key. When you have completed all the questions in a section, check your answers against the key. As you did with the official samples, reread and rework the questions on which your answers do not coincide, not to memorize facts but to sharpen your ability to reason as the test-makers do. Following the answer key for the English Expression questions you will find corrected, reworded or expanded sentences. If you are not very secure in your mastery of English usage and grammar, study the review provided in Part Four.

12 TIPS FOR EXAMINATION DAY

1. Leave home early enough to get to the exam 10 to 15 minutes ahead of time. Once there, find a seat that's comfortable for you and settle down before the test begins.

2. Approach the test with confidence. A positive attitude is a great strategic asset.

3. Listen carefully to the examiner's instructions and question any procedures that are not clear to you.

4. When the exam begins, read carefully. Read every word of the directions. Read every word of every question. Read all the answer choices for each question before making your selection. It is statistically true that the most errors are made when the correct answer is the last choice given. Too many people mark the first answer that seems correct without reading through all the choices to find out which answer is *best*.

5. Mark your answers by completely blackening the space of your choice.

6. Mark only one answer for each question.

7. If you change your mind about an answer, erase completely so that only the new answer will register on the scoring machine.

8. Check often to be sure that the answer number corresponds to the question number.

9. Pace yourself. Do not dwell too long on any question. If you guess at the answer, mark the question in the test booklet and come back to it at the end of the exam if time allows.

10. Stay alert. Be sure you darken the space for the letter you have chosen.

11. If you find that time is running out, try to pick up your pace, but do not panic. It is possible to earn a high score without answering every question.

12. If you finish before time is called, check to be certain that there is only one answer for each question; then give extra attention to the questions you guessed at.

AFTER THE EXAM

Passing the written examination is only the first step along the path to becoming a Foreign Service Officer. The next step is the Oral Assessment, a day-long series of activities that includes oral and written as well as individual and group exercises. Part Three of this book provides essential information about this crucial segment of the Foreign Service examination process. Here you will find a detailed description of the day's activities together with suggestions on what to wear, on how to act, and on what you can do to prepare for the oral and written exercises you will face.

Part Two

THREE MODEL FOREIGN SERVICE OFFICER EXAMS

ANSWER SHEET FOR FIRST MODEL FOREIGN SERVICE OFFICER EXAM

Knowledge Questions

1 Ⓐ Ⓑ Ⓒ Ⓓ   15 Ⓐ Ⓑ Ⓒ Ⓓ   29 Ⓐ Ⓑ Ⓒ Ⓓ   43 Ⓐ Ⓑ Ⓒ Ⓓ   57 Ⓐ Ⓑ Ⓒ Ⓓ

2 Ⓐ Ⓑ Ⓒ Ⓓ   16 Ⓐ Ⓑ Ⓒ Ⓓ   30 Ⓐ Ⓑ Ⓒ Ⓓ   44 Ⓐ Ⓑ Ⓒ Ⓓ   58 Ⓐ Ⓑ Ⓒ Ⓓ

3 Ⓐ Ⓑ Ⓒ Ⓓ   17 Ⓐ Ⓑ Ⓒ Ⓓ   31 Ⓐ Ⓑ Ⓒ Ⓓ   45 Ⓐ Ⓑ Ⓒ Ⓓ   59 Ⓐ Ⓑ Ⓒ Ⓓ

4 Ⓐ Ⓑ Ⓒ Ⓓ   18 Ⓐ Ⓑ Ⓒ Ⓓ   32 Ⓐ Ⓑ Ⓒ Ⓓ   46 Ⓐ Ⓑ Ⓒ Ⓓ   60 Ⓐ Ⓑ Ⓒ Ⓓ

5 Ⓐ Ⓑ Ⓒ Ⓓ   19 Ⓐ Ⓑ Ⓒ Ⓓ   33 Ⓐ Ⓑ Ⓒ Ⓓ   47 Ⓐ Ⓑ Ⓒ Ⓓ   61 Ⓐ Ⓑ Ⓒ Ⓓ

6 Ⓐ Ⓑ Ⓒ Ⓓ   20 Ⓐ Ⓑ Ⓒ Ⓓ   34 Ⓐ Ⓑ Ⓒ Ⓓ   48 Ⓐ Ⓑ Ⓒ Ⓓ   62 Ⓐ Ⓑ Ⓒ Ⓓ

7 Ⓐ Ⓑ Ⓒ Ⓓ   21 Ⓐ Ⓑ Ⓒ Ⓓ   35 Ⓐ Ⓑ Ⓒ Ⓓ   49 Ⓐ Ⓑ Ⓒ Ⓓ   63 Ⓐ Ⓑ Ⓒ Ⓓ

8 Ⓐ Ⓑ Ⓒ Ⓓ   22 Ⓐ Ⓑ Ⓒ Ⓓ   36 Ⓐ Ⓑ Ⓒ Ⓓ   50 Ⓐ Ⓑ Ⓒ Ⓓ   64 Ⓐ Ⓑ Ⓒ Ⓓ

9 Ⓐ Ⓑ Ⓒ Ⓓ   23 Ⓐ Ⓑ Ⓒ Ⓓ   37 Ⓐ Ⓑ Ⓒ Ⓓ   51 Ⓐ Ⓑ Ⓒ Ⓓ   65 Ⓐ Ⓑ Ⓒ Ⓓ

10 Ⓐ Ⓑ Ⓒ Ⓓ   24 Ⓐ Ⓑ Ⓒ Ⓓ   38 Ⓐ Ⓑ Ⓒ Ⓓ   52 Ⓐ Ⓑ Ⓒ Ⓓ   66 Ⓐ Ⓑ Ⓒ Ⓓ

11 Ⓐ Ⓑ Ⓒ Ⓓ   25 Ⓐ Ⓑ Ⓒ Ⓓ   39 Ⓐ Ⓑ Ⓒ Ⓓ   53 Ⓐ Ⓑ Ⓒ Ⓓ   67 Ⓐ Ⓑ Ⓒ Ⓓ

12 Ⓐ Ⓑ Ⓒ Ⓓ   26 Ⓐ Ⓑ Ⓒ Ⓓ   40 Ⓐ Ⓑ Ⓒ Ⓓ   54 Ⓐ Ⓑ Ⓒ Ⓓ   68 Ⓐ Ⓑ Ⓒ Ⓓ

13 Ⓐ Ⓑ Ⓒ Ⓓ   27 Ⓐ Ⓑ Ⓒ Ⓓ   41 Ⓐ Ⓑ Ⓒ Ⓓ   55 Ⓐ Ⓑ Ⓒ Ⓓ   69 Ⓐ Ⓑ Ⓒ Ⓓ

14 Ⓐ Ⓑ Ⓒ Ⓓ   28 Ⓐ Ⓑ Ⓒ Ⓓ   42 Ⓐ Ⓑ Ⓒ Ⓓ   56 Ⓐ Ⓑ Ⓒ Ⓓ   70 Ⓐ Ⓑ Ⓒ Ⓓ

TEAR HERE

English Expression Questions

1 Ⓐ Ⓑ Ⓒ Ⓓ Ⓔ　　23 Ⓐ Ⓑ Ⓒ Ⓓ Ⓔ　　45 Ⓐ Ⓑ Ⓒ Ⓓ Ⓔ　　67 Ⓐ Ⓑ Ⓒ Ⓓ Ⓔ　　89 Ⓐ Ⓑ Ⓒ Ⓓ Ⓔ

2 Ⓐ Ⓑ Ⓒ Ⓓ Ⓔ　　24 Ⓐ Ⓑ Ⓒ Ⓓ Ⓔ　　46 Ⓐ Ⓑ Ⓒ Ⓓ Ⓔ　　68 Ⓐ Ⓑ Ⓒ Ⓓ Ⓔ　　90 Ⓐ Ⓑ Ⓒ Ⓓ Ⓔ

3 Ⓐ Ⓑ Ⓒ Ⓓ Ⓔ　　25 Ⓐ Ⓑ Ⓒ Ⓓ Ⓔ　　47 Ⓐ Ⓑ Ⓒ Ⓓ Ⓔ　　69 Ⓐ Ⓑ Ⓒ Ⓓ Ⓔ　　91 Ⓐ Ⓑ Ⓒ Ⓓ Ⓔ

4 Ⓐ Ⓑ Ⓒ Ⓓ Ⓔ　　26 Ⓐ Ⓑ Ⓒ Ⓓ Ⓔ　　48 Ⓐ Ⓑ Ⓒ Ⓓ Ⓔ　　70 Ⓐ Ⓑ Ⓒ Ⓓ Ⓔ　　92 Ⓐ Ⓑ Ⓒ Ⓓ Ⓔ

5 Ⓐ Ⓑ Ⓒ Ⓓ Ⓔ　　27 Ⓐ Ⓑ Ⓒ Ⓓ Ⓔ　　49 Ⓐ Ⓑ Ⓒ Ⓓ Ⓔ　　71 Ⓐ Ⓑ Ⓒ Ⓓ Ⓔ　　93 Ⓐ Ⓑ Ⓒ Ⓓ Ⓔ

6 Ⓐ Ⓑ Ⓒ Ⓓ Ⓔ　　28 Ⓐ Ⓑ Ⓒ Ⓓ Ⓔ　　50 Ⓐ Ⓑ Ⓒ Ⓓ Ⓔ　　72 Ⓐ Ⓑ Ⓒ Ⓓ Ⓔ　　94 Ⓐ Ⓑ Ⓒ Ⓓ Ⓔ

7 Ⓐ Ⓑ Ⓒ Ⓓ Ⓔ　　29 Ⓐ Ⓑ Ⓒ Ⓓ Ⓔ　　51 Ⓐ Ⓑ Ⓒ Ⓓ Ⓔ　　73 Ⓐ Ⓑ Ⓒ Ⓓ Ⓔ　　95 Ⓐ Ⓑ Ⓒ Ⓓ Ⓔ

8 Ⓐ Ⓑ Ⓒ Ⓓ Ⓔ　　30 Ⓐ Ⓑ Ⓒ Ⓓ Ⓔ　　52 Ⓐ Ⓑ Ⓒ Ⓓ Ⓔ　　74 Ⓐ Ⓑ Ⓒ Ⓓ Ⓔ　　96 Ⓐ Ⓑ Ⓒ Ⓓ Ⓔ

9 Ⓐ Ⓑ Ⓒ Ⓓ Ⓔ　　31 Ⓐ Ⓑ Ⓒ Ⓓ Ⓔ　　53 Ⓐ Ⓑ Ⓒ Ⓓ Ⓔ　　75 Ⓐ Ⓑ Ⓒ Ⓓ Ⓔ　　97 Ⓐ Ⓑ Ⓒ Ⓓ Ⓔ

10 Ⓐ Ⓑ Ⓒ Ⓓ Ⓔ　　32 Ⓐ Ⓑ Ⓒ Ⓓ Ⓔ　　54 Ⓐ Ⓑ Ⓒ Ⓓ Ⓔ　　76 Ⓐ Ⓑ Ⓒ Ⓓ Ⓔ　　98 Ⓐ Ⓑ Ⓒ Ⓓ Ⓔ

11 Ⓐ Ⓑ Ⓒ Ⓓ Ⓔ　　33 Ⓐ Ⓑ Ⓒ Ⓓ Ⓔ　　55 Ⓐ Ⓑ Ⓒ Ⓓ Ⓔ　　77 Ⓐ Ⓑ Ⓒ Ⓓ Ⓔ　　99 Ⓐ Ⓑ Ⓒ Ⓓ Ⓔ

12 Ⓐ Ⓑ Ⓒ Ⓓ Ⓔ　　34 Ⓐ Ⓑ Ⓒ Ⓓ Ⓔ　　56 Ⓐ Ⓑ Ⓒ Ⓓ Ⓔ　　78 Ⓐ Ⓑ Ⓒ Ⓓ Ⓔ　　100 Ⓐ Ⓑ Ⓒ Ⓓ Ⓔ

13 Ⓐ Ⓑ Ⓒ Ⓓ Ⓔ　　35 Ⓐ Ⓑ Ⓒ Ⓓ Ⓔ　　57 Ⓐ Ⓑ Ⓒ Ⓓ Ⓔ　　79 Ⓐ Ⓑ Ⓒ Ⓓ Ⓔ　　101 Ⓐ Ⓑ Ⓒ Ⓓ Ⓔ

14 Ⓐ Ⓑ Ⓒ Ⓓ Ⓔ　　36 Ⓐ Ⓑ Ⓒ Ⓓ Ⓔ　　58 Ⓐ Ⓑ Ⓒ Ⓓ Ⓔ　　80 Ⓐ Ⓑ Ⓒ Ⓓ Ⓔ　　102 Ⓐ Ⓑ Ⓒ Ⓓ Ⓔ

15 Ⓐ Ⓑ Ⓒ Ⓓ Ⓔ　　37 Ⓐ Ⓑ Ⓒ Ⓓ Ⓔ　　59 Ⓐ Ⓑ Ⓒ Ⓓ Ⓔ　　81 Ⓐ Ⓑ Ⓒ Ⓓ Ⓔ　　103 Ⓐ Ⓑ Ⓒ Ⓓ Ⓔ

16 Ⓐ Ⓑ Ⓒ Ⓓ Ⓔ　　38 Ⓐ Ⓑ Ⓒ Ⓓ Ⓔ　　60 Ⓐ Ⓑ Ⓒ Ⓓ Ⓔ　　82 Ⓐ Ⓑ Ⓒ Ⓓ Ⓔ　　104 Ⓐ Ⓑ Ⓒ Ⓓ Ⓔ

17 Ⓐ Ⓑ Ⓒ Ⓓ Ⓔ　　39 Ⓐ Ⓑ Ⓒ Ⓓ Ⓔ　　61 Ⓐ Ⓑ Ⓒ Ⓓ Ⓔ　　83 Ⓐ Ⓑ Ⓒ Ⓓ Ⓔ　　105 Ⓐ Ⓑ Ⓒ Ⓓ Ⓔ

18 Ⓐ Ⓑ Ⓒ Ⓓ Ⓔ　　40 Ⓐ Ⓑ Ⓒ Ⓓ Ⓔ　　62 Ⓐ Ⓑ Ⓒ Ⓓ Ⓔ　　84 Ⓐ Ⓑ Ⓒ Ⓓ Ⓔ　　106 Ⓐ Ⓑ Ⓒ Ⓓ Ⓔ

19 Ⓐ Ⓑ Ⓒ Ⓓ Ⓔ　　41 Ⓐ Ⓑ Ⓒ Ⓓ Ⓔ　　63 Ⓐ Ⓑ Ⓒ Ⓓ Ⓔ　　85 Ⓐ Ⓑ Ⓒ Ⓓ Ⓔ　　107 Ⓐ Ⓑ Ⓒ Ⓓ Ⓔ

20 Ⓐ Ⓑ Ⓒ Ⓓ Ⓔ　　42 Ⓐ Ⓑ Ⓒ Ⓓ Ⓔ　　64 Ⓐ Ⓑ Ⓒ Ⓓ Ⓔ　　86 Ⓐ Ⓑ Ⓒ Ⓓ Ⓔ　　108 Ⓐ Ⓑ Ⓒ Ⓓ Ⓔ

21 Ⓐ Ⓑ Ⓒ Ⓓ Ⓔ　　43 Ⓐ Ⓑ Ⓒ Ⓓ Ⓔ　　65 Ⓐ Ⓑ Ⓒ Ⓓ Ⓔ　　87 Ⓐ Ⓑ Ⓒ Ⓓ Ⓔ　　109 Ⓐ Ⓑ Ⓒ Ⓓ Ⓔ

22 Ⓐ Ⓑ Ⓒ Ⓓ Ⓔ　　44 Ⓐ Ⓑ Ⓒ Ⓓ Ⓔ　　66 Ⓐ Ⓑ Ⓒ Ⓓ Ⓔ　　88 Ⓐ Ⓑ Ⓒ Ⓓ Ⓔ　　110 Ⓐ Ⓑ Ⓒ Ⓓ Ⓔ

TEAR HERE

FIRST MODEL
FOREIGN SERVICE OFFICER EXAM

KNOWLEDGE QUESTIONS

70 questions—2 hours

1. Organization structure deals with the relationship between functions and the personnel performing these functions. It is usually advisable to think first of functions, then of the individuals performing these functions. Most implicit in this approach is the recognition that
   (A) conditions outside the organization may necessitate changes in the organization structure
   (B) functions need not always be coordinated for an organization to effectively carry out its objectives
   (C) functions tend to change with time while the interests and abilities of personnel are usually permanent
   (D) personnel emphasis often results in unusual combinations of duties that are difficult to manage

Questions 2 to 4 are based on the following choices:

   (A) Specific tariffs
   (B) Ad valorem tariffs
   (C) Compound tariffs (specific or ad valorem, whichever is lower)
   (D) Quotas

2. If both domestic prices and the prices of imports fall, they tend to be more protective than before.

3. When import prices rise, they give greater protection than before.

4. They do not provide an incentive for exporting countries to decrease their prices.

5. Which pairs an important person in history with an idea he supported?
   (A) Adam Smith—Wealth is created by the working class.
   (B) Mohandas Gandhi—India can free itself from England only by developing its own modernized industry.
   (C) Martin Luther—Only through good works can man attain salvation.
   (D) Thomas Jefferson—If a government fails to protect the rights of the people, they have the right to change it.

6. Who would feel an adverse effect of inflation most immediately?
   (A) An investor in enterprises involving real estate
   (B) A retired individual living on an insurance annuity
   (C) An individual who has most of his capital invested in common stock
   (D) A member of a union which has an escalator clause in its contract with management

7. Which one was NOT a result of the British-French-Israeli action against Egypt in October 1956?
   (A) A deadlock in the U.N. because of the Soviet veto
   (B) A drastic decline in British influence in the Middle East
   (C) An increase in United States and Soviet influence in the area
   (D) An increase in the influence of President Nasser with the Arab masses

8. A United States citizen is arrested in Germany for possession of heroin. Which of the following situations is he most likely to face?
   (A) He will be released as soon as the fact that he is not a citizen of Germany is verified.
   (B) He will be imprisoned for the maximum period allowed by German law for this offense without judicial process because he is not a citizen of Germany.
   (C) He will be released to the custody of the United States consular officer for prosecution under United States law.
   (D) He will be prosecuted under the laws of Germany and will be sentenced accordingly.

9. Chinese residents of Southeast Asian countries often are regarded with suspicion and hostility by the indigenous population. Arrange the following explanations for this phenomenon in decreasing order of significance.
   I. Most Southeast Asian countries were invaded by China at some point in their precolonial history.
   II. Southeast Asians often are suspicious of Chinese clannishness and tendency to preserve a separate cultural identity.
   III. Many Southeast Asians remember and resent the Chinese role as economic middleman during the colonial era.
   IV. The Chinese frequently are wealthy and control a disproportionately large share of the local economy.
   (A) II, I, IV, III
   (B) III, IV, I, II
   (C) IV, II, III, I
   (D) IV, I, III, II

10. It is estimated that prices will rise by 5% during the coming year. Interest on the current outstanding debt for the coming year may be expected to
    (A) depend on new capital programs
    (B) increase by about 5%
    (C) increase by more than 5% because of the generally more rapid increase in construction costs
    (D) remain unchanged

11. Which of the following statements concerning the power to declare war by the United States is correct?
    (A) Congress is forbidden to declare war until it has received a request from the President for a declaration of war.
    (B) A congressional resolution declaring war does not require the President's signature.
    (C) A congressional resolution declaring war requires the President's signature.
    (D) The power of Congress to override a presidential veto does not apply in the case of a declaration of war.

12. All of the following statements express policies of the United States government during the Cold War EXCEPT
    (A) "Our policy with regard to Europe is not to interfere with her internal concerns but to consider each European government de facto as the legitimate government and to cultivate friendly relations with it."
    (B) "If we find it impossible to enlist Soviet cooperation in the solution of world problems, we should be prepared to join with the British and other Western countries in an attempt to build up a world of our own."
    (C) "The role of this country should consist of friendly aid in the drafting of a European economic program to get Europe on its feet and to provide financial support for such a program so far as it may be practical for us to do so."
    (D) "The United States seeks no territorial expansion or selfish advantage and has no plans for aggression against any other state, large or small, but is committed to the mutual security of non-Communist nations in Europe."

13. All of the following problems were common to the postwar settlements of World War I and World War II EXCEPT
    (A) the Italo-Yugoslav boundary
    (B) the Polish boundaries
    (C) Russian intransigence at postwar conferences
    (D) reparations from the defeated countries

Questions 14 to 16 are based on the following diagram showing a firm's cost and revenue:

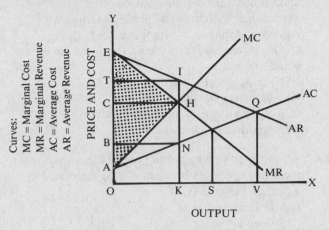

Curves:
MC = Marginal Cost
MR = Marginal Revenue
AC = Average Cost
AR = Average Revenue

14. The most profitable output for the firm to produce is
(A) OS
(B) OV
(C) OK
(D) OA

15. The amount of profits will be shown by
(A) INQ
(B) TICH
(C) ACH
(D) either AEH or BTIN

16. If the government levied a tax per unit of output, the price per unit for the firm would
(A) rise by the amount of the tax
(B) rise by more than the amount of the tax
(C) rise by less than the amount of the tax
(D) remain the same

17. In which one of the following are the items regarding the United Nations INCORRECTLY paired?
(A) United for Peace Resolution—Right of the General Assembly to act because of a Security Council veto
(B) UNESCO—Rehabilitation of Korea following the Korean War
(C) Procedural Matters—Vote of any seven members of the Security Council

(D) Trusteeship Council—Supervision of designated territories whose peoples have not attained self-government

18. According to the Constitution of the United States, which action might be legal?
(A) Florida refuses admission to immigrants from Cuba.
(B) Texas levies a tax on jewelry imported from Mexico.
(C) New York grants the right to vote to 18-year-olds.
(D) Congress levies a tax on wheat being shipped to India.

19. "A man who lived from 1865 to 1945 would have witnessed developments which in European history occupied several centuries: absolute monarchy, constitutional monarchy, liberalism, imperialist expansion, military dictatorship, totalitarian fascism, foreign occupation."
The above description best fits
(A) India
(B) China
(C) Japan
(D) Egypt

20. Which one of the following constituted a violation by the Soviet Union of agreements made at the Yalta Conference?
(A) Acquiring the Kurile Islands from Japan
(B) Entering the war against Japan
(C) Preventing free democratic elections in Eastern Europe
(D) Occupying the eastern zone of Germany

21. The most effective power of the U.S. Congress in influencing executive action in foreign policy making is its
(A) role in the treaty-making process
(B) exclusive authority to declare war
(C) control over the appropriations process
(D) role in confirming presidential appointments

Questions 22 to 24 are based on the map below:

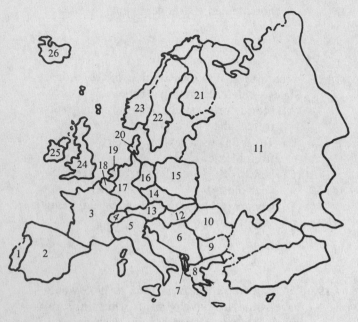

22. The country in which the United States and the former Soviet Union confronted one another both in diplomacy and in chess is
(A) 21
(B) 26
(C) 10
(D) 15

23. The country which immediately comes to mind in connection with the word *appeasement* is
(A) 4
(B) 12
(C) 13
(D) 14

24. Two countries which maintained their neutrality throughout both World Wars are
(A) 4 and 22
(B) 12 and 25
(C) 22 and 23
(D) 4 and 18

25. "Let One Hundred Flowers Bloom, Let One Hundred Schools of Thought Contend." This is the title of a speech given in the attempt to soften the harsh realities of dictatorship by
(A) Joseph Stalin
(B) Francisco Franco
(C) Fidel Castro
(D) Mao Tse-tung

26. "The political system of the allied powers is essentially different from that of America. We should consider any attempt on their part to extend their system to any portion of this hemisphere as dangerous to our peace and safety."
This statement is representative of the ideas expressed in
(A) the Freeport Doctrine
(B) Manifest Destiny
(C) the Constitution of the Confederacy
(D) the Monroe Doctrine

27. All of the following are in general use as payment arrangements between a U.S. seller and a foreign buyer EXCEPT
(A) bills of exchange
(B) open accounts
(C) consular invoices
(D) cash

28. In the context of international relations, the term "good offices" is used in connection with the
(A) priority system for assigning floor space to delegations at the United Nations
(B) selective system for assigning locations to foreign embassies in Washington
(C) procedure for mediation of disputes between nations
(D) maintenance of liaison between the United States and the former Soviet Union

29. Which of the following neither is, nor was, concerned with economic and military aid for Europe?
(A) GATT
(B) Marshall Plan
(C) NATO
(D) OECD

30. The basic assumptions underlying the doctrines of laissez-faire and natural rights are also the basic assumptions underlying the
(A) divine right theory and natural law
(B) mercantile theory and divine right theory
(C) social contract theory and natural law
(D) social contract theory and state socialism

31. Gross national product is defined as
(A) total goods produced
(B) total goods and services produced
(C) total goods and services produced, less taxes
(D) net national products plus dividends

32. The present international political system is most accurately characterized as a
    (A) loose concert of power tending toward a world empire
    (B) unit-veto system tending toward a balance of power
    (C) tight bipolar system tending toward a universal system
    (D) loose bipolar system tending toward a multi-polar or unit-veto system

33. The Federal Reserve can do all of the following EXCEPT
    (A) set the discount rate
    (B) open market operations
    (C) set the reserve requirements
    (D) set the prime rate

34. "During the decade 1840–1850, they left their native land in large numbers because of the famine and came to the United States to settle, for the greater part, in seaboard cities." This description best applies to emigrants from
    (A) Germany
    (B) Ireland
    (C) Russia
    (D) Italy

35. Which of the following novels is a polemic against slavery?
    (A) *The Nigger of the "Narcissus"*
    (B) *The Way of All Flesh*
    (C) *Of Human Bondage*
    (D) *Uncle Tom's Cabin*

36. "Man is born free, and everywhere he is in irons" is a quotation from the writings of
    (A) Karl Marx
    (B) Jean Jacques Rousseau
    (C) John Locke
    (D) François Voltaire

37. Avoiding conflict by recruiting potential or existing leaders of the opposition is a technique known as
    (A) pre-emption
    (B) co-optation
    (C) isolation
    (D) assignation

38. An increase in consumer spending leads to a proportionally larger increase in capital expenditure. This is an example of which of the following?
    (A) Inflation
    (B) Deflation
    (C) Accelerator
    (D) Multiplier

39. Country P, through legislative enactment, defines its monetary unit in terms of sisal. Sisal is coined in limitless quantities at slight cost and is free to move into and out of the country in any quantity. In addition, all legal tender is redeemable, at no loss, in sisal coinage upon demand. The monetary standard which most applies to this situation is
    (A) Full Sisal Coin Standard
    (B) Limited Sisal Bullion Standard
    (C) Sisal Exchange Standard
    (D) Full Sisal Control Standard

40. A 19th-century naturalist, philosopher, and writer who had a profound effect on political philosophy and action in the 20th century and the book through which this influence was imparted are
    (A) Henry David Thoreau and *Civil Disobedience*
    (B) Charles Darwin and *Origin of the Species*
    (C) Adam Smith and *Wealth of Nations*
    (D) Charles M. Sheldon and *In His Steps*

41. Often in financial statement analysis the current ratio is used. This ratio is
    (A) current assets divided by current liabilities
    (B) current liabilities divided by current assets
    (C) current assets less inventory divided by current liabilities
    (D) current assets less current liabilities divided by working capital

Questions 42 to 44 are based on the map below:

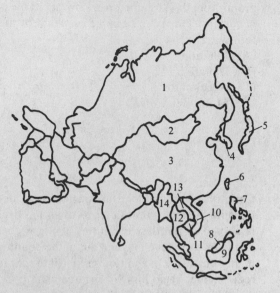

42. From among the choices offered, the ONLY country not to have been under colonial rule in modern times is
(A) 7
(B) 9
(C) 10
(D) 12

43. The countries which were once known as French Indo-China are
(A) 10, 11, and 12
(B) 10, 11, and 13
(C) 11, 12, and 13
(D) 12, 13, and 14

44. The country which is overwhelmingly Moslem, though not controlled by Fundamentalists nor considered an Islamic state, is
(A) 2
(B) 7
(C) 9
(D) 14

45. The single event which revolutionized the teaching of science and mathematics in the schools of America was the
(A) downing of Gary Powers' U-2 spy plane
(B) dropping of atomic bombs at Hiroshima and Nagasaki
(C) launching of the Soviet satellite Sputnik
(D) orbiting of the earth by Yuri Gagarin

46. Which of the following normally occurs when a commercial bank makes a loan to a business firm?

(A) The bank's liabilities and assets increase.
(B) The bank's liabilities and assets decrease.
(C) The bank's liabilities increase and its assets decrease.
(D) The bank's liabilities decrease and its assets increase.

47. A change in the dollar:pound sterling exchange ratio from 3:1 to 4:1 is best described as
(A) depreciation of the pound
(B) devaluation of the dollar
(C) depreciation of the two currencies
(D) depreciation of the dollar relative to the pound

48. The safety of diplomatic missions and their accredited personnel in a foreign country is the responsibility of
(A) the security forces of the country which sent the mission
(B) the special United Nations security forces
(C) the host country or its appointed designates
(D) a joint force of host country and security personnel of the country from which the mission comes

49. Sometimes "the impossible" can only be accomplished by the most "improbable" person. Thus, only a leader with well-established credentials as a hard-liner can get away with making overtures to "the other side." Of the following, one visit does NOT fit into this category.
(A) The visit of Nixon to China
(B) The visit of John Paul II to the Temple in Rome
(C) The visit of Willy Brandt to the United States
(D) The visit of Sadat to Jerusalem

50. The responsibility for specific types of decisions generally is best delegated to
(A) the highest organizational level at which there is an individual possessing the ability, desire, impartiality, and access to relevant information needed to make these decisions
(B) the lowest organizational level at which there is an individual possessing the ability, desire, impartiality, and access to relevant information needed to make these decisions

(C) a group of executives, rather than a single executive, if these decisions deal with an emergency

(D) the organizational level midway between that which will have to carry out these decisions and that which will have to authorize the resources for their implementation

51. An American student in London becomes friendly with ''the wrong crowd'' and soon is involved in a bungled bank robbery. The robbers are apprehended, and the American student calls the American consulate for help. The consul can offer advice and encouragement to the jailed student, but he/she CANNOT

(A) request release of the student for trial in the United States as a United States citizen

(B) attend the trial as an observer

(C) communicate with the student's parents to reassure them that the student is being treated fairly

(D) visit the student in prison if the student is convicted

52. The Boxers, whose name comes down in history because of their role as the aggressors in the Boxer Rebellion in China in 1900, drew that name from

(A) their attempt to box China in from the rest of the world, in other words, their isolationism

(B) their attempt to box missionaries into tiny isolated enclaves

(C) the fact that they relied heavily on hand-to-hand combat

(D) the Chinese Secret Society of the Righteous and Harmonious Fists to which they belonged and in which they practiced boxing and calisthenic rituals which they believed made them impervious to bullets

53. The Boxer Rebellion was limited to North China because

(A) it was a rogue operation, not sanctioned by the government

(B) viceroys in South China refused to obey the Empress Dowager and protected their foreigners

(C) poverty and foreign aggression were serious problems only in North China

(D) missionaries had attracted few converts in South China

54. The historical basis for the Sanctuary Movement in the United States Southwest is

(A) the nonestablishment clause of the First Amendment

(B) St. Thomas More's search for sanctuary in the cathedral

(C) the role of ancient Greek temples as a refuge for criminals

(D) the international law principle that clerics should always receive safe passage

55. The Department of Justice has been actively prosecuting the church workers who are involved in the Sanctuary Movement because the Justice Department claims that

(A) the Sanctuary Movement is simply abetting illegal immigration

(B) many of those seeking sanctuary are simply common criminals seeking to escape justice at home

(C) the churches and shelters do not meet standards of health and sanitation

(D) because of separation of church and state, the United States does not recognize the sanctity of the confessional

56. International observers supervised the election in El Salvador in 1982 and declared that the elections were reasonably free and democratic. Because of the nature of the elections, the United States considers El Salvador to be a democratic country and officially approves of its regime. One consequence of this approval is that

(A) El Salvador is prohibited from opening trade relations with the Soviet Union

(B) refugees from El Salvador cannot be given political asylum in the United States

(C) emigrants from El Salvador have automatic entry into the United States

(D) El Salvador is automatically a party to the Contadora Agreement

57. In the terminology of international relations, a client state is a state which

(A) is governed by another state

(B) is self-governing but is totally dominated by another state and always does the bidding of the dominating state

(C) is autonomous but buys all imported goods from the same source

(D) is extremely dependent on another state for support in matters of defense and economics

58. Mikhail Gorbachev declared a policy of "Glasnost" in Soviet Russia. The policy allowed for carefully controlled openness of cultural expression and for private entrepreneurship. Under earlier leadership, attempts at some degree of "Glasnost" in the satellite nations were promptly squelched by Soviet intervention in all EXCEPT
    (A) Czechoslovakia
    (B) Romania
    (C) Hungary
    (D) Poland

59. The history of many nations in Southern Africa is marked by violence, much of it between blacks and whites and much between blacks and blacks. The history of South Africa is remarkable because of the extent of the violence of whites against whites. This violence culminated in
    (A) the ceding of the Cape Colony to Britain by Germany
    (B) partition of the country into "homelands"
    (C) independence of Transvaal and the Orange Free State
    (D) the Boer War

60. Precursors of the European Economic Community and the European Free Trade Association were the
    I. Franco-Prussian Alliance
    II. Hanseatic League
    III. Zollverein
    IV. League of Nations
    (A) I and II only
    (B) II and III only
    (C) II and IV only
    (D) I and IV only

61. Occasionally an individual who was at one time a militant activist against the establishment spends a period in reflection and study and does a total turnabout, encouraging peaceful coexistence and positive cooperation. Such a person has the potential of changing the attitudes and behavior of large groups of followers. Two members of the black community who offered this promise after their "conversions" were/are
    (A) Lew Alcindor and Kareem Abdul Jabbar
    (B) Eldridge Cleaver and Malcolm X
    (C) W.E.B. DuBois and Martin Luther King, Jr.
    (D) Gwendolyn Brooks and Matthew Henson

Questions 62 and 63 are based on the following paragraph from the Constitution of the United States:

Article I, Section 8, paragraph 12 of the U.S. Constitution states: "The Congress shall have Power to raise and support Armies, but no Appropriation of Money to that Use shall be for a longer Term than two Years."

62. The two-year funding restriction imposed by this article affects the Defense Department most directly in its
    (A) preparation of its annual budget
    (B) guarantee of pay to members of the volunteer army
    (C) development of sophisticated new aircraft
    (D) construction of domestic missile silos

63. The most likely reason that the framers of the Constitution worded Article I, Section 8, paragraph 12 in this way is that they
    (A) did not want to commit funds they had not yet raised
    (B) believed that if we were truly defenseless no one would attack us
    (C) did not want to give the military the power that the guarantee of long-term funding might bestow
    (D) wanted to allow each Congress to appropriate funds on the basis of its own priorities and its own philosophies

64. It has been suggested that tax reform in Japan would ease our own balance of trade problems. U.S. economists suggest that Japan should make mortgage interest deductible, end the exemption of taxation on interest income, and expand mortgage availability at lower rates and with longer maturities. These measures should stimulate a housing boom in Japan as an alternative to the export orientation of its economy. The idea is intriguing but impractical and unlikely to occur because
    (A) Japan has not asked for our advice and the United States has no business meddling in Japan's internal economics
    (B) Japan has severe restrictions on the height of buildings
    (C) conversion of industries for domestic consumption is difficult and expensive
    (D) Japan is unconcerned with our financial woes

65. Individuals who are actively involved in righting injustices against their own people often extend their interests and activities into working for other causes. Thus, Martin Luther King, Jr., who actively and eloquently worked and argued for civil rights for American blacks, also was an active participant in the movement protesting our involvement in Vietnam. Similarly, the abolitionist Frederick Douglass also took an active role in
    (A) defending free immigration for famine-struck refugees from Ireland
    (B) the struggle of Massachusetts factory workers to organize for higher wages and a 10-hour work day
    (C) seeking equal rights for women by speaking at the Seneca Falls Convention of 1848
    (D) seeking better conditions for mental patients by working with Dorothea Dix.

66. Alice Walker, well-known as the author of *The Color Purple,* is most appropriately placed in a grouping with
    (A) Jean Toomer and Virginia Woolf
    (B) Zora Neale Hurston and Nikki Giovanni
    (C) Shirley Chisholm and Coretta King
    (D) Flannery O'Connor and Lorraine Hansberry

67. The United States Constitution has created amazing stability of life in the United States MAINLY because
    (A) Supreme Court justices have been so wise
    (B) it is so difficult to change
    (C) it cleverly balances rights of people, states, and federal government
    (D) of the separation of powers

68. Native Americans have been much admired for their skill at arts and crafts and at artistic design, but are seldom given adequate credit for their intellectual achievements. All of the following are Native Americans who are correctly paired with their achievements EXCEPT
    (A) Sequoya—developer of the Cherokee phonetic alphabet and creator of a literate Indian nation
    (B) General Eli Parker—civil engineer and draftsman of the articles of Lee's surrender at Appomattox
    (C) George Catlin—author and artist
    (D) Dr. Charles Eastman—physician, YMCA director, organizer of Boy Scouts and Camp Fire Girls

69. Excesses of one sort often lead to a backlash which results in excesses of another sort. Which of the following is the most likely result of the excessive materialism and uninhibited sexual freedom of the 1970s?
    (A) The rapid spread of the disease AIDS
    (B) Much highly restrictive legislation
    (C) The resurgence of religious fundamentalism
    (D) A rash of bankruptcies

70. A manufacturing company finds itself in financial difficulty, but wishes to weather the storm and to remain in business. The first step is to reduce the budget. For the long-run survival of the company, which of the following is the LEAST desirable way to trim the budget?
    (A) Cut back on research and development
    (B) Defer raises across the board
    (C) Omit allocations for capital improvements to plant
    (D) Lay off a portion of the work force

END OF KNOWLEDGE QUESTIONS

IF YOU FINISH BEFORE TIME IS CALLED, CHECK OVER YOUR
WORK ON THIS PART ONLY. DO NOT CONTINUE UNTIL THE
SIGNAL IS GIVEN.
THERE WILL BE A TEN MINUTE BREAK BETWEEN PARTS.

ENGLISH EXPRESSION

110 questions—60 minutes

Directions: Some of the following sentences contain problems in grammar, usage, diction (choice of words), and idiom. Some sentences are correct. No sentence contains more than one error.

You will find that the error, if there is one, is underlined and lettered. Assume that all other elements of the sentence are correct and cannot be changed. In choosing answers, follow the requirements of standard written English. If there is an error, select the one underlined part that must be changed in order to make the sentence correct, and blacken the corresponding space on the answer sheet. If there is no error, mark answer space E.

1. In planning your future, one must be as
    ———   A   ——— B
    honest with yourself as possible, make care-

    ful decisions about the best course

    to follow to achieve a particular purpose,
    ———————————————————————
                    C
    and, above all, have the courage

    to stand by those decisions. No error
    ———————————————— ————
              D   E

2. Even though history does not actually re-
    —————
      A
    peat itself, knowledge of history can give
                         ——   ————
                          B   C
    current problems a familiar, less formidable
                                 ————
                                   D
    look. No error
          ————
            E

3. The Curies had almost exhausted their re-
               ————————————
                      A
    sources, and for a time it seemed
             ———————————————
                      B
    unlikely that they ever would find the
    ——————————————————
                 C
    solvent to their financial problems.
    ——————————————————
                 D
    No error
    ————
      E

4. If the rumors are correct, Haworth
       ——————————
             A
    will not be convicted, for each of the of-
    ——————————————
                 B

ficers on the court realizes that Chatham

and Norris may be the real culprit and that
                    ———————————————
                             C
their testimony is not completely trust-
————
  D
worthy. No error
        ————
          E

5. The citizens of Washington,

    like Los Angeles, prefer to commute by
    ———————
        A
    automobile, even though motor vehicles

    contribute nearly as many contaminants
               ——————————
                     B
    to the air as do all other sources combined.
              ———————————   ————————
                    C   D
    No error
    ————
      E

6. By the time Ralph Rogers completes his tes-
    ——————————————————————
                    A
    timony, every major executive of our com-

    pany but Mark Jamieson and I
                            ———————
                               B
    will have been accused of complicity in
    —————————— ———————————
          C   D
    the stock swindle. No error
                       ————
                         E

7. Within six months the store was operating
    ——————————
          A
    profitably and efficient: shelves
    ——————————————
              B
    were well stocked, goods were selling rap-
    ——————————————
              C
    idly, and the cash register

    was ringing constantly. No error
    —————————————— ————
              D   E

8. Shakespeare's comedies have an advantage

    over Shaw in that Shakespeare's were
    ————————
      A   B

58

written <u>primarily</u> to entertain and <u>not to</u>
      C   D

argue for a cause. <u>No error</u>
               E

9. Any true insomniac <u>is well aware of</u> the
                             A

futility of <u>such measures as</u> drinking hot
               B

milk, <u>regular hours, deep breathing</u>, count-
               C

ing sheep, and <u>concentrating on</u> black vel-
                  D

vet. <u>No error</u>
     E

10. <u>I</u> would <u>appreciate</u> your <u>treating</u> me <u>as if I</u>
        A   B   C

<u>was</u> your brother. <u>No error</u>
 D   E

11. Enough change toward conservatism to se-

cure a better balance and to accept more

<u>openly</u> the fundamentals of character and
A

<u>their</u> mastery <u>are</u> to be commended, but
 B   C

<u>not</u> a return to the unnecessarily harsh and
D

harmful practices of a generation ago.

<u>No error</u>
E

12. The appearance of the beggar was

<u>in one respect</u> <u>similar to</u> the elegant gentle-
     A   B

man, for the beggar, too, <u>walked</u>
                       C

<u>with dignity</u>. <u>No error</u>
   D   E

13. The interest of American industry

for <u>developing</u> <u>previously</u> wasted intel-
     A   B

lectual resources <u>suggests</u> that we
                C

<u>may have reached</u> a new plateau in our eco-
         D

nomic development. <u>No error</u>
               E

14. <u>That</u> scientist must be <u>ingenious</u> to be able
   A   B

to <u>arrive at</u> such <u>valid</u> conclusions. <u>No error</u>
     C   D   E

15. She was <u>promoted</u> because she had made
         A

<u>less</u> errors <u>than</u> the other <u>secretary</u>. <u>No error</u>
 B   C   D   E

16. She <u>flouts</u> her mink coat <u>whenever</u> she goes
     A   B

out with us so that <u>we'll</u> think <u>she's</u> very
                 C   D

wealthy. <u>No error</u>
       E

17. We objected to <u>him</u> reprimanding us for
             A

<u>our good</u>, especially when he said it <u>hurt</u>
 B   C

<u>him</u> more than us. <u>No error</u>
  D   E

18. The boy, <u>as well as</u> <u>his mother</u>, <u>desperately</u>
          A   B   C

<u>need</u> help. <u>No error</u>
 D   E

19. Many a box of oranges <u>have</u> been sent to
    A   B

<u>New York</u> by <u>enthusiastic</u> Californians.
   C   D

<u>No error</u>
E

20. <u>Let</u> me say once and for all that between
A

you and <u>I</u> <u>there</u> can be no <u>further</u> friend-
       B C   D

ship. <u>No error</u>
    E

21. He <u>proved</u> to his own <u>satisfaction</u> that he
    A   B

was as shrewd as, if not <u>shrewder than</u>, she.
     C   D

<u>No error</u>
E

22. The <u>award</u> should go to the pupil <u>who</u> we
    _A _B
    think the <u>parents</u> had <u>intended</u> it for.
    _C _D
    <u>No error</u>
    _E

23. If you <u>saw</u> the <u>number</u> of pancakes he
    _A _B
    <u>consumed</u> at breakfast this morning, you
    _C
    <u>would have understood</u> why he is so over-
    _D
    weight. <u>No error</u>
    _E

24. Ceremonies <u>were opened</u> by a drum and
    _A
    bugle <u>corps</u> of Chinese <u>school</u> children
    _B _C
    <u>parading</u> up Mott Street in colorful uni-
    _D
    forms. <u>No error</u>
    _E

25. Neither the Brontë sisters <u>nor</u> their brother
    _A _B
    Branwell <u>are</u> remembered as <u>healthy</u> or
    _C _D
    happy. <u>No error</u>
    _E

26. When my <u>commanding</u> officer first
    _A
    <u>looked up</u> from his desk, he <u>took</u>
    _B _C
    Lieutenant Baxter to be <u>I</u>. <u>No error</u>
    _D _E

27. Lifeguards <u>have been known</u> to <u>effect</u>
    _A _B
    rescues <u>even</u> <u>during</u> tumultuous storms.
    _C _D
    <u>No error</u>
    _E

28. The <u>mayor</u> <u>expressed</u> concern about the
    _A _B
    large <u>amount</u> of people injured at street
    _C
    <u>crossings</u>. <u>No error</u>
    _D _E

29. "<u>Leave us</u> <u>face</u> the fact that <u>we're in</u>
    _A _B _C
    <u>trouble!</u>" he shouted. <u>No error</u>
    _D _E

30. <u>Due to</u> <u>his being hospitalized</u>, the <u>star</u> half-
    _A _B _C
    back was <u>unable to play</u> in the champion-
    _D
    ship game. <u>No error</u>
    _E

31. I know that you <u>will enjoy</u> <u>receiving</u> flowers
    _A _B
    that <u>smell</u> so <u>sweetly</u>. <u>No error</u>
    _C _D _E

32. He is <u>at least</u> ten years <u>older</u> <u>then</u> <u>she</u> is.
    _A _B _C _D
    <u>No error</u>
    _E

33. I <u>found</u> one of <u>them</u> books that <u>tells</u> you
    _A _B _C
    how to build a <u>model</u> airplane. <u>No error</u>
    _D _E

34. <u>Drawing up</u> the plan <u>promised</u> <u>to be</u> a <u>year's</u>
    _A _B _C _D
    work. <u>No error</u>
    _E

35. There are <u>less</u> derelicts in the
    _A
    <u>downtown</u> area since the <u>crumbling</u>
    _B _C
    building was <u>razed</u>. <u>No error</u>
    _D _E

Directions: In each of the following sentences, some part of the sentence or the entire sentence is underlined. Beneath each sentence you will find five ways of phrasing the underlined part. The first of these repeats the original; the other four are different. If you think the original is better than any of the alternatives, choose answer A; otherwise choose one of the others. Select the best version and blacken the corresponding space on your answer sheet.

This is a test of correctness and effectiveness of expression. In choosing answers, follow the requirements of standard written English; that is, pay attention to grammar, choice of words, sentence construction, and punctuation. Choose the answer that produces the most effective sentence—clear and exact, without awkwardness or ambiguity. Do not make a choice that changes the meaning of the original sentence.

36. The tribe of warriors believed that boys and girls should be reared separate, and, as soon as he was weaned, the boys were taken from their mothers.

   (A) reared separate, and, as soon as he was weaned, the boys were taken from their mothers

   (B) reared separate, and, as soon as he was weaned, a boy was taken from his mother

   (C) reared separately, and, as soon as he was weaned, the boys were taken from their mothers

   (D) reared separately, and, as soon as a boy was weaned, they were taken from their mothers

   (E) reared separately, and, as soon as a boy was weaned, he was taken from his mother

37. Despite Vesta being only the third largest, it is by far the brightest of the known asteroids.

   (A) Despite Vesta being only the third largest, it is by far the brightest of the known asteroids.

   (B) Vesta, though only the third largest asteroid, is by far the brightest of the known ones.

   (C) Being only the third largest, yet Vesta is by far the brightest of the known asteroids.

   (D) Vesta, though only the third largest of the known asteroids, is by far the brightest.

   (E) Vesta is only the third largest of the asteroids, it being, however, the brightest one.

38. As a result of the discovery of the Dead Sea Scrolls, our understanding of the roots of Christianity has had to be revised considerably.

   (A) has had to be revised considerably

   (B) have had to be revised considerably

   (C) has had to undergo revision to a considerable degree

   (D) have had to be subjected to considerable revision

   (E) has had to be revised in a considerable way

39. Because it is imminently suitable to dry climates, adobe has been a traditional building material throughout the southwestern states.

   (A) it is imminently suitable to

   (B) it is eminently suitable for

   (C) it is eminently suitable when in

   (D) of its eminent suitability with

   (E) of being imminently suitable in

40. Such of his stories as was original were accepted.

   (A) Such of his stories as was original were accepted.

   (B) Such of his stories as were original was accepted.

   (C) Such of his stories as were original were accepted.

   (D) Such of his stories as were original were excepted.

   (E) His stories such as were original were excepted.

41. We can't do their job since its difficult to do even ours.

   (A) its difficult to do even ours.

   (B) its difficult to do even our's.

   (C) its' difficult to do even ours'.

   (D) it's difficult to do even ours.

   (E) its difficult to do ours even.

42. Do you think that Alice has shown more progress than any girl in the class?

   (A) more progress than any girl in the class?

   (B) greater progress than any girl in the class?

   (C) more progress than any girl in the class has shown?

   (D) more progress than any other girl in the class?

   (E) more progress from that shown by any girl in the class?

43. Although she was unable to attend the concert, she insisted on me going.

   (A) on me going.

   (B) on I going.

   (C) for me to go.

   (D) upon me going.

   (E) on my going.

44. Everyone, including Anne and Helen, was there in time for the ceremony.
    - (A) Everyone, including Anne and Helen, was there
    - (B) Everyone including Anne and Helen, was there
    - (C) Everyone, including Anne and Helen, were there
    - (D) Everyone including Anne, and Helen, was there
    - (E) Everyone including Anne and Helen was there

45. I was really very much excited at the news, that's why I dropped the vase.
    - (A) at the news, that's why
    - (B) by the news, that's why
    - (C) at the news; that's why
    - (D) at the news, that is why
    - (E) at the news that's why

46. My brother and I look so much alike that the professor supposed me to be him.
    - (A) supposed me to be him.
    - (B) supposed me to be he.
    - (C) supposed I to be him.
    - (D) supposed I to be he.
    - (E) thought me to be he.

47. With a sigh of relief, she set the completed report on the desk; then she herself laid down and fell asleep.
    - (A) she set the completed report on the desk; then she herself laid down
    - (B) she sat the completed report on the desk; then she herself laid down
    - (C) she sat the completed report on the desk; then she herself lay down
    - (D) she set the completed report on the desk; then she herself lay down
    - (E) she set the completed report on the desk; then herself she laid down

48. Is the climate of Italy somewhat like Florida?
    - (A) somewhat like Florida?
    - (B) somewhat similar to Florida?
    - (C) somewhat like that of Florida?
    - (D) something like Florida?
    - (E) similar to Florida?

49. Everyone except Ruth and I knows her.
    - (A) Everyone except Ruth and I knows her.
    - (B) Everyone except Ruth and I know her.
    - (C) Everyone besides Ruth and me knows her.
    - (D) Everyone knows her except Ruth and I.
    - (E) Everyone knows her except Ruth and me.

50. Being an intelligent person, the slur was disregarded by him.
    - (A) Being an intelligent person, the slur was disregarded by him.
    - (B) Being that he was an intelligent person, the slur was disregarded by him.
    - (C) Being an intelligent person, he disregarded the slur.
    - (D) Being that he was an intelligent person, he disregarded the slur.
    - (E) As an intelligent person, the slur was disregarded by him.

51. The reason I plan to go is because she will be disappointed if I don't.
    - (A) because she will be disappointed
    - (B) that she will be disappointed
    - (C) because she will have a disappointment
    - (D) on account of she will be disappointed
    - (E) because she shall be disappointed

52. The usher won't leave us come into the auditorium once the lecture has begun.
    - (A) The usher won't leave us come
    - (B) The usher won't let us come
    - (C) The usher refuses to leave us come
    - (D) The usher won't leave us enter
    - (E) The usher won't allow that we come

53. Let's you and me settle the matter between ourselves.
    - (A) Let's you and me settle the matter between ourselves.
    - (B) Let's I and you settle the matter between ourselves.
    - (C) Let's both of us settle the matter among ourselves.
    - (D) Let's me and you settle the matter between ourselves.
    - (E) Let you and me settle the matter among ourselves.

54. The Potsdam Conference of 1945 was the final wartime conference of World War II,

which was held in a Berlin suburb and attended by Joseph Stalin, Harry Truman, and Clement Atlee.
(A) World War II, which was held in a Berlin suburb and attended
(B) World War II, and was held in a Berlin suburb and was attended
(C) World War II; was held in a Berlin suburb and it was attended
(D) World War II. It was held in a Berlin suburb and was attended
(E) World War II, and it was held in a Berlin suburb and attended

55. The work can be a challenging and exciting experience, which demands a degree of flexibility, adaptability, and self-sufficiency.
(A) experience, which demands
(B) experience. It demands
(C) experience, demanding
(D) experience; which demands
(E) experience and demands

Directions: In each of the following questions you are given a complete sentence to be rephrased according to the directions which follow it. You should rephrase the sentence mentally to save time, although you may make notes in your test book if you wish.

Below each sentence and its directions are listed words or phrases that may occur in your revised sentence. When you have thought out a good sentence, look in the choices A through E for the word or entire phrase that is included in your revised sentence, and blacken the corresponding space on the answer sheet. The word or phrase you choose should be the most accurate and most nearly complete of all the choices given, and should be part of a sentence that meets the requirements of standard written English.

Of course, a number of different sentences can be obtained if the sentence is revised according to directions, and not all of these possibilities can be included in only five choices. If you should find that you have thought of a sentence that contains none of the words or phrases listed in the choices, you should attempt to rephrase the sentence again so that it includes a word or phrase that is listed.

Although the directions may at times require you to change the relationship between parts of the sentence or to make slight changes in meaning in other ways, make only those changes that the directions require; that is, keep the meaning the same, or as nearly the same as the directions permit. If you think that more than one good sentence can be made according to the directions, select the sentence that is most exact, effective, and natural in phrasing and construction.

56. The archaeologists could only mark out the burial site, for then winter came.
Begin with Winter came before.
(A) could do nothing more
(B) could not do anything
(C) could only do
(D) could do something
(E) could do anything more

57. The white reader often receives some insight into the reasons why black men are angry from descriptions by a black writer of the injustice they encounter in a white society.
Begin with A black writer often gives.
(A) when describing
(B) by describing
(C) he has described
(D) in the descriptions
(E) because of describing

58. The agreement between the university officials and the dissident students provides for student representation on every university committee and on the board of trustees.
Substitute provides that for provides for.
(A) be
(B) are
(C) would have
(D) would be
(E) is to be

59. A tap on the door having interrupted her musings, she decided to finish washing her hair.
Begin the sentence with Since a tap on the door.
(A) had interrupted
(B) occurred to interpret
(C) broke up
(D) interrupted
(E) was interrupting

60. That book is interesting; it is full of stories of adventure.
Change the semicolon to because.
(A) it is filled with
(B) there is in it
(C) it is stuffed with
(D) we find in it
(E) it has many

61. Returning as a mature person to the town of his birth, he was greeted by those who had shunned him as a boy.

    Begin the sentence with <u>When he returned</u>.

    (A) to the town where he was born
    (B) to his birthplace town
    (C) to the town where he was given birth
    (D) to his birthtown
    (E) to the place of his birth

62. My whole family was invited by them to the cookout; my father, my mother, my sister and I were invited.

    Begin with <u>They invited</u>.

    (A) cookout, my mother, my father, my sister and me.
    (B) cookout, my mother, my father, my sister and I.
    (C) cookout—my mother, my father, my sister and I.
    (D) cookout—my mother, my father, my sister and me.
    (E) cookout including my mother, my father, my sister and I.

63. The gate opened and the two men emerged.

    Change <u>The gate</u> to <u>As soon as the gate</u>.

    (A) , here the two men emerged.
    (B) , we found that the two men emerged.
    (C) , the two men had emerged.
    (D) , only the two men emerged.
    (E) , the two men emerged.

64. Summer was now coming on with hasty steps, and I was aware that my day of decision was fast approaching.

    Change <u>Summer was</u> to <u>Now that summer was</u>.

    (A) steps, I realized
    (B) steps, because
    (C) steps, it dawned on me
    (D) steps, at last
    (E) steps, I found

65. When he had swum until his strength was exhausted, Tom threw up his arms and sank.

    Begin the sentence with <u>He swam</u>.

    (A) exhausted, Tom threw
    (B) exhausted. Tom, however,
    (C) exhausted, so Tom

    (D) exhausted. Tom then
    (E) exhausted while Tom

66. Differences of climate and of surroundings have, in the course of ages, caused differences of speech.

    Begin the sentence with <u>Because of differences</u>.

    (A) speech differences have come to pass.
    (B) differences of speech have occurred.
    (C) speech differences have been caused.
    (D) differences of speech have remained.
    (E) we come upon differences of speech.

67. The special rewards of a Foreign Service career include the pride and satisfaction of representing the United States abroad, the challenge of working in an action-oriented profession, and the opportunity for growth and change.

    Begin the sentence with <u>Foreign Service careers</u>.

    (A) include pride and satisfaction
    (B) includes such rewards
    (C) are special rewards
    (D) are rewarding for their
    (E) offer such special rewards

68. That man is a famous man in England as well as Russia.

    Begin with <u>He is</u>.

    (A) not only of fame in England but also in Russia.
    (B) also famous in England as well as in Russia.
    (C) famous not only in England but also in Russia.
    (D) not only famous in England but also in Russia.
    (E) of a famous reputation in England as well as in Russia.

69. He likes swimming and he also likes playing tennis.

    Change <u>swimming</u> to <u>to swim</u>.

    (A) and playing tennis.
    (B) and he likes playing tennis.
    (C) and he likes to play tennis.
    (D) and to play tennis.
    (E) also to play tennis.

70. The search for the lost ring was abandoned as we had been raking the beach for hours.

Change <u>as</u> to <u>after</u>.

(A) raking the beach
(B) the beach had been raked
(C) having the beach raked
(D) the time that the beach was raked
(E) we had raked the beach

71. Her brother at no time has been dependable and he never will be dependable.

Begin with <u>Her brother has never</u>.

(A) been dependable and he never will be.
(B) tried to be dependable and never will be.
(C) been dependable and never will be.
(D) shown dependability and never will be.
(E) at any time been dependable and never will be.

72. The chairman of a committee of Congress is the individual on the committee having the greatest seniority as well as being a member of the majority party.

Begin with <u>The member of the majority party</u>.

(A) has seniority as chairman
(B) serves as chairman
(C) serves as congressional chairman
(D) will be the senior chairman
(E) serves as party chairman

73. About eleven cents of every tax dollar is spent for interest which constitutes the second largest item of the federal budget.

Begin with <u>Interest</u>.

(A) it costing about eleven cents
(B) and spending about eleven cents
(C) constituting about eleven cents
(D) consuming about eleven cents
(E) with about eleven cents

74. The Sirens were mythical creatures who sang for sailors and beguiled them towards the rocks where they were shipwrecked.

Omit <u>and</u>.

(A) sailors; beguiled them
(B) sailors, beguiled the sailors
(C) sailors, also beguiling them
(D) sailors. They beguiled them
(E) sailors, beguiling them

75. A dictator is an absolute ruler of a country. He may be a ruler who was legally elected and who has declared that an emergency necessitates his absolute rule, or he may be a ruler who has seized power by force.

Write as one sentence ending with <u>is called a dictator</u>.

(A) or one who
(B) or he may be a ruler who
(C) or one ruler who
(D) or an absolute ruler who
(E) and a ruler who

76. He was euphoric because of his recent achievement; therefore, he continued his studies.

Begin with <u>Euphoric</u>.

(A) achievement, and he
(B) achievement, so he
(C) achievement; therefore, he
(D) achieving; therefore, he
(E) achievement, he

77. Whether a play is realistic or unrealistic is dependent upon the style in which it is written.

Begin with <u>The style</u>.

(A) depends on
(B) is dependent upon
(C) is determined by
(D) determines whether
(E) will determine

78. These codes of behavior were important not only to those who hoped for acceptance by high society but also to those who aspired for nothing more elegant than Mr. Smith's cookouts.

Substitute <u>both</u> for <u>not only</u>.

(A) also
(B) as well as
(C) but
(D) too
(E) and

79. A register of all the varieties of flora and fauna of a region represents its plants and animals in the same way as a listing of all the elements of the general customs of a people represents its culture.

Begin with Just as.

(A) like a listing
(B) so a list
(C) therefore a list
(D) in the same way a listing
(E) while a listing

80. Because the pleasure boat's mechanic had been careless, forty lives were lost that fateful summer afternoon.

Being with Forty lives.

(A) in view of the pleasure boat's mechanic being careless.
(B) due to the mechanic's carelessness.
(C) by the pleasure boat's mechanic being careless.
(D) although the pleasure boat's mechanic had been careless.
(E) because the pleasure boat's mechanic had been careless.

81. The puppies, frightened by the banging of the front door, all rolled or jumped from the sofa and scrambled back to their box.

Begin with Scrambling back to their box.

(A) the front door, had jumped and rolled
(B) had rolled by the front door
(C) the door, had all jumped
(D) the front door, had all rolled
(E) the front door, all frightened

82. The disease, another of many said to be increasing rapidly, is marked by exhaustion and progressive paralysis.

Change The disease, another of to The disease is one of.

(A) rapidly, is marked
(B) is marked rapidly
(C) rapidly, but is marked
(D) rapidly and is marked
(E) but is rapidly marked

83. Running across the lush meadow, she tossed her head back and smiled at the sun.

Begin with She tossed.

(A) sun while running
(B) sun all the while running
(C) while the sun
(D) as if running
(E) sun even while she ran

84. Considerable energy has been expended by those who criticize the present system.

Begin with Those who.

(A) had expended
(B) had to expend
(C) have expended
(D) expenditure
(E) in expenditure

85. It occurred to her as she stepped into the bright sunshine that she had forgotten her sun hat.

Begin with As she stepped.

(A) to her that
(B) her but that
(C) to her with
(D) her with
(E) to her sun hat

86. Frederick Douglass, a black American leader, was a talented journalist and a powerful statesman.

Begin with Frederick Douglass was not only.

(A) leader, was a
(B) leader, journalist
(C) leader, a talented
(D) leader and also
(E) leader but also

87. The three composers who produced the culmination of the Classical Era were Haydn, Mozart, and Beethoven.

Begin with Haydn.

(A) were three composers
(B) were the three
(C) were composers
(D) was the composers
(E) were the only

88. The boys burst into the room sniffing the air like a pack of hungry hounds.

Begin with The boys sniffed.

(A) hounds after having
(B) hounds after had burst
(C) hounds burst into the room
(D) hounds the pack of boys
(E) hounds, the boys

89. One final doubt mars this vision of paradise.

Begin with This vision of paradise.

(A) is not moved by
(B) is marred over by
(C) could be marred by
(D) must have been marred by
(E) is marred by

90. The business of the old men of the tribe was to teach the young men the wisdom of ancient ways devised by ancestors who had become gods.

Begin with The wisdom of ancient ways.

(A) gods, were taught to the old men
(B) ancestors were taught
(C) gods, was taught to the young men
(D) gods, were taught to the young men
(E) ancestors who had been taught

Directions: In each of the following questions you are given four sentences and a question that asks for the best sequence to make a clear, sensible paragraph. Choose the correct option that reflects the ordering of the sentences that represents the best order for a clear, sensible paragraph.

91. I. Nations and regions are empowered to determine for themselves the relative weights to give to equality, growth, provision of basic needs, dignity, etc. and also to be able to implement development as they have defined it.

II. Under this definition, development is a process of empowerment, where people and, on the international level, nations, gain the power to control some of the basic factors affecting their lives.

III. One definition of underdevelopment characterizes it as vulnerability and, consequently, development as emancipation from that vulnerability.

IV. On the personal level, development also encompasses gaining the ability to define for oneself and to implement one's own plan for mental and physical well-being.

Which of the following presents the best sequence of the sentences above to make a clear, sensible paragraph?

(A) I, II, III, IV
(B) III, I, II, IV
(C) III, II, I, IV
(D) IV, II, III, I
(E) I, IV, III, II

92. I. The name generally given to this new spirit of peaceful accommodation was detente.

II. Both were aware that each could severely wound, if not destroy, the other with long-range nuclear missiles.

III. Yet this "balance of terror" produced a kind of mutual accommodation: each country appeared to accept the status quo and to recognize that there was little to gain from building threatening new weapons or from interfering in what the other country viewed as its sphere of influence.

IV. In the early 1970s, after more than twenty-five years of Cold War and arms competition between the United States and the Soviet Union, there occurred a noticeable relaxation of tension between the two countries.

Which of the following presents the best sequence of the sentences above to make a clear, sensible paragraph?

(A) IV, II, I, III
(B) IV, II, III, I
(C) I, II, III, IV
(D) II, III, I, IV
(E) II, III, IV, I

93.

I. Sometimes young people make the mistake of picking a job just because a much-admired relative or friend likes that job.

II. It is risky to choose an occupation just because you admire or are fond of someone who has chosen it.

III. You may admire Joe Montana, Louis Nizer, or a good homicide detective.

IV. But this does not mean that you can count on being successful or happy as a professional ball player, criminal lawyer, or detective.

Which of the following presents the best sequence of the sentences above to make a clear, sensible paragraph?

(A) I, II, III, IV
(B) III, IV, I, II
(C) I, IV, III, II
(D) III, II, I, IV
(E) I, III, II, IV

94.

I. Sri Lanka must diversify its exports while concentrating more of its agricultural energy on the production of staple foods.

II. Because so much land and manpower is devoted to cultivating cash crops, staple foods like rice, sugar, and flour must be imported.

III. These three crops are oriented almost entirely towards export and do little to feed the impoverished nation.

IV. Sri Lanka has an ever-widening trade deficit, a predominantly agricultural economy, and dependency for its foreign exchange upon three cash crops: tea, rubber, and coconuts.

Which of the following presents the best sequence of the sentences above to make a clear, sensible paragraph?

(A) I, II, III, IV
(B) II, III, I, IV
(C) III, II, IV, I
(D) IV, III, I, II
(E) IV, III, II, I

95.

I. If future organizations are to be unstable, shifting coalitions, then individual skills and abilities, particularly those emphasizing innovativeness, creativity, flexibility, and the latest technological knowledge, are crucial, and individual training is most appropriate.

II. This approach seems better designed for overcoming hierarchical barriers, for developing a degree of interpersonal relationships which make communication along the chain of command possible, and for retaining a modicum of innovation and/or flexibility.

III. But if there is to be little change in organizational structure, then the main thrust of training should be group-oriented or organizational development.

IV. The kind of training that an organization should emphasize depends upon the present and future structure of the organization.

Which of the following presents the best sequence of the sentences above to make a clear, sensible paragraph?

(A) I, II, III, IV
(B) II, III, I, IV
(C) IV, I, III, II
(D) III, I, II, IV
(E) IV, III, II, I

96.

I. In Tanzania, these divisions have not appeared for several reasons.

II. Many nations have emerged from the anticolonial struggle with one strong ruling party.

III. In most of these nations, soon after independence, the support for and/or unity of this party rapidly diminished as divisions arose between interest groups which had supported independence.

IV. Struggles were often between tribes or were between the wealthy western-educated elite and the rest of society.

Which of the following presents the best sequence of the sentences above to make a clear, sensible paragraph?

(A) I, II, III, IV
(B) II, I, IV, III
(C) II, I, III, IV
(D) II, III, IV, I
(E) III, IV, II, I

97.
I. An Italian at the close of the war might well have said: "We have poured out more blood and treasure to gain southern Tyrol and a few coast towns on the Adriatic than we did in all the wars for national liberty and union during the nineteenth century."

II. But many Italians felt that the war had cost Italy more than had been gained.

III. "Perhaps a stronger government might have won for us richer spoils of victory."

IV. Italy supposedly was more fortunate than its former allies, Germany and Austria-Hungary, because it was on the winning side when World War I ended.

Which of the following presents the best sequence of the sentences above to make a clear, sensible paragraph?

(A) IV, II, I, III
(B) IV, I, II, III
(C) IV, III, I, II
(D) I, II, III, IV
(E) I, III, IV, II

98.
I. The textbook doctrine proposed cave development deep below the water table, by random circulation of slowly percolating groundwater ("phreatic" origin).

II. Biospeleology advanced slowly in the United States from 1930 to 1950, even though this was the time of a lively debate over the origin of caves.

III. Other theories placed the zone of cave development at or above the local water table ("vadose" origin).

IV. The central point was whether caves form above or below the local water table.

Which of the following presents the best sequence of the sentences above to make a clear, sensible paragraph?

(A) IV, I, III, II
(B) IV, II, I, III
(C) I, III, II, IV
(D) I, IV, III, II
(E) II, IV, I, III

99.
I. It is only with respect to those laws which offend fundamental values of human life that moral defense of civil disobedience can be rationally supported.

II. However, disobedience of laws not the subject of dissent, but merely used to dramatize dissent, is regarded as morally as well as legally unacceptable.

III. Civil disobedience is by definition a violation of the law.

IV. The theory of civil disobedience recognizes that its actions, regardless of their justification, must be punished.

Which of the following presents the best sequence of the sentences above to make a clear, sensible paragraph?

(A) II, I, IV, III
(B) I, II, III, IV
(C) III, IV, II, I
(D) III, II, I, IV
(E) IV, III, II, I

100.
I. Revolutions have tended to result in authoritarian regimes.

II. However, when the masses rioted and staged a violent revolution, the new government ended up being extremely authoritarian.

III. In fact, in European history since 1789, the more involved the people became in a change of governments, the more likely the new government was to be an authoritarian one.

IV. When the change in government was controlled by the middle class, a relatively peaceful coup d'état took place and a regime no more authoritarian than the one before it came into power.

Which of the following presents the best sequence of the sentences above to make a clear, sensible paragraph?

(A) I, IV, III, II
(B) I, III, IV, II
(C) IV, I, III, II
(D) I, II, IV, III
(E) III, IV, I, II

101.

I. The proponents of the evolutionary theory adamantly insist that special creation be excluded from any possible consideration as an explanation for origins on the basis that it does not qualify as a scientific theory.

II. On the other hand, they would view as unthinkable the consideration of evolution as anything less than pure science.

III. These considerations alone convince most people that molecules-to-man evolution has actually occurred.

IV. Almost all science books and school texts present evolution as an established fact.

Which of the following presents the best sequence of the sentences above to make a clear, sensible paragraph?

(A) I, II, III, IV
(B) I, II, IV, III
(C) III, IV, I, II
(D) IV, III, I, II
(E) IV, III, II, I

102.

I. The State today is in more danger from suppression than from violence, because, in the end, suppression leads to violence.

II. Whoever pleads for justice helps to keep the peace; and whoever tramples upon the plea for justice, temperately made in the name of peace, only outrages peace and kills something fine in the heart of man that was put there when we received our humanity.

III. When that is killed, brute meets brute on each side of the line.

IV. Violence is the child of suppression.

Which of the following presents the best sequence of the sentences above to make a clear, sensible paragraph?

(A) I, IV, III, II
(B) II, I, III, IV
(C) I, IV, II, III
(D) II, IV, I, III
(E) IV, I, III, II

103.

I. In a living organism, the rate of assimilation of cosmic radiation and the rate of disintegration of radiocarbon are in precise equilibrium.

II. Radiocarbon dating, the process by which the age of long-preserved organic remains is determined, is derived from this knowledge.

III. At death, however, assimilation ceases and disintegration proceeds at the known immutable rate.

IV. The rate of disintegration of radioactive bodies is independent of the nature of the chemical compound in which the radioactive body resides and of the temperature, pressure, and other physical characteristics of its environment.

Which of the following presents the best sequence of the sentences above to make a clear, sensible paragraph?

(A) I, III, IV, II
(B) I, II, III, IV
(C) II, I, IV, III
(D) IV, III, I, II
(E) IV, III, II, I

104.

I. Today China remains one of the great cultures of the world, while the Mayan culture has all but disappeared.

II. The culture of China two thousand years ago was somewhat similar to that of the ancient Mayas.

III. Both cultures had made great advances in medicine and religion, and both had highly developed social and political structures.

IV. Yet, during those twenty centuries, the geographical conditions around which these cultures developed have not shown much change.

Which of the following presents the best sequence of the sentences above to make a clear, sensible paragraph?

(A) I, II, III, IV
(B) I, II, IV, III
(C) II, I, III, IV
(D) II, III, IV, I
(E) II, III, I, IV

105.
I. The target is wrong, for in attacking the tests, critics divert attention from the fault that lies with ill-informed or incompetent users.

II. The standardized educational or psychological tests that are widely used to aid in selecting, classifying, assigning, or promoting students, employees, and military personnel have been the target of recent attacks.

III. Whether the results will be valuable, meaningless, or even misleading depends partly upon the tool itself but largely upon the user.

IV. The tests themselves are merely tools, with characteristics that can be measured with reasonable precision under specified conditions.

Which of the following presents the best sequence of the sentences above to make a clear, sensible paragraph?

(A) I, II, III, IV
(B) I, IV, III, II
(C) II, I, III, IV
(D) IV, III, II, I
(E) IV, II, I, III

106.
I. Aristotle's philosophy supported the status quo, and so it prevailed until well into the nineteenth century.

II. Plato, the feminist, suggested that "the gifts of nature are equally diffused in the two sexes" and proposed that women's education be equal to that of men.

III. Aristotle felt that women were not fit to govern and therefore were not worthy of the kind of education offered to men.

IV. Plato's philosophy was rivaled, however, by that of Aristotle.

Which of the following presents the best sequence of the sentences above to make a clear, sensible paragraph?

(A) I, III, II, IV
(B) II, IV, I, III
(C) III, II, IV, I
(D) II, IV, III, I
(E) III, I, II, IV

107.
I. Program management is an administrative system combining planning and control techniques to guide and coordinate all of the activities that contribute to one overall program or project.

II. The concept of "program management" was first developed in order to handle some of the complex projects undertaken by the U.S. Department of Defense in the 1950s.

III. It has been used by the federal government to manage space exploration and other programs involving many contributing organizations.

IV. It is also used by state and local governments and by some large firms to provide administrative integration of work from a number of sources, be they individuals, departments, or outside companies.

Which of the following presents the best sequence of the sentences above to make a clear, sensible paragraph?

(A) I, II, III, IV
(B) II, I, III, IV
(C) I, III, IV, II
(D) II, III, IV, I
(E) I, III, II, IV

108.
I. In some countries, such as Botswana, Lesotho, and Swaziland, South Africa has rarely had to interfere directly in national affairs.

II. In other cases, such as in Mozambique, Zimbabwe, and Angola, governments that are more hostile to South Africa have been brought to power, and South Africa has imposed its will through force.

III. The South African government has consistently been able to keep its neighbors, if not in a state of peaceful coexistence, at least in a state of fear and dependency toward South Africa.

IV. These countries' economic dependency on South Africa and the interests of their ruling classes have brought about governments that are unlikely to threaten South Africa nor to leave South Africa's political-economic sphere of influence.

Which of the following presents the best sequence of the sentences above to make a clear, sensible paragraph?

(A) I, II, IV, III
(B) III, I, II, IV
(C) I, IV, III, II
(D) III, IV, I, II
(E) III, I, IV, II

109.   I. Similarly, in today's society marijuana is often used simultaneously or sequentially with other psychoactive drugs.

  II. When drug interactions occur, the simultaneous presence of two or more drugs in the body can exert effects that are greater than those that would result from the simple addition of the effects of each drug used separately.

  III. The practice of occasionally adulterating marijuana complicates analysis of the effects of marijuana use in noncontrolled settings.

  IV. Behavioral changes that are attributed to marijuana may actually derive from the adulterants.

Which of the following presents the best sequence of the sentences above to make a clear, sensible paragraph?

(A) II, I, III, IV
(B) II, IV, I, III
(C) III, IV, I, II
(D) IV, III, II, I
(E) IV, I, II, III

110.   I. A major task imposed upon education and on the schools was that which we call Americanization.

  II. No other people had ever absorbed such large and varied racial stock so rapidly or so successfully.

  III. Each decade after 1840 saw from two to eight million immigrants pour into America.

  IV. It was the public school that proved itself the most efficacious of all agencies of Americanization—Americanization not only of the children but, through them, of the parents as well.

Which of the following presents the best sequence of the sentences above to make a clear, sensible paragraph?

(A) I, III, II, IV
(B) II, III, I, IV
(C) I, II, III, IV
(D) III, IV, II, I
(E) IV, II, III, I

END OF ENGLISH EXPRESSION QUESTIONS

IF TIME PERMITS, CHECK OVER YOUR WORK ON THE
ENGLISH EXPRESSION QUESTIONS ONLY.

CORRECT ANSWERS FOR FIRST MODEL FOREIGN SERVICE OFFICER EXAM

Knowledge Questions

1. D	15. D	29. A	43. B	57. D
2. A	16. C	30. C	44. C	58. B
3. B	17. B	31. B	45. C	59. D
4. D	18. C	32. D	46. A	60. B
5. D	19. C	33. D	47. D	61. B
6. B	20. C	34. B	48. C	62. C
7. A	21. C	35. D	49. C	63. D
8. D	22. B	36. B	50. B	64. A
9. D	23. D	37. B	51. A	65. C
10. D	24. A	38. C	52. D	66. B
11. C	25. D	39. A	53. B	67. B
12. A	26. D	40. A	54. C	68. C
13. C	27. C	41. A	55. A	69. C
14. C	28. C	42. D	56. B	70. A

Key to Maps

Europe—*Questions 22 to 24*

1. Portugal	8. Greece	15. Poland	20. Denmark
2. Spain	9. Bulgaria	16. German Democratic Republic	21. Finland
3. France	10. Romania		22. Sweden
4. Switzerland	11. Soviet Union	17. Federal Republic of Germany	23. Norway
5. Italy	12. Hungary		24. Great Britain
6. Yugoslavia	13. Austria	18. Belgium	25. Ireland
7. Albania	14. Czechoslovakia	19. Netherlands	26. Iceland

East Asia—*Questions 42 to 44*

1. Soviet Union	5. Japan	9. Indonesia	13. Laos
2. Mongolia	6. Taiwan	10. Vietnam	14. Burma
3. China	7. Philippines	11. Kampuchea	
4. Korea	8. Malaysia	12. Thailand	

English Expression Questions

1. B	23. A	45. C	67. E	89. E
2. E	24. E	46. A	68. C	90. C
3. D	25. C	47. D	69. D	91. C
4. C	26. D	48. C	70. E	92. B
5. A	27. E	49. E	71. C	93. A
6. B	28. C	50. C	72. B	94. E
7. B	29. A	51. B	73. D	95. C
8. A	30. A	52. B	74. E	96. D
9. C	31. D	53. A	75. A	97. A
10. D	32. C	54. D	76. E	98. E
11. C	33. B	55. C	77. D	99. C
12. B	34. E	56. E	78. E	100. B
13. A	35. A	57. B	79. B	101. D
14. B	36. E	58. A	80. E	102. C
15. B	37. D	59. A	81. D	103. A
16. A	38. A	60. E	82. C	104. E
17. A	39. B	61. E	83. A	105. C
18. D	40. C	62. D	84. C	106. D
19. B	41. D	63. E	85. A	107. B
20. B	42. D	64. A	86. E	108. E
21. E	43. E	65. D	87. B	109. C
22. B	44. A	66. B	88. A	110. A

English Expression Questions: Correctly Stated Sentences

1. **(B)** In planning your future, *you* must be as honest with yourself as possible, make careful decisions about the best course to follow to achieve a particular purpose, and, above all, have the courage to stand by those decisions.

2. **(E)** This sentence is correct.

3. **(D)** The Curies had almost exhausted their resources, and for a time it seemed unlikely that they ever would find the *solution* to their financial problems.

4. **(C)** If the rumors are correct, Haworth will not be convicted, for each of the officers on the court realizes that Chatham and Norris may be the real *culprits* and that their testimony is not completely trustworthy.

5. **(A)** The citizens of Washington, like *those* of Los Angeles, prefer to commute by automobile, even though motor vehicles contribute nearly as many contaminants to the air as do all other sources combined.

6. **(B)** By the time Ralph Rogers completes his testimony, every major executive of our company but Mark Jamieson and *me* will have been accused of complicity in the stock swindle.

7. **(B)** Within six months the store was operating profitably and *efficiently*: shelves were well stocked, goods were selling rapidly, and the cash register was ringing constantly.

8. **(A)** Shakespeare's comedies have an advantage over *Shaw's* in that Shakespeare's were written primarily to entertain and not to argue for a cause.

9. **(C)** Any true insomniac is well aware of the futility of such measures as drinking hot milk, *keeping* regular hours, practicing deep breathing, counting sheep, and concentrating on black velvet.

10. **(D)** I would appreciate your treating me as if I *were* your brother.

11. **(C)** Enough change toward conservatism to secure a better balance and to accept more openly the fundamentals of character and their mastery *is* to be commended, but not a return to the unecessarily harsh and harmful practices of a generation ago.

12. **(B)** The appearance of the beggar was in one respect similar to *that of* the elegant gentleman, for the beggar too, walked with dignity.

13. **(A)** The interest of American industry *in* developing previously wasted intellectual resources suggests that we may have reached a new plateau in our economic development.

14. **(B)** That scientist must be *ingenious* to be able to arrive at such valid conclusions.

15. **(B)** She was promoted because she made *fewer* errors than the other secretary.

16. **(A)** She *flaunts* her mink coat whenever she goes out with us so that we'll think she's very wealthy.

17. **(A)** We objected to *his* reprimanding us for our good, especially when he said it hurt him more than us.

18. **(D)** The boy, as well as his mother, desperately *needs* help.

19. **(B)** Many a box of oranges *has* been sent to New York by enthusiastic Californians.

20. **(B)** Let me say once and for all that between you and *me* there can be no further friendship.

21. **(E)** This sentence is correct.

22. **(B)** The award should go to the pupil *whom* we think the parents had intended it for. Better still—The award should go to the pupil *for whom* the parents had intended it.

23. **(A)** If you *had seen* the number of pancakes he consumed at breakfast this morning, you would have understood why he is so overweight.

24. **(E)** This sentence is correct.

25. **(C)** Neither the Bronte sisters nor their brother Branwell *is* remembered as healthy or happy.

26. **(D)** When my commanding officer first looked up from his desk, he took Lieutenant Baxter to be *me*.

27. **(E)** This sentence is correct.

28. **(C)** The mayor expressed concern about the large *number* of people injured at street crossings.

29. **(A)** "*Let* us face the fact that we're in trouble!" he shouted.

30. **(A)** *Because he was* hospitalized, the star halfback was unable to play in the championship game.

31. **(D)** I know that you will enjoy receiving flowers that smell so *sweet*.

32. **(C)** He is at least ten years older *than* she is.

33. **(B)** I found one of *those* books that tells you how to build a model airplane.

34. **(E)** This sentence is correct.

35. **(A)** There are *fewer* derelicts in the downtown area since the crumbling building was razed.

36. **(E)** The tribe of warriors believed that boys and girls should be reared *separately,* and, as soon as *a boy* was weaned, *he* was taken from *his mother*.

37. **(D)** *Vesta, though only the third largest of the known asteroids, is by far the brightest.*

38. **(A)** As a result of the discovery of the Dead Sea Scrolls, our understanding of the roots of Christianity has had to be revised considerably.

39. **(B)** Because it is *eminently* suitable *for* dry climates, adobe has been a traditional building material throughout the southwestern states.

40. **(C)** Such of his stories as *were* original were accepted.

41. **(D)** We can't do their job since *it's* difficult to do even ours.

42. **(D)** Do you think that Alice has shown more progress than any *other* girl in the class?

43. **(E)** She insisted on *my* going.

44. **(A)** Everyone, including Anne and Helen, was there in time for the ceremony.

45. **(C)** I was really very much excited at the news; that's why I dropped the vase.

46. **(A)** My brother and I look so much alike that the professor supposed me to be him.

47. **(D)** With a sigh of relief, she set the completed report on the desk; then she herself *lay* down and fell asleep.

48. **(C)** Is the climate of Italy somewhat like *that* of Florida?

49. **(E)** Everyone *knows her except Ruth and me.*

50. **(C)** Being an intelligent person, *he disregarded the slur.*

51. **(B)** The reason I plan to go is *that* she will be disappointed if I don't.

52. **(B)** The usher won't *let* us come into the auditorium once the lecture has begun.

53. **(A)** Let's you and me settle the matter between ourselves.

54. **(D)** The Potsdam Conference of 1945 was the final wartime conference of World War II. *It* was held in a Berlin suburb and *was* attended by Joseph Stalin, Harry Truman, and Clement Atlee.

55. **(C)** The work can be a challenging and exciting experience, *demanding* a degree of flexibility, adaptability, and self-sufficiency.

56. **(E)** Winter came before the archaeologists *could do anything more* than mark out the burial site.

57. **(B)** A black writer often gives the white reader some insight into the reasons why black men are angry *by describing* the injustice blacks encounter in a white society.

58. **(A)** The agreement between the university officials and the dissident students provides that students *be* represented on every university committee and on the board of trustees.

59. **(A)** Since a tap on the door *had interrupted* her musings, she decided to finish washing her hair.

60. **(E)** That book is interesting because *it has many* stories of adventure.

61. **(E)** When he returned *to the place of his birth,* he was greeted by those who had shunned him as a boy.

62. **(D)** They invited my whole family to the *cookout— my mother, my father, my sister and me.*

63. **(E)** As soon as the gate opened, *the two men emerged.*

64. **(A)** Now that summer was coming on with hasty steps, *I realized* that my day of decision was fast approaching.

65. **(D)** He swam until his strength was *exhausted. Tom then* threw up his arms and sank.

66. **(B)** Because of differences of climate and of surroundings, in the course of ages *differences of speech have occurred.*

67. **(E)** Foreign Service careers *offer such special rewards* as the pride and satisfaction of representing the United States abroad, the challenge of working in an action-oriented profession, and the opportunity for growth and change.

68. **(C)** He is *famous not only in England but also in Russia.*

69. **(D)** He likes to swim *and to play tennis.*

70. **(E)** The search for the lost ring was abandoned after *we had raked the beach* for hours.

71. **(C)** Her brother has never *been dependable and never will be.*

72. **(B)** The member of the majority party with the greatest seniority *serves as chairman* of a Congressional committee.

73. **(D)** Interest constitutes the second largest item of the federal budget *consuming about eleven cents* of every tax dollar.

74. **(E)** The Sirens were mythical creatures who sang for *sailors, beguiling them* towards the rocks where they were shipwrecked.

75. **(A)** An absolute ruler of a country who was legally elected and has declared that an emergency necessitates his absolute rule *or one who* has seized power by force is called a dictator.

76. **(E)** Euphoric because of his recent *achievement, he* continued his studies.

77. **(D)** The style in which a play is written *determines whether* it is realistic or unrealistic.

78. **(E)** These codes of behavior were important both to those who hoped for acceptance by high society *and* to those who aspired for nothing more elegant than Mr. Smith's cookouts.

79. **(B)** Just as a register of all the varieties of flora and fauna of a region represents its plants and animals, *so a list* of all the elements of the general customs of a people represents its culture.

80. **(E)** Forty lives were lost that fateful summer afternoon *because the pleasure boat's mechanic had been careless.*

81. **(D)** Scrambling back to their box, the puppies, frightened by the banging of *the front door, had all rolled* or jumped from the sofa.

82. **(C)** The disease is one of many said to be increasing *rapidly and is marked* by exhaustion and progressive paralysis.

83. **(A)** She tossed her head back and smiled at the *sun while running* across the lush meadow.

84. **(C)** Those who criticize the present system *have expended* considerable energy.

85. **(A)** As she stepped into the bright sunlight it occurred *to her that* she had forgotten her sunhat.

86. **(E)** Frederick Douglass was not only a black American *leader but also* a talented journalist and a powerful statesman.

87. **(B)** Haydn, Mozart, and Beethoven *were the three* composers who produced the culmination of the Classical Era.

88. **(A)** The boys sniffed the air like a pack of hungry *hounds after having* burst into the room.

89. **(E)** This vision of paradise *is marred by* one final doubt.

90. **(C)** The wisdom of ancient ways, devised by ancestors who had become *gods, was taught to the young men* by the old men of the tribe.

ANSWER SHEET FOR SECOND MODEL FOREIGN SERVICE OFFICER EXAM

Knowledge Questions

1 Ⓐ Ⓑ Ⓒ Ⓓ   15 Ⓐ Ⓑ Ⓒ Ⓓ   29 Ⓐ Ⓑ Ⓒ Ⓓ   43 Ⓐ Ⓑ Ⓒ Ⓓ   57 Ⓐ Ⓑ Ⓒ Ⓓ

2 Ⓐ Ⓑ Ⓒ Ⓓ   16 Ⓐ Ⓑ Ⓒ Ⓓ   30 Ⓐ Ⓑ Ⓒ Ⓓ   44 Ⓐ Ⓑ Ⓒ Ⓓ   58 Ⓐ Ⓑ Ⓒ Ⓓ

3 Ⓐ Ⓑ Ⓒ Ⓓ   17 Ⓐ Ⓑ Ⓒ Ⓓ   31 Ⓐ Ⓑ Ⓒ Ⓓ   45 Ⓐ Ⓑ Ⓒ Ⓓ   59 Ⓐ Ⓑ Ⓒ Ⓓ

4 Ⓐ Ⓑ Ⓒ Ⓓ   18 Ⓐ Ⓑ Ⓒ Ⓓ   32 Ⓐ Ⓑ Ⓒ Ⓓ   46 Ⓐ Ⓑ Ⓒ Ⓓ   60 Ⓐ Ⓑ Ⓒ Ⓓ

5 Ⓐ Ⓑ Ⓒ Ⓓ   19 Ⓐ Ⓑ Ⓒ Ⓓ   33 Ⓐ Ⓑ Ⓒ Ⓓ   47 Ⓐ Ⓑ Ⓒ Ⓓ   61 Ⓐ Ⓑ Ⓒ Ⓓ

6 Ⓐ Ⓑ Ⓒ Ⓓ   20 Ⓐ Ⓑ Ⓒ Ⓓ   34 Ⓐ Ⓑ Ⓒ Ⓓ   48 Ⓐ Ⓑ Ⓒ Ⓓ   62 Ⓐ Ⓑ Ⓒ Ⓓ

7 Ⓐ Ⓑ Ⓒ Ⓓ   21 Ⓐ Ⓑ Ⓒ Ⓓ   35 Ⓐ Ⓑ Ⓒ Ⓓ   49 Ⓐ Ⓑ Ⓒ Ⓓ   63 Ⓐ Ⓑ Ⓒ Ⓓ

8 Ⓐ Ⓑ Ⓒ Ⓓ   22 Ⓐ Ⓑ Ⓒ Ⓓ   36 Ⓐ Ⓑ Ⓒ Ⓓ   50 Ⓐ Ⓑ Ⓒ Ⓓ   64 Ⓐ Ⓑ Ⓒ Ⓓ

9 Ⓐ Ⓑ Ⓒ Ⓓ   23 Ⓐ Ⓑ Ⓒ Ⓓ   37 Ⓐ Ⓑ Ⓒ Ⓓ   51 Ⓐ Ⓑ Ⓒ Ⓓ   65 Ⓐ Ⓑ Ⓒ Ⓓ

10 Ⓐ Ⓑ Ⓒ Ⓓ   24 Ⓐ Ⓑ Ⓒ Ⓓ   38 Ⓐ Ⓑ Ⓒ Ⓓ   52 Ⓐ Ⓑ Ⓒ Ⓓ   66 Ⓐ Ⓑ Ⓒ Ⓓ

11 Ⓐ Ⓑ Ⓒ Ⓓ   25 Ⓐ Ⓑ Ⓒ Ⓓ   39 Ⓐ Ⓑ Ⓒ Ⓓ   53 Ⓐ Ⓑ Ⓒ Ⓓ   67 Ⓐ Ⓑ Ⓒ Ⓓ

12 Ⓐ Ⓑ Ⓒ Ⓓ   26 Ⓐ Ⓑ Ⓒ Ⓓ   40 Ⓐ Ⓑ Ⓒ Ⓓ   54 Ⓐ Ⓑ Ⓒ Ⓓ   68 Ⓐ Ⓑ Ⓒ Ⓓ

13 Ⓐ Ⓑ Ⓒ Ⓓ   27 Ⓐ Ⓑ Ⓒ Ⓓ   41 Ⓐ Ⓑ Ⓒ Ⓓ   55 Ⓐ Ⓑ Ⓒ Ⓓ   69 Ⓐ Ⓑ Ⓒ Ⓓ

14 Ⓐ Ⓑ Ⓒ Ⓓ   28 Ⓐ Ⓑ Ⓒ Ⓓ   42 Ⓐ Ⓑ Ⓒ Ⓓ   56 Ⓐ Ⓑ Ⓒ Ⓓ   70 Ⓐ Ⓑ Ⓒ Ⓓ

TEAR HERE

English Expression Questions

1 Ⓐ Ⓑ Ⓒ Ⓓ Ⓔ   23 Ⓐ Ⓑ Ⓒ Ⓓ Ⓔ   45 Ⓐ Ⓑ Ⓒ Ⓓ Ⓔ   67 Ⓐ Ⓑ Ⓒ Ⓓ Ⓔ   89 Ⓐ Ⓑ Ⓒ Ⓓ Ⓔ
2 Ⓐ Ⓑ Ⓒ Ⓓ Ⓔ   24 Ⓐ Ⓑ Ⓒ Ⓓ Ⓔ   46 Ⓐ Ⓑ Ⓒ Ⓓ Ⓔ   68 Ⓐ Ⓑ Ⓒ Ⓓ Ⓔ   90 Ⓐ Ⓑ Ⓒ Ⓓ Ⓔ
3 Ⓐ Ⓑ Ⓒ Ⓓ Ⓔ   25 Ⓐ Ⓑ Ⓒ Ⓓ Ⓔ   47 Ⓐ Ⓑ Ⓒ Ⓓ Ⓔ   69 Ⓐ Ⓑ Ⓒ Ⓓ Ⓔ   91 Ⓐ Ⓑ Ⓒ Ⓓ Ⓔ
4 Ⓐ Ⓑ Ⓒ Ⓓ Ⓔ   26 Ⓐ Ⓑ Ⓒ Ⓓ Ⓔ   48 Ⓐ Ⓑ Ⓒ Ⓓ Ⓔ   70 Ⓐ Ⓑ Ⓒ Ⓓ Ⓔ   92 Ⓐ Ⓑ Ⓒ Ⓓ Ⓔ
5 Ⓐ Ⓑ Ⓒ Ⓓ Ⓔ   27 Ⓐ Ⓑ Ⓒ Ⓓ Ⓔ   49 Ⓐ Ⓑ Ⓒ Ⓓ Ⓔ   71 Ⓐ Ⓑ Ⓒ Ⓓ Ⓔ   93 Ⓐ Ⓑ Ⓒ Ⓓ Ⓔ
6 Ⓐ Ⓑ Ⓒ Ⓓ Ⓔ   28 Ⓐ Ⓑ Ⓒ Ⓓ Ⓔ   50 Ⓐ Ⓑ Ⓒ Ⓓ Ⓔ   72 Ⓐ Ⓑ Ⓒ Ⓓ Ⓔ   94 Ⓐ Ⓑ Ⓒ Ⓓ Ⓔ
7 Ⓐ Ⓑ Ⓒ Ⓓ Ⓔ   29 Ⓐ Ⓑ Ⓒ Ⓓ Ⓔ   51 Ⓐ Ⓑ Ⓒ Ⓓ Ⓔ   73 Ⓐ Ⓑ Ⓒ Ⓓ Ⓔ   95 Ⓐ Ⓑ Ⓒ Ⓓ Ⓔ
8 Ⓐ Ⓑ Ⓒ Ⓓ Ⓔ   30 Ⓐ Ⓑ Ⓒ Ⓓ Ⓔ   52 Ⓐ Ⓑ Ⓒ Ⓓ Ⓔ   74 Ⓐ Ⓑ Ⓒ Ⓓ Ⓔ   96 Ⓐ Ⓑ Ⓒ Ⓓ Ⓔ
9 Ⓐ Ⓑ Ⓒ Ⓓ Ⓔ   31 Ⓐ Ⓑ Ⓒ Ⓓ Ⓔ   53 Ⓐ Ⓑ Ⓒ Ⓓ Ⓔ   75 Ⓐ Ⓑ Ⓒ Ⓓ Ⓔ   97 Ⓐ Ⓑ Ⓒ Ⓓ Ⓔ
10 Ⓐ Ⓑ Ⓒ Ⓓ Ⓔ   32 Ⓐ Ⓑ Ⓒ Ⓓ Ⓔ   54 Ⓐ Ⓑ Ⓒ Ⓓ Ⓔ   76 Ⓐ Ⓑ Ⓒ Ⓓ Ⓔ   98 Ⓐ Ⓑ Ⓒ Ⓓ Ⓔ
11 Ⓐ Ⓑ Ⓒ Ⓓ Ⓔ   33 Ⓐ Ⓑ Ⓒ Ⓓ Ⓔ   55 Ⓐ Ⓑ Ⓒ Ⓓ Ⓔ   77 Ⓐ Ⓑ Ⓒ Ⓓ Ⓔ   99 Ⓐ Ⓑ Ⓒ Ⓓ Ⓔ
12 Ⓐ Ⓑ Ⓒ Ⓓ Ⓔ   34 Ⓐ Ⓑ Ⓒ Ⓓ Ⓔ   56 Ⓐ Ⓑ Ⓒ Ⓓ Ⓔ   78 Ⓐ Ⓑ Ⓒ Ⓓ Ⓔ   100 Ⓐ Ⓑ Ⓒ Ⓓ Ⓔ
13 Ⓐ Ⓑ Ⓒ Ⓓ Ⓔ   35 Ⓐ Ⓑ Ⓒ Ⓓ Ⓔ   57 Ⓐ Ⓑ Ⓒ Ⓓ Ⓔ   79 Ⓐ Ⓑ Ⓒ Ⓓ Ⓔ   101 Ⓐ Ⓑ Ⓒ Ⓓ Ⓔ
14 Ⓐ Ⓑ Ⓒ Ⓓ Ⓔ   36 Ⓐ Ⓑ Ⓒ Ⓓ Ⓔ   58 Ⓐ Ⓑ Ⓒ Ⓓ Ⓔ   80 Ⓐ Ⓑ Ⓒ Ⓓ Ⓔ   102 Ⓐ Ⓑ Ⓒ Ⓓ Ⓔ
15 Ⓐ Ⓑ Ⓒ Ⓓ Ⓔ   37 Ⓐ Ⓑ Ⓒ Ⓓ Ⓔ   59 Ⓐ Ⓑ Ⓒ Ⓓ Ⓔ   81 Ⓐ Ⓑ Ⓒ Ⓓ Ⓔ   103 Ⓐ Ⓑ Ⓒ Ⓓ Ⓔ
16 Ⓐ Ⓑ Ⓒ Ⓓ Ⓔ   38 Ⓐ Ⓑ Ⓒ Ⓓ Ⓔ   60 Ⓐ Ⓑ Ⓒ Ⓓ Ⓔ   82 Ⓐ Ⓑ Ⓒ Ⓓ Ⓔ   104 Ⓐ Ⓑ Ⓒ Ⓓ Ⓔ
17 Ⓐ Ⓑ Ⓒ Ⓓ Ⓔ   39 Ⓐ Ⓑ Ⓒ Ⓓ Ⓔ   61 Ⓐ Ⓑ Ⓒ Ⓓ Ⓔ   83 Ⓐ Ⓑ Ⓒ Ⓓ Ⓔ   105 Ⓐ Ⓑ Ⓒ Ⓓ Ⓔ
18 Ⓐ Ⓑ Ⓒ Ⓓ Ⓔ   40 Ⓐ Ⓑ Ⓒ Ⓓ Ⓔ   62 Ⓐ Ⓑ Ⓒ Ⓓ Ⓔ   84 Ⓐ Ⓑ Ⓒ Ⓓ Ⓔ   106 Ⓐ Ⓑ Ⓒ Ⓓ Ⓔ
19 Ⓐ Ⓑ Ⓒ Ⓓ Ⓔ   41 Ⓐ Ⓑ Ⓒ Ⓓ Ⓔ   63 Ⓐ Ⓑ Ⓒ Ⓓ Ⓔ   85 Ⓐ Ⓑ Ⓒ Ⓓ Ⓔ   107 Ⓐ Ⓑ Ⓒ Ⓓ Ⓔ
20 Ⓐ Ⓑ Ⓒ Ⓓ Ⓔ   42 Ⓐ Ⓑ Ⓒ Ⓓ Ⓔ   64 Ⓐ Ⓑ Ⓒ Ⓓ Ⓔ   86 Ⓐ Ⓑ Ⓒ Ⓓ Ⓔ   108 Ⓐ Ⓑ Ⓒ Ⓓ Ⓔ
21 Ⓐ Ⓑ Ⓒ Ⓓ Ⓔ   43 Ⓐ Ⓑ Ⓒ Ⓓ Ⓔ   65 Ⓐ Ⓑ Ⓒ Ⓓ Ⓔ   87 Ⓐ Ⓑ Ⓒ Ⓓ Ⓔ   109 Ⓐ Ⓑ Ⓒ Ⓓ Ⓔ
22 Ⓐ Ⓑ Ⓒ Ⓓ Ⓔ   44 Ⓐ Ⓑ Ⓒ Ⓓ Ⓔ   66 Ⓐ Ⓑ Ⓒ Ⓓ Ⓔ   88 Ⓐ Ⓑ Ⓒ Ⓓ Ⓔ   110 Ⓐ Ⓑ Ⓒ Ⓓ Ⓔ

TEAR HERE

SECOND MODEL
FOREIGN SERVICE OFFICER EXAM

KNOWLEDGE QUESTIONS

70 questions—2 hours

1. By Supreme Court decisions, the principle has been established that a state can be prevented from infringing upon freedom of speech and of the press
   (A) only if its constitution provides a guarantee against such infringement
   (B) because freedom of speech and of the press are considered to be basic liberties protected by the Fourteenth Amendment against state action
   (C) under the "due process" clause of the Fifth Amendment
   (D) only in specific instances

2. In the years immediately following the Congress of Vienna, the Great Powers of Europe generally followed the policy of
   (A) granting democratic reforms to prevent revolutions
   (B) suppressing democratic movements
   (C) cooperating to bring about the downfall of Napoleon
   (D) checking Russian expansion in the Balkans

3. If Country K can produce Commodity A with 1 unit of input and Commodity B with 3 units of input, and Country P can produce Commodity A with 5 units of input and Commodity B with 10 units of input, it would be most likely that
   (A) Country K would produce both commodities and Country P neither
   (B) Country P would gain from trade, Country K would not
   (C) Country K would gain from trade, Country P would not
   (D) each country would gain by trading with the other

4. If each of the following groups of artists could collaborate on a work, which group would most probably create an American folk opera based upon themes drawn from the early history of the nation?
   (A) Leonard Bernstein, Jack Kerouac, and Pearl Primus
   (B) Aaron Copland, Carl Sandburg, and Agnes de Mille
   (C) Lukas Foss, Ernest Hemingway, and George Balanchine
   (D) Paul Hindemith, Henry Miller, and Anthony Tudor

5. A diplomatic pouch shares extraterritorial privileges with an embassy or consulate; that is, it is exempt from customs inspection and from local jurisdiction. This special status is granted to a diplomatic pouch to provide a government with some confidential means for transmitting confidential messages and documents. If a consular official sends diamonds to his home country in a diplomatic pouch, he is
   (A) fully within his rights and privileges granted by extraterritoriality
   (B) in violation of moral law
   (C) in violation of international law
   (D) in violation of the laws of all countries through which the pouch must travel

6. "His attitude is as provincial as an isolationist country's unwillingness to engage in any international trade whatever, on the ground that it will be required to buy something from outsiders which could possibly be produced by local talent, although not as well and not as cheaply." This statement is most descriptive of the attitude of the division chief in a government agency who

(A) wishes to restrict promotions to supervisory positions in his division exclusively to employees in his division

(B) refuses to delegate responsible tasks to subordinates qualified to perform these tasks

(C) believes that informal on-the-job training of new staff members is superior to formal training methods

(D) frequently makes personal issues out of matters that should be handled on an impersonal basis.

Questions 7 and 8 are based on the diagram below:

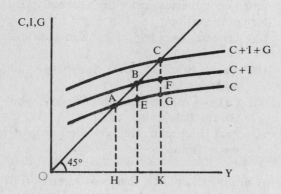

7. Equilibrium national income would be
(A) OK
(B) BJ
(C) FK
(D) OJ

8. Savings plus taxes would be
(A) FG
(B) BE
(C) CG
(D) AH

9. A major result of the Commercial Revolution (1450–1650) was the
(A) prohibition of trade with the Orient
(B) growth in the power of the feudal lords
(C) increase in trade of the Italian city-states
(D) rise to power of European nations bordering on the Atlantic.

10. Which of the following are true of the majority of immigrants who came to the United States between 1880 and 1920?
  I. They came under contract and worked primarily as domestics.
  II. They arrived able to speak and write the English language.
  III. They were from Southern and Eastern Europe.
  IV. They settled in large cities.
(A) I and II only
(B) I and III only
(C) II and IV only
(D) III and IV only

11. The United States has declared war at some time or other against all of the following countries *except*
(A) England
(B) Russia
(C) Spain
(D) Italy

12. In the middle of the twentieth century, political boundaries in Africa were determined primarily by
(A) geographic realities
(B) economic factors
(C) tribal organization
(D) 19th-century European power politics

13. Which of the following contributed most to increasing the yield of rice in Asian countries in the 1960s?
(A) Use of fertilizers
(B) Increased use of irrigation
(C) Rotation of crops
(D) Development of new strains

14. A writ of *certiorari* grants a litigant's petition to have
(A) his case heard by the Supreme Court
(B) his case retried in the court of original jurisdiction
(C) the court of appeals rehear the appeal
(D) the lower court's decision reversed

15. ''With two films, *Z* and *State of Siege,* he has emerged as the contemporary director who has best mastered the technique of transforming odious political situations into tension-filled feature films, and he has moved the political film from a genre with sectarian appeal to one with a mass audience.''

The film director described above is
   (A) Costa Gavras
   (B) Jean-Luc Godard
   (C) Michelangelo Antonioni
   (D) Ingmar Bergman

16. All of the following innovations in higher education in the United States are fairly recent EXCEPT the
   (A) introduction of open admissions policies
   (B) inclusion of Black Studies programs
   (C) accreditation of programs by regional accrediting agencies
   (D) increase in the number of community colleges

17. The event that initiated the voluntary participation of states in multilateral, high-level political conferences and eventually led to the formation of the League of Nations and the United Nations was
   (A) the Hague Conference
   (B) the Congress of Vienna
   (C) the Geneva Conference
   (D) the Paris Peace Conference

18. The number of voters participating in the 1920 United States presidential election increased relatively more than the total population increased from 1916 to 1920 primarily because
   (A) the increase in the urban population made it relatively easy for a larger percent to vote
   (B) improvements in educational methods increased popular interest in politics
   (C) the Nineteenth Amendment was ratified in 1920
   (D) voters turned out in large numbers to vote against the League of Nations

19. Missile bases of a number of European countries are located at
   (A) Venezuela
   (B) Argentina
   (C) Guyana
   (D) French Guiana

20. The Supreme Court of the United States
   (A) has the right to reverse decisions previously handed down by the Court
   (B) may deal directly with a problem even before it is faced with it in the tangible form of a legal controversy
   (C) must avoid passing judgment on federal laws that state courts have declared contrary to the Constitution
   (D) must muster a two-thirds vote of its membership to declare a law unconstitutional

Questions 21 and 22 are based on the following production-possibility schedules:

For Country A					
Food	50	40	30	20	10	0
Clothing	0	6	12	18	24	30

For Country B					
Food	100	80	60	40	20	0
Clothing	0	18	36	54	72	90

21. Both schedules indicate
   (A) decreasing costs
   (B) constant costs
   (C) first decreasing costs, then increasing costs
   (D) first increasing costs, then decreasing costs

22. If there are no restrictions on trade between the two countries, it is most likely that
   (A) both countries will produce both commodities
   (B) no trade will take place
   (C) Country A will produce only food; Country B will produce both commodities
   (D) Country A will produce only food; Country B will produce only clothing

23. The interest which Russia has historically manifested in the Dardanelles arises from a desire to have an outlet to the
   (A) Black Sea
   (B) Adriatic Sea
   (C) North Sea
   (D) Mediterranean Sea

24. Which of the following assassinations was the direct cause of a major war?
    (A) Olaf Palme in Sweden
    (B) Anwar Sadat in Egypt
    (C) Archduke Francis Ferdinand in Bosnia
    (D) Mohandas Gandhi in India

25. With per capita incomes as low as they are in southern Asia, it will not be easy to raise the rate of savings and investment. These countries are caught in something like a vicious circle of poverty. Not much can be saved from low incomes; but since not much is saved and consequently invested in production equipment, income continues to remain low. It has been estimated that with population increasing at current Indian rates a net saving of five percent of national income would be just about sufficient to maintain per capita incomes at their present level.

    Given an output-capital ratio of 1:3, the rate of population increase in India must be approximately
    (A) 1/3%
    (B) 1%
    (C) 1 2/3%
    (D) 3%

26. The objective of the International Monetary Fund is to
    (A) underwrite loans to governments for industrial projects
    (B) eliminate trade barriers in the form of protective tariffs
    (C) discourage a multilateral system of international payment
    (D) correct maladjustments in international exchange rates

27. Which of the following has the same effect as an export on the U.S. balance of payments?
    (A) An American takes a Sabena flight from Boston to Brussels.
    (B) An American purchases preferred stock in a Korean auto manufacturing firm.
    (C) An American receives a birthday check from relatives in the Netherlands.
    (D) An American purchases goods produced in a Taiwanese plant which was built with American funds.

28. Perry's visit to Japan (1854) was made primarily in order to
    (A) obtain Japanese markets for United States merchants
    (B) prevent the Japanese domination of China
    (C) break the British monopoly of Japanese trade
    (D) settle the controversy over the seal fisheries

29. Which one of the following was the FIRST official step taken by the United States in support of resistance to Communist aggression?
    (A) Joint action with the Allies in support of Italy's claims against Yugoslavia
    (B) Secretary of State Marshall's plan to strengthen Western Europe
    (C) President Truman's plan to aid Greece and Turkey
    (D) The signing of the North Atlantic Alliance

30. Which of the following has contributed most to the increase in real wages in the United States since 1900?
    (A) Rising prices
    (B) Increasing productivity
    (C) Increasing strength of labor unions
    (D) Increasing use of the corporate form of business organization

31. The Nazi-Soviet Nonaggression Pact in 1939 was followed almost immediately by
    (A) Germany's attack on the Soviet Union
    (B) Germany's attack on Poland
    (C) the Munich Agreement
    (D) the Atlantic Charter

32. Which of the following events is the result of the three others mentioned?
    (A) the formation of the Holy Alliance
    (B) pronouncement of the Monroe Doctrine
    (C) revolts in Spanish territories in the Americas
    (D) Russian claims on the Pacific Coast of North America

33. "Dependent on outside sources for iron ore, recent development of hydroelectric power, large consumption of wheat products, rainfall scarce in southern portion"—this description applies chiefly to
    (A) the former West Germany
    (B) Italy
    (C) Sweden
    (D) the former Soviet Union

34. All of the following were included in Woodrow Wilson's "Fourteen Points" EXCEPT
(A) freedom of the press
(B) freedom of the seas
(C) reduction of armaments
(D) the establishment of a general federation of nations

35. When President Reagan spoke of the excesses of government being pushed onto our children, he was referring specifically to
(A) high taxes
(B) required cuts in aid to education
(C) future costs of interest payments on the national debt
(D) the plight of the homeless

Questions 36 to 39 are based on the map below:

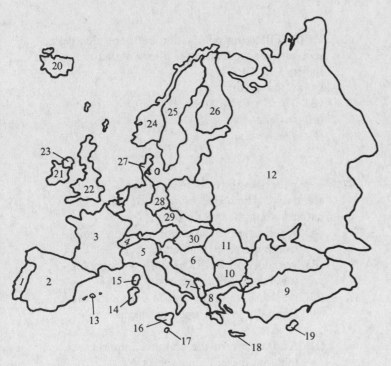

36. 9 and 12 have in common
I. language
II. government
III. location on two continents
IV. state religions
(A) I and II only
(B) III only
(C) I, II, and III only
(D) I, II, III, and IV

37. During World War II, a prominent politician in this country turned traitor and collaborated with the Nazi invaders of his country to head a puppet government. This country was
(A) 24
(B) 25
(C) 26
(D) 27

38. The name of this man, which name has now come into the language to refer specifically to a traitor/collaborator, was
(A) Vichy
(B) Quisling
(C) Turncoat
(D) Maginot

39. The area labeled 23 is
(A) a land best known for its bucolic tranquility
(B) engaged in a bitter struggle for its independence from 21
(C) the site of a religious conflict masquerading as a political conflict
(D) the site of a political conflict masquerading as a religious conflict

40. If a nation uses exchange controls to eliminate a balance of payments deficit, which one of the following is the nation likely to employ?
(A) Limiting its imports to the amount of its exports
(B) Lowering the nation's internal price level by passage of law
(C) Limiting its exports to the amount of its imports
(D) Increasing the value of its currency

41. John F. Kennedy once said, "A rising tide lifts all the boats." He probably did NOT mean
(A) that a fixed tax surcharge affects all citizens equally
(B) that an improvement in the economy would be beneficial to all
(C) that a grounded tanker will come free once the tide comes in
(D) that improved morale in the workplace would improve productivity

42. All of the following high-achievers were black EXCEPT
    (A) Dr. Daniel Hale Williams, who performed open-heart surgery in Chicago in 1893
    (B) Eli Whitney, who invented the cotton gin
    (C) Garrett A. Morgan, who invented electric traffic signals
    (D) Benjamin Banneker, who laid out Washington, D.C. when the original designer, Pierre L'Enfant, had an argument with Thomas Jefferson and took the plans to France

43. President Andrew Johnson opposed giving blacks preferential treatment in granting them instant citizenship while foreign immigrants were forced to undergo citizenship education and to wait the requisite number of years for citizenship. In contrast to the views of Andrew Johnson, the climate surrounding the era of Lyndon Johnson produced legislation granting preferential treatment to blacks. Such legislation culminated in
    (A) Brown v. Board of Education
    (B) Affirmative Action legislation
    (C) discrediting of the doctrine of separate but equal
    (D) laws guaranteeing equal pay for equal work

44. While in their American airport awaiting departure, the leader of a teen tour to Israel gathers the members of the tour around him and says, "If any of you has ANY drugs on your person or in your luggage—marijuana, crack, hash, or anything else—go into the restroom and flush every bit of it, no matter how little, right now." There may be a number of valid reasons for the leader of a teen tour to make this demand, but the most important reason for the leader to make the statement to this group is that
    (A) teenagers who are using drugs are hard to supervise
    (B) the airport is in the United States and possession of any amount of any drugs in the United States is a crime
    (C) Israeli officials tend to deal especially harshly with American teenagers caught in any offense
    (D) Israel has extremely strict drug laws to which everyone is subject while in the State of Israel

45. "The people are drafted into a huge army of ideological warriors. Even in peacetime, an attempt to defect for a civilian is regarded by law as high treason and is equated with the defection of a soldier to the enemy lines during a war." This reasoning is/was the rationale for
    (A) the new immigration laws in the United States
    (B) the demilitarized zone between North and South Korea
    (C) the Berlin Wall
    (D) the Warsaw Ghetto

46. The period from 1905 to 1914 saw massive immigration to the United States from
    (A) southern and eastern Europe
    (B) the Middle East and the Balkan states
    (C) Ireland and Scotland
    (D) Japan and Indochina

47. Of the following publications, all are clearly recognized as reflecting the biases of their publishers EXCEPT
    (A) *Commentary*
    (B) *The Christian Science Monitor*
    (C) *Insight*
    (D) *The Nation*

48. If a nation were to increase its exports substantially, which one of the following alternatives would be most probable?
    (A) A reduction in the nation's imports equal to the increase in its exports
    (B) A reduction in the nation's imports less the increase in its exports
    (C) An increase in the nation's imports substantially greater than the increase in exports
    (D) An increase in the nation's imports less than the increase in exports

49. The occurrence of export-biased technical change in the same nation discussed in question 48 would tend to
    (A) bring about a rise in the level of unemployment in the nation
    (B) bring about deflation in that nation
    (C) turn the terms of trade against the nation
    (D) turn the terms of trade against those countries the nation trades with

50. Over the past few years, a number of accused Nazi war criminals have been deported from the United States despite the fact that these individuals have lived here peacefully for many years and had attained U.S. citizenship. The basis for expelling these persons was that
    (A) under international law all persons must stand trial in the country in which they committed their crimes
    (B) war criminals are not welcome here
    (C) the countries that wished to try them threatened the United States with economic sanctions if the accused were not returned
    (D) the individuals had lied about their criminal past when applying for immigrant visas

51. An administrator with overall responsibility for all administrative operations in a large operating agency is considering organizing the agency's personnel office around either of the following two alternative concepts:
    Alternative I—a corps of specialists for each branch of personnel subject matter, whose skills, counsel, or work products are coordinated only by the agency personnel officer.
    Alternative II—a crew of so-called "personnel generalists," who individually work with particular segments of the organization but deal with all subspecialties of the personnel function.
    The one of the following which most tends to be a *drawback* of Alternative I, as compared with Alternative II, is that
    (A) training and employee relations work call for education, interests, and talents that differ from those required for classification and compensation work
    (B) personnel office staff may develop only superficial familiarity with the specialized areas to which they have been assigned
    (C) supervisors may fail to get continuing, overall personnel advice on an integrated basis
    (D) the personnel specialists are likely to become so interested in and identified with the operating view as to particular cases that they lose their professional objectivity and become merely advocates of what some supervisor wants

52. The Constitution of the United States
    (A) places greater priority on national security than it does on the right of free expression
    (B) while recognizing the need for security, places that need in a subordinate position to freedom of speech
    (C) establishes elaborate machinery for determining which speech will not damage national security
    (D) allows for self-policing and informal checks and balances in determining that which will damage national security

53. Each branch of the government has a role in the balancing of free speech and freedom of the press with the national security. Which of the following branches is INCORRECTLY paired with a role in the process?
    (A) Legislative—enacts legislation declaring specific activities to be criminal disclosure
    (B) Judiciary—enjoins publication of information which the government has declared to be critical
    (C) Legislative—classifies documents as to the degree of sensitivity of each
    (D) Judiciary—adjudicates suits brought against the press

54. An international treaty once negotiated by the administration, ratified by Congress and signed by the President, has the force of law and is binding on future administrations. However, the United States has a congressional election every two years and a presidential election every four years. Elections can, of course, change the sentiments in Congress and in the White House. Knowing this, foreign governments
    (A) do not even attempt to enter into treaties with the United States
    (B) wait until the end of a President's term to begin negotiations on treaties that they hope to enter into
    (C) contribute heavily to the campaigns of congressmen they expect to be sympathetic to their treaties
    (D) begin negotiations as soon as possible after inauguration day

55. An international agreement advocated by one President but rejected by his successor was the
    (A) U.N. Convention on the Law of the Sea
    (B) Panama Canal Treaty
    (C) agreement to notify other countries immediately after a nuclear accident
    (D) League of Nations

56. The chief responsibility for enforcing International Law lies with
    (A) the International Court of Justice in the Hague
    (B) a special tribunal set up to deal with each major transgression of International Law
    (C) the courts of the aggrieved nation
    (D) each individual nation, which is responsible for its own enforcement

57. Each of the following famous black persons is correctly paired with his or her contributions or accomplishments EXCEPT
    (A) William H. Hastie—producer of spoofs at Harvard
    (B) Dr. Mary McCleod Bethune—advisor to Franklin D. Roosevelt and to Harry S. Truman
    (C) Gwendolyn Brooks—Pulitzer Prize-winning poet and novelist
    (D) Tom Bradley—mayor of Los Angeles

Questions 58 to 60 are based on the map below:

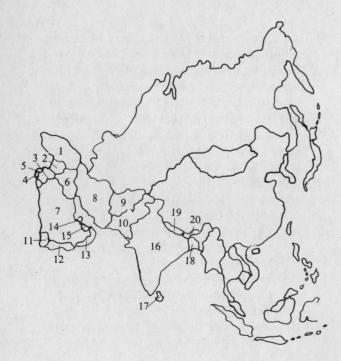

58. These two countries share a common religion and were once one. Their separation made geographical and political sense. They are
    (A) 16 and 17
    (B) 10 and 18
    (C) 18 and 19
    (D) 10 and 20

59. This nation fancies itself peacemaker and power broker of the Middle East. Through its activities, it has tried to ingratiate itself with other major powers and surrounding states (except Israel). This nation is
    (A) 1
    (B) 2
    (C) 3
    (D) 14

60. The "top of the world" is in
    (A) 16
    (B) 18
    (C) 19
    (D) 20

61. "A person charged in any State with Treason, Felony, or other Crime, who shall flee from Justice, and be found in another State, shall on Demand of the executive Authority of the State from which he fled, be delivered up, to be removed to the State having Jurisdiction of the Crime."

    The above quotation sums up extradition arrangements
    (A) among all states under International Law
    (B) among all the member states of NATO
    (C) among states under the U.S. Constitution
    (D) under the Fugitive Slave Act

62. The manner of avoiding deficit trading which would BEST serve the interests of the United States is
    (A) isolationism and self-sufficiency
    (B) making investments abroad instead of loans
    (C) encouraging foreign investments in the United States
    (D) imposing higher tariffs to discourage imports

63. Under international law, a nation can claim to have responded in self-defense to an armed attack when shots have been fired, when an army with guns has invaded, or when war has been declared against it on paper. Determination of identity of aggressor nation and defensive nation becomes significant
    (A) in punishing for war crimes
    (B) in determining the status of prisoners of war
    (C) only in the writing of histories
    (D) after the war, in determining the status and distribution of captured territory

64. In his book *The Souls of Black Folk*, which was published in 1903, W.E.B. DuBois urged patriotic, nonviolent activism as the route by which American blacks might best achieve civil rights and political and economic equality. He felt that Booker T. Washington's route of advancement through work and money neglected the crucial areas of dignity and manhood. W.E.B. DuBois' ideas as stated in this book probably influenced the movements and activities of
    I. Mohandas Gandhi
    II. Martin Luther King, Jr.
    III. John L. Lewis
    IV. Allen W. Dulles
    (A) I only
    (B) I and II only
    (C) II and III only
    (D) III and IV only

65. One of the most important concerns of personnel administrators in a foreign outpost of any level is morale. The most important reason for maintaining high morale and general contentment throughout the staff is
    (A) the high cost of turnover
    (B) unhappy staffers will discourage their friends and future recruitment will be more difficult
    (C) happy employees are more productive
    (D) unhappy employees tend to be riper targets for breaches of security through carelessness or for their personal gain

66. Article VI of the U.S. Constitution states: "The Senators and Representatives before mentioned, and the Members of the several State Legislatures, and all executive and judicial Officers, both of the United States and of the several States, shall be bound by Oath

or Affirmation to support this Constitution; but no religious Test shall ever be required as a Qualification to any Office or public Trust under the United States."
This article effectively
    (A) serves as a nonestablishment clause
    (B) gives freedom of religion to officeholders but denies it to the citizenry at large
    (C) denies the exercise of religion to officeholders
    (D) declares that the United States is an atheistic country

67. As originally conceived in 1935, the Social Security System was to be a contributory, self-supporting system. Moneys paid in by a large force of wage earners would go into a trust fund to pay retirement, survivor's, and disability benefits to a far smaller population. However, in the early 1980s the Social Security Trust Fund found itself facing deficiencies because drafters of the Act had not considered certain contingencies in their budget projections. These included:
    I. declining death rate
    II. inflation
    III. population cycles resulting in a smaller work force
    IV. increase in number of early retirements
    (A) I and II only
    (B) I and III only
    (C) I, III, and IV only
    (D) I, II, III, and IV

68. During the Falklands War in 1982, Argentina failed to receive support—economic, military, moral, or vocal—from the Third World countries of Asia and Africa. While economic and military support were outside the ability of most of these countries to supply, Argentina was distressed at its abandonment by these countries on the floor of the U.N. General Assembly. The most likely reason for this abandonment was that
    (A) the Third World countries of Asia and Africa do not like Argentina
    (B) the countries feared reprisals from Britain
    (C) these Third World nations were trying to establish reputations as neutrals
    (D) nations with fragile boundaries of their own feared setting a precedent of settling territorial disputes by military means

69. All of the following novels served to awaken black consciousness and to alert whites to the Negro condition EXCEPT
(A) *Cry, the Beloved Country*
(B) *Roots*
(C) *Of Human Bondage*
(D) *Native Son*

70. Identities of all the combatants in the Spanish Civil War were never clearly delineated, but, in the end, members of the major coalitions know who they were. Of the following alliances, the ONLY one which is certainly correct is
(A) Nationalists, Loyalists, Clergy
(B) Anarchists, Communists, Falangists
(C) Republicans, Monarchists, Partisans
(D) Socialists, Anarchists, Loyalists

END OF KNOWLEDGE QUESTIONS

IF YOU COMPLETE THIS PART BEFORE TIME IS CALLED,
CHECK OVER YOUR ANSWERS. DO NOT CONTINUE UNTIL
YOU ARE TOLD TO DO SO.
THERE WILL BE A TEN MINUTE BREAK BETWEEN PARTS.

ENGLISH EXPRESSION

110 questions—60 minutes

Directions: Some of the following sentences contain problems in grammar, usage, diction (choice of words), and idiom. Some sentences are correct.

No sentence contains more than one error.

You will find that the error, if there is one, is underlined and lettered. Assume that all other elements of the sentence are correct and cannot be changed. In choosing answers, follow the requirements of standard written English. If there is an error, select the one underlined part that must be changed in order to make the sentence correct, and blacken the corresponding space on the answer sheet. If there is no error, mark answer space E on your answer sheet.

1. Granting this to be true, what would you
   A   B
   imply from the statement that he has
   C   D
   made? No error
         E

2. The child felt very bad when his teacher
              A   B
   criticized him before the entire class.
                  C   D
   No error
   E

3. He had a large amount of friends until he
      A   B   C
   lost all his money. No error
   D   E

4. Being that she was a newcomer to our
   A   B
   organization, Rose was shy. No error
         C   D   E

5. The florist asked three of us, Dan, Edward,
                    A
   and I, to carry the plants down to the
       B   C   D
   loading dock. No error
                E

6. My father, along with hundreds
              A
   of other workers, have been on strike since
         B   C
   New Year's Day. No error
   D   E

7. Jack likes all sports: tennis, basketball,
        A   B
   football, and etc. No error
   C   D   E

8. That Bill's reasoning was fallacious was
   A   B
   soon apparent to all. No error
        C   D   E

9. Neither John nor his children is likely to
   A   B   C
   attend the ceremonies. No error
             D   E

10. He will give the message to whoever opens
       A   B   C   D
    the door. No error
             E

11. The constant rise of prices and wages bring
        A   B   C
    about inflation. No error
          D   E

12. That was the same identical damaged article
                        A   B
    that was returned to the store last month.
    C   D
    No error
    E

13. If I weren't dressed in this uniform, I
         A   B
    wouldn't feel so conspicuous. No error
    C   D   E

14. It was not quite clear whether it was his
        A   B
    friend or him who had requested the favor.
             C   D
    No error
    E

15. After he had paid the fee and saw the
                  A   B
    pictures, he was quite satisfied. No error
    C   D   E

16. <u>Further</u> acquaintance with the memoirs
    A

    of Elizabeth Barrett Browning and Robert

    Browning <u>enable</u> us to appreciate the <u>depth</u>
    B   C

    of influence that two people of talent can

    have on <u>one another.</u> <u>No error</u>
    D   E

17. Because he <u>has always been</u> popular and
    A

    <u>with abundant wealth,</u> he <u>thoroughly en-</u>
    B   C

    joyed his <u>college years.</u> <u>No error</u>
    D   E

18. <u>Having studied</u> your report carefully, I
    A

    <u>am convinced</u> that <u>neither</u> of your solutions
    B   C

    <u>are correct.</u> <u>No error</u>
    D   E

19. If he is successful in his attempt <u>to cross the</u>
    A

    lake, he <u>will have swum</u> a <u>distance of</u>
    B   C

    twelve miles. <u>No error</u>
    D   E

20. <u>In spite of</u> his youth, <u>no faster</u> runner than
    A   B

    <u>him</u> <u>will be</u> found on our Olympic team.
    C   D

    <u>No error</u>
    E

21. <u>Because of</u> the poor lighting, they
    A

    <u>mistakenly supposed</u> the <u>intruder</u> to be <u>I</u>.
    B   C   D

    <u>No error</u>
    E

22. <u>None of</u> the <u>diplomats</u> at the conference was
    A   B

    able either <u>to comprehend</u> or <u>solve</u> the prob-
    C   D

    lem. <u>No error</u>
    E

23. It was <u>agreed</u> by a majority of the signers of
    A

    the <u>compact</u> that truth <u>as well as</u> justice was
    B   C

    to be <u>there</u> rule of life. <u>No error</u>
    D   E

24. Everybody was <u>up</u> early on Monday
    A

    <u>because</u> our <u>local</u> store was having <u>it's</u> an-
    B   C   D

    nual sale. <u>No error</u>
    E

25. A careful driver <u>watches</u> the road and goes
    A

    <u>slowly</u> or quickly <u>depending upon</u> the con-
    B   C

    dition of the road, the <u>visibility</u>,
    D

    and the traffic. <u>No error</u>
    E

26. What <u>affect</u> the law will have on our <u>drivers</u>
    A   B

    and <u>how</u> it will affect our lives <u>remain</u> to be
    C   D

    seen. <u>No error</u>
    E

27. If I <u>was</u> you, I should be <u>careful</u> of <u>who</u> my
    A   B   C

    friends <u>are.</u> <u>No error</u>
    D   E

28. Merriher, <u>who</u> I never thought was even
    A

    in the running, not only <u>won handily</u> but
    B   C

    also <u>broke</u> a record. <u>No error</u>
    D   E

29. Although his story had <u>aspects of truth</u>
    A   B

    about it, I <u>couldn't hardly</u> believe
    C

    what he said. <u>No error</u>
    D   E

30. I would gladly <u>have attended</u> your wedding
    A

    gladly <u>if</u> you <u>invited</u> me by mail or by <u>phone</u>.
    B   C   D

    <u>No error</u>
    E

31. I don't understand your fondness for them;
        ‾A‾   ‾‾‾B‾‾‾   ‾C‾
     I can't stand the both of them. No error
                       ‾‾‾‾D‾‾‾   ‾‾E‾‾

32. A torrential downpour, in addition to long
        ‾‾‾A‾‾‾‾   ‾‾‾‾‾B‾‾‾‾‾

     stretches of road construction that made it

     necessary to slow down to fifteen miles an

     hour, have so delayed us that we shall not be
           ‾C‾

     on hand for the ceremony. No error
     ‾‾D‾‾   ‾‾E‾‾

33. The professor, along with a committee of
                    ‾‾‾‾A‾‾‾‾   ‾‾B‾‾‾‾‾

     honor students, have compiled a reading list.
                    ‾‾C‾‾   ‾‾‾D‾‾‾

     No error
     ‾‾E‾‾

34. It was he, not I, who became nauseous
            ‾A‾   ‾B‾   ‾‾‾C‾‾‾

     because of the boat's motion. No error
                   ‾‾‾D‾‾‾‾   ‾‾E‾‾

35. Although Richard graduated high school
                      ‾‾‾A‾‾‾‾

     with honors, he failed three subjects as a
     ‾‾‾B‾‾‾‾   ‾‾C‾‾   ‾‾D‾‾

     college freshman. No error
                       ‾‾E‾‾

Directions: In each of the followng sentences, some part of the sentence or the entire sentence is underlined. Beneath each sentence you will find five ways of phrasing the underlined part. The first of these repeats the original; the other four are different. If you think the original is better than any of the alternatives choose answer A; otherwise choose one of the others. Select the best version and blacken the corresponding space on your answer sheet.

This is a test of correctness and effectiveness of expression. In choosing answers, follow the requirements of standard written English; that is, pay attention to grammar, choice of words, sentence construction, and punctuation. Choose the answer that produces the most effective sentence—clear and exact, without awkwardness or ambiguity. Do not make a choice that changes the meaning of the original sentence.

36. At first Shakespeare's plays were performed
     more for the roles they provided the actors
     than for the truth of their characterizations
     or the beauty of their verse.
     (A) were performed more for the roles they
         provided

(B) were more performed because of pro-
    viding good roles for
(C) had been performed more for the roles
    they could provide
(D) had been performed more for the roles
    that are provided in them for
(E) had been performed more because of
    the roles they provided

37. Desiring to insure the continuity of their
     knowledge, magical lore is transmitted by
     the chiefs to their descendants.
     (A) magical lore is transmitted by the chiefs
     (B) transmission of magical lore is made by
         the chiefs
     (C) the chiefs' magical lore is transmitted
     (D) the chiefs transmit magical lore
     (E) the chiefs make transmission of magical
         lore

38. Both diplomats have this point in common:
     their forte lies not so much in administra-
     tive routine or social activities as much as
     securing the greatest advantage to their
     country at the conference table.
     (A) as much as
     (B) as much as in
     (C) as in
     (D) but it is
     (E) but is in

39. If the parent would have shown more inter-
     est, her daughter would have been in college
     today.
     (A) If the parent would have shown more
         interest
     (B) If the parent had shown more interest
     (C) If the parent would have showed more
         interest
     (D) If the parent would have been showing
         more interest
     (D) Should the parent have shown more in-
         terest

40. Having eaten a hearty luncheon, the judge
     was ready to seriously consider the circum-
     stances.
     (A) to seriously consider the circumstances.
     (B) to seriously deliberate the circum-
         stances.
     (C) to consider seriously the circumstances.
     (D) to consider the circumstances seriously.
     (E) to consider the serious circumstances.

41. Crossing the bridge, <u>a glimpse of the islands was caught</u>.
    (A) a glimpse of the islands was caught.
    (B) a glimpse of the islands were caught.
    (C) we caught a glimpse of the islands.
    (D) the islands were caught a glimpse of.
    (E) we caught a glimpse of the islands' view.

42. This book has been <u>laying here for weeks</u>.
    (A) laying here for weeks.
    (B) laying here weeks.
    (C) laying down here for weeks.
    (D) lieing here for weeks.
    (E) lying here for weeks.

43. When the officer <u>will return</u>, I'll tell him you called.
    (A) will return,
    (B) will return
    (C) will have returned,
    (D) returns,
    (E) shall return,

44. <u>After he graduated school</u>, he entered the army,
    (A) After he graduated school,
    (B) After he was graduated from school,
    (C) When he graduated school,
    (D) After he graduated school
    (E) As he was graduated from school,

45. I think they, <u>as a rule, are much more conniving than us</u>.
    (A) as a rule, are much more conniving than us.
    (B) as a rule are much more conniving than us.
    (C) as a rule, are much more conniving than we.
    (D) as a rule; are much more conniving than us.
    (E) are, as a rule, much more conniving than us.

46. Sitting around the fire, <u>mystery stories were told by each of us</u>.
    (A) mystery stories were told by each of us.
    (B) mystery stories were told by all of us.
    (C) each of us told mystery stories.
    (D) stories of mystery were told by each of us.
    (E) mystery stories were told by us all.

47. The loud noise of the subway trains and the trolley cars <u>frighten people from the country</u>.
    (A) frighten people from the country.
    (B) frighten country people.
    (C) frighten persons from the country.
    (D) frightens country people.
    (E) frighten people who come from the country.

48. Inspecting the final report, <u>the director could find no fault</u> with the <u>committee's</u> recommendations.
    (A) the director could find no fault
    (B) the director could not find no faults
    (C) no fault could be found by the director
    (D) no fault was found by the director
    (E) the director's findings agreed

49. <u>Instead of him going home</u>, he went to a movie.
    (A) Instead of him going home
    (B) Instead that he went home
    (C) Instead of going home
    (D) Instead of his going home
    (E) Instead that he was going home

50. <u>I could not but help feel</u> that her reasons for coming here were not honest.
    (A) I could not but help feel
    (B) I could not feel
    (C) I could help feel
    (D) I could not help feel
    (E) I could feel

51. <u>She never has and she never will do any work</u>.
    (A) She never has and she never will do any work.
    (B) She never has and she never will do no work.
    (C) She never has, and she never will do any work.
    (D) Never has she and never will she do any work.
    (E) She never has done and she never will do any work.

52. <u>He is not as talented as his wife</u>.
    (A) He is not as talented as his wife.
    (B) He is not so talented than his wife.
    (C) He is not talented like his wife is.
    (D) As his wife, he is not as talented.
    (E) He doesn't have the talent of his wife.

53. Did you see James's hat?
    (A) Did you see James's hat?
    (B) Did you see James hat?
    (C) Have you seen Jame's hat?
    (D) Have you seen James hat?
    (E) Have you saw James hat?

54. Security Officers perform investigative and protective services in the United States and overseas; are responsible for the security of U.S. facilities, operations, and personnel abroad; and combat criminal, intelligence, and terrorist activities worldwide which might threaten American lives and property.
    (A) and combat criminal, intelligence, and terrorist activities worldwide
    (B) combatting criminal, intelligence, and terrorist activities worldwide
    (C) and combat worldwide criminal, intelligence, and terrorist activities
    (D) and they combat criminal, intelligence, and terrorist activities worldwide
    (E) and combat criminal, intelligence, and worldwide terrorist activities

55. The congressman attached an amendment to an appropriations bill providing that a condition of any agreement between the United States and Mexico would be that "neither slavery nor involuntary servitude shall ever exist" in any part of the territory to be acquired from Mexico.
    (A) in any part of the territory to be acquired from Mexico.
    (B) in any portion of Mexican territory.
    (C) in any territory acquired from Mexico.
    (D) in any part of the territory which we had acquired from Mexico.
    (E) in any part of the territory occupied by Mexico.

Directions: In each of the following questions, you are given a complete sentence to be rephrased according to the directions which follow it. You should rephrase the sentence mentally to save time, although you may make notes in your test book if you wish.

Below each sentence and its directions are listed words or phrases that may occur in your revised sentence. When you have thought out a good sentence, look in the choices A through E for the word or entire phrase that is included in your revised sentence and blacken the corresponding space on the answer sheet. The word or phrase you choose should be the most accurate and most nearly complete of all the choices given and should be part of a sentence that meets the requirements of standard written English.

Of course, a number of different sentences can be obtained if the sentence is revised according to the directions, and not all of these possibilities can be included in only five choices. If you should find that you have thought of a sentence that contains none of the words or phrases listed in the choices, you should attempt to rephrase the sentence again so that it includes a word or phrase that is listed.

Although the directions may at times require you to change the relationship between parts of the sentence or to make slight changes in meaning in other ways, *make only those changes that the directions require*: that is, keep the meaning the same, or as nearly the same as the directions permit. If you think that more than one good sentence can be made according to the directions, select the sentence that is most exact, effective, and natural in phrasing and construction.

56. Four months have passed since his dismissal, during which time Alan has looked for work daily.
    Begin with Each day.
    (A) will have passed
    (B) that have passed
    (C) that passed
    (D) were to pass
    (E) has passed

57. The reason Frank is going to Arizona is explained by the fact that he is in need of a climate which is dry.
    Change is explained by the fact that to is that.
    (A) he must have a climate which is dry.
    (B) a dry climate is what he needs.
    (C) a climate which is dry is what he needs.
    (D) the climate is dry.
    (E) he needs a dry climate.

58. Perhaps by noon we shall have shot five rabbits.
    Begin the sentence with When noon arrives.
    (A) we may shoot
    (B) we might have shot
    (C) we will have shot
    (D) we may have shot
    (E) we shot

59. There is a bank on which the wild thyme grows.

Change There is a bank to I know a bank.

(A) whereon
(B) in which
(C) whereby
(D) from which
(E) by which

60. A decision was made by Oliver Wendell Holmes to become a writer as his father was a successful author.

Begin with Oliver Wendell Holmes.

(A) decided to become a writer on account of
(B) decided to become a writer since
(C) decided to become a writer in view of the fact that
(D) decided to become a writer while
(E) decided to become a writer although

61. If the gods wish to destroy someone, they will make him mad first.

Begin with Whomever the gods wish to destroy.

(A) they will make him mad first.
(B) they will first try to make him mad.
(C) they will first make him angry.
(D) first they make him mad.
(E) they first make mad.

62. Faulkner's novels' language resembles the language of Proust's novels.

Begin with The language of Faulkner's novels.

(A) is somewhat like that of Proust.
(B) is somewhat like Proust.
(C) is somewhat like that of Proust's.
(D) is somewhat as Proust's.
(E) is somewhat like Proust's novels.

63. Try to be patient considering that we can assist only one of you at a time.

Change considering that to since.

(A) we can assist but one of you
(B) we can't assist but one of you
(C) we can't only assist one of you
(D) we can't only assist but one of you
(E) we can't assist one of you

64. It will be two weeks tomorrow that the book will be on the shelf.

Begin with By tomorrow.

(A) the book will have lied
(B) the book will have lain
(C) the book will have laid
(D) the book will be laying
(E) the book shall have laid

65. Asia is a continent that has value equal to Africa's and has a fuller development than Africa.

Eliminate is a continent that.

(A) is as valuable as and is more fully developed
(B) is as valuable and more fully developed
(C) is as valued and more fully developed
(D) is so valuable as and more fully developed
(E) is just as valuable and more fully developed

66. Blame could not be attached to either the diplomats or our President for the fiasco.

Begin with Neither the diplomats.

(A) or our President was to blame
(B) nor our President were to blame
(C) or our President was to blame
(D) nor our President was to blame
(E) and our President were to blame

67. Rather than ignoring the rules, it would be advisable for you to consider all aspects.

Begin with Instead of.

(A) you ignoring the rules,
(B) you being ignorant of the rules,
(C) your ignoring the rules,
(D) your being ignorant of the rules,
(E) the rules being ignored by you,

68. With promptness, you might have arrived in time for the first act.

Begin with If you.

(A) would have been prompt
(B) were prompt
(C) had been prompt
(D) showed promptness
(E) could have been prompt

69. By the recurrence of identical sounds, the emotions are aided in being awakened.

Begin with The recurrence.

(A) has a great deal to do with awakening the emotions.
(B) gives help in awakening the emotions.
(C) help to awaken the emotions.
(D) helps to awaken the emotions.
(E) is of help in awakening the emotions.

70. Jerry was running in the rain and he tripped on a stick.

Begin with Running in the rain,

(A) Jerry tripped on a stick.
(B) a stick tripped Jerry.
(C) a stick caused Jerry to trip.
(D) a stick made Jerry trip.
(E) Jerry was tripped on a stick.

71. He wrote all kinds of plays including plays that were comedies, histories, and tragedies.

Change all kinds of plays to several kinds of plays.

(A) . They were comedies,
(B) . They are comedies,
(C) , comedies
(D) : comedies
(E) ; comedies

72. The speed limit was reduced to fifty-five miles per hour on open highways in America primarily because it had been determined that a significant amount of gasoline would be saved.

Omit primarily because.

(A) thus saving
(B) in order to save
(C) thereby determining that
(D) and that was how
(E) ; and we saved

73. The main reason that interstellar travel is considered improbable in the near future is that the fuel for such a lengthy trip has not yet been compounded.

Begin with The fuel for such a lengthy trip.

(A) compounded because
(B) compounded and
(C) compounded, and
(D) compounded, while
(E) compounded; therefore

74. Hardcover novels have declined so in popularity that it is beginning to make economic sense to publish first in paperback.

Begin with Publishing first

(A) because
(B) therefore
(C) in spite of the fact that
(D) moreover
(E) although

75. Prior to and during the Depression, high protective tariff barriers were erected throughout the Western world in futile attempts to protect and stimulate domestic industries.

Begin with The attempts by

(A) led to Depression.
(B) protected and stimulated domestic industries.
(C) constituted an exercise in futility.
(D) proved futile.
(E) erected high protective tariff barriers.

76. I learned the art of spiritual peace during my forty years in China from many friends, who, though illiterate, were wise and sophisticated.

Begin with During my forty years in China.

(A) wisdom among many friends
(B) peace, were wise and sophisticated
(C) peace from many friends
(D) learned the art of the peaceful spirit
(E) the art of peace, though illiterate

77. When man lived in a cave with only stone implements at his disposal, his mind no less than his actions was grooved into simple channels.

Begin with Living in a cave.

(A) mankind was both mind and action
(B) man was actively and simply grooved
(C) man of mind and action was grooved
(D) man, mind, actions, all were grooved
(E) man, in both his mind and his actions

78. Certainty that the students alone were to blame for the discipline problems in the high school caused the school board to retain the principal.

Change the noun <u>certainty</u> to the adjective <u>sure.</u>

(A) was retained
(B) will retain
(C) retained
(D) has been retained
(E) had retained

79. Greece has a claim upon our attention because we are by our spiritual and mental inheritance partly Greek.

Begin with <u>Because our spiritual.</u>

(A) inheritance is partly Greek, Greece
(B) inheritance are partly Grecian, Greece
(C) inheriting for the most part Greece, and the Greek
(D) inheritance for the most part is Greek, Greece
(E) inheritance is partly Greek; Greece

80. The ideas of Camus belong in the broad stream of contemporary thought called Existentialism.

Change the proper name, <u>Camus,</u> to its possessive form.

(A) Camus's ideas
(B) His ideas (Camus')
(C) His (Camus's) ideas
(D) Camus' ideas
(E) Ideas from Camus

81. The film ended and the sobbing crowd arose.

Change <u>The film</u> to <u>As soon as the film.</u>

(A) ended; the sobbing
(B) ended and the sobbing
(C) ended, the sobbing
(D) ended before the sobbing
(E) ended: the sobbing

82. We recommend that you buy that red dress over there even though it is a bit shopworn.

Change <u>even though</u> to <u>which.</u>

(A) consequently
(B) nevertheless
(C) we hope
(D) we doubt
(E) understandably

83. The results of the poll had little or no effect on the actions of the legislature.

Begin with <u>The actions of the legislature.</u>

(A) was barely effected
(B) was barely affected
(C) was hardly under effect
(D) were hardly affected
(E) were hardly effected

84. We could find no precedent for the judge's outrageous ruling in this case.

Begin with <u>No precedent.</u>

(A) can be found
(B) could be found
(C) is being found
(D) cannot be found
(E) can find

85. Such fallacious reasoning can quickly and easily be detected by an experienced debater.

Begin with <u>An experienced debater.</u>

(A) easily detect such
(B) easy detection but
(C) easily but fallaciously
(D) easy and quick detecting
(E) easily detected such

86. I am completely exhausted, so please turn down the record player.

Eliminate <u>so.</u>

(A) exhausted; please
(B) exhausted, please
(C) exhausted and please
(D) exhausted: please
(E) exhausting; pleasing

87. Just why some individuals choose one way of adjusting to their difficulties and others choose another way is not known.

Begin with <u>It is.</u>

(A) completely unknown why some people
(B) not knowable why some individuals
(C) not known why some individuals
(D) complete and unknown why some people
(E) not known why just some people

88. Control of the Mississippi had always been the goal of nations having ambitions in the New World.

    Begin with <u>Nations having ambitions</u>.

    (A) had forever maintained the right to control the Mississippi.
    (B) had always had the goal of controlling the Mississippi.
    (C) had forever had the goal to control of the Mississippi.
    (D) had always had the goal of Mississippi control.
    (E) had always maintained control of the Mississippi.

89. There is a very simple way in which technical terminology can lose contact with reality.

    Begin with <u>Technical terminology can</u>.

    (A) in reality with
    (B) with reality in
    (C) really in contact with
    (D) in contact with
    (E) with contact in

90. Today Venice seems to provide artists with such obvious subjects to paint that we are apt to forget that it was not always so.

    Delete the conjunction <u>that</u>.

    (A) painting; we are
    (B) to paint, however being
    (C) to paint, we are
    (D) to paint—we are
    (E) to paint; we are

Directions: In each of the following questions you are given four sentences and a question that asks for the best sequence to make a clear, sensible paragraph. Choose the correct option that reflects the ordering of the sentences that represents the best order for a clear, sensible paragraph.

91. I. The laws of war are those portions of international law that deal with the inception of war, the conduct of war, and the cessation of war.

    II. They regulate the relations between states at war and the relationships of those states which claim to be neutral powers.

    III. The popular view of war is that war is uncontrolled violence and barbarism, near the bottom in the annals of man's inhumanity to man.

    IV. Actually, war is a political act, usually undertaken only when it appears that all other alternatives have failed.

    Which of the following presents the best sequence of the sentences above to make a clear, sensible paragraph?

    (A) I, IV, II, III
    (B) III, I, II, IV
    (C) III, IV, I, II
    (D) IV, III, I, II
    (E) IV, I, II, III

92. I. Inertial guidance systems are used today in airplanes, submarines, and spacecraft.

    II. Inertial systems serve a need on fast-moving vehicles moving in a three-dimensional plane, where position information is required by the pilot almost constantly.

    III. These are very important items to have readily available, whether one is in a high-speed vehicle with very low visibility due to poor weather or in a spacecraft traveling in lunar orbit.

    IV. They display for the pilot his pitch, roll and yaw angles, heading, speed, and latitude and longitude.

    Which of the following presents the best sequence of the sentences above to make a clear, sensible paragraph?

    (A) I, IV, III, II
    (B) II, IV, I, III
    (C) III, II, I, IV
    (D) III, I, II, IV
    (E) IV, I, II, III

93. I. The intensified agricultural production required in these countries has potential adverse side effects on other resources.

    II. Some other problems include waterlogging, soil erosion, increased population of pests, and agricultural pollution.

    III. The disruptive effects of absent reservoirs are self-evident.

    IV. In most Asian countries, where rice is the principal food crop, increased cultivation has barely met the demands of the growing populations.

Which of the following presents the best sequence of the sentences above to make a clear, sensible paragraph?

(A) I, II, III, IV
(B) I, III, II, IV
(C) IV, II, III, I
(D) IV, I, III, II
(E) IV, I, II, III

94.   I. The business of the private security sector is not only to sell safety and security but to educate people in the many ways they can protect themselves.

II. This important service makes private security a natural ally of the police and a formidable foe of the criminal.

III. Together they can fashion a program that will foster public understanding and enlist public assistance in combating crime.

IV. Both police and private security stand to gain, but more importantly, the public stands to gain the most.

Which of the following presents the best sequence of the sentences above to make a clear, sensible paragraph?

(A) I, II, III, IV
(B) I, III, IV, II
(C) II, III, IV, I
(D) IV, I, II, III
(E) IV, III, II, I

95.   I. Thus, even Third World nations must get most of their news from the big four Western news agencies, and they are thereby susceptible to cultural imperialism.

II. These stories are written and filed the day before they are transmitted, and the stories are not updated during the day.

III. The news agencies of Third World countries can afford to keep few, if any, foreign correspondents.

IV. Even attempts to pool Third World resources have had limited success; Interlink, the wire service of Inter Press Service (IPS), the Third World's largest news agency and the world's sixth largest (after the big four and Tass, the news agency of the former Soviet Union), carries only about ten stories a day.

Which of the following presents the best sequence of the sentences above to make a clear, sensible paragraph?

(A) II, I, III, IV
(B) II, III, IV, I
(C) III, I, II, IV
(D) IV, III, II, I
(E) III, IV, II, I

96.   I. When television is good, nothing—not the theater, not magazines, nor newspapers—is better.

II. I invite you to sit down in front of your television set when your station goes on the air and stay there without a book, correspondence, handicrafts project, or anything else to distract you and keep your eyes glued to that set until the station signs off.

III. I can assure you that you will observe a vast wasteland.

IV. But when television is bad, nothing is worse.

Which of the following presents the best sequence of the sentences above to make a clear, sensible paragraph?

(A) I, II, III, IV
(B) I, IV, II, III
(C) II, I, III, IV
(D) II, III, IV, I
(E) III, IV, I, II

97.   I. The larger arsenals for chemical-biological warfare may be restricted to the major powers, but there is little doubt that an increasing capability is proliferating in some of the smaller and developing countries.

II. The reasons are that the nations, including some of the smaller ones, are already downstream too far.

III. And it is most difficult to dispense with this first reaction.

IV. The first reaction one has to the question of viable approaches to the control of chemical and biological weapons is that there are no such approaches.

Second Model Foreign Service Officer Exam / 101

Which of the following presents the best sequence of the sentences above to make a clear, sensible paragraph?

(A) I, II, IV, III
(B) I, II, III, IV
(C) IV, III, II, I
(D) IV, I, II, III
(E) IV, II, I, III

98. I. No one person decides anything; each decision of any importance is the product of an intricate process of brokerage involving individuals inside and outside the organization who feel some reason to be affected by the decision or who have special knowledge to contribute to it.

II. The increase in the extent to which each individual is personally responsible to others is most noticeable in a large bureaucracy.

III. The more varied the organization's constituency, the more outside ''vetogroups'' will need to be taken into account.

IV. But even if no outside consultations were involved, sheer size would produce a complex process of decision.

Which of the following presents the best sequence of the sentences above to make a clear, sensible paragraph?

(A) I, II, III, IV
(B) II, I, IV, III
(C) II, I, III, IV
(D) III, II, I, IV
(E) IV, III, II, I

99. I. In its beginning, the conflict between Christianity and Islam was violent.

II. But throughout this long period there were sometimes peaceful and more rational dialogues and debates.

III. The dialogue with Islam has a long history.

IV. One could cite here the Muslim conquests in the seventh and eighth centuries, the Crusades, the Inquisition in Spain, religious persecution, and the missionary movements.

Which of the following presents the best sequence of the sentences above to make a clear, sensible paragraph?

(A) I, II, III, IV
(B) I, III, IV, II
(C) III, II, IV, I
(D) III, I, II, IV
(E) III, I, IV, II

100. I. The common-sense character of the merit system seems so natural to most Americans that many people wonder why it should ever have been inoperative.

II. The criteria may not have always been appropriate and competition has not always been fair, but competition there was, and the responsibilities and the rewards—with exceptions of course—have gone to those who could measure up in terms of intelligence, knowledge, or perseverance.

III. After all, the American economic system, the most phenomenal the world has ever known, is also founded on a rugged selective process that emphasizes the personal qualities of capacity, industriousness, and productivity.

IV. This has been true not only in the economic area, in the money-making process, but also in achievement in the professions and other walks of life.

Which of the following presents the best sequence of the sentences above to make a clear, sensible paragraph?

(A) I, II, III, IV
(B) I, III, II, IV
(C) I, IV, II, III
(D) II, III, IV, I
(E) II, IV, I, III

101. I. If we make a long, dedicated search that fails, we will not have wasted our time.

II. We will have developed important technology, with applications to many other aspects of our own civilization.

III. We will surely have added greatly to our knowledge of the physical universe.

IV. Whether the search for extraterrestrial intelligence succeeds or fails, its consequences will be extraordinary.

Which of the following presents the best sequence of the sentences above to make a clear, sensible paragraph?

(A) IV, I, II, III
(B) II, IV, I, III
(C) III, II, I, IV
(D) II, III, IV, I
(E) III, I, II, IV

102.

I. Professionals in the business and the conscientious test publishers know the limitations as well as the values.

II. But they have no jurisdiction over users; a test can be administered by almost anyone, whether he knows how to interpret it or not.

III. They write these things into test manuals and in critiques of available tests.

IV. Nor can the difficulty be controlled by limiting sales to qualified users; some attempts to do so have been countered by restraint-of-trade suits.

Which of the following presents the best sequence of the sentences above to make a clear, sensible paragraph?

(A) I, II, III, IV
(B) I, III, IV, II
(C) I, IV, II, III
(D) I, III, II, IV
(E) III, I, II, IV

103.

I. That is, it must be possible to conceive of an experiment, the failure of which would disprove the theory.

II. Neither is supported by events, processes, or properties which can now be observed.

III. In reality, neither creation nor evolution qualifies as scientific theory.

IV. In addition, a scientific theory must be subject to or capable of falsification.

Which of the following presents the best sequence of the sentences above to make a clear, sensible paragraph?

(A) I, II, III, IV
(B) III, II, I, IV
(C) II, III, I, IV
(D) III, II, IV, I
(E) IV, I, II, III

104.

I. Yet, the land cannot be moved.

II. Land, property, real estate, or territory, by whatever name one chooses to call it, is a powerful force for both contentment and for strife.

III. Because of this last reality, wars have been fought.

IV. The location of the land determines the quality and quantity of the sustenance it provides, the nature of the shelter and the ease with which it may be obtained, and indeed, the very quality of life.

Which of the following presents the best sequence of the sentences above to make a clear, sensible paragraph?

(A) I, II, III, IV
(B) II, III, IV, I
(C) II, IV, I, III
(D) II, I, III, IV
(E) IV, III, II, I

105.

I. That is the history of the race.

II. You tell me that law is above freedom of utterance.

III. And I reply that you can have no wise laws nor free enforcement of wise laws until there is free expression of the wisdom of the people—and alas, their folly with it.

IV. But if there is freedom, folly will die of its own poison.

Which of the following presents the best sequence of the sentences above to make a clear, sensible paragraph?

(A) I, II, III, IV
(B) II, III, IV, I
(C) II, I, III, IV
(D) II, IV, III, I
(E) IV, III, II, I

106.

I. The technique begins with the assembling of a list of all the activities needed to accomplish an overall task.

II. The time required for each activity is estimated by simple statistical techniques by the persons who will be responsible for the work, and the time required to complete the entire string of activities along each sequential path through the network is then calculated.

III. One of the specific administrative techniques for program management is Program Evaluation Review Technique (PERT).

IV. The next step consists of arranging these activities in a sequential network showing both how much time each activity will take and which activities must be completed before others can begin.

Which of the following presents the best sequence of the sentences above to make a clear, sensible paragraph?

(A) I, II, IV, III
(B) II, I, IV, III
(C) I, IV, III, II
(D) III, I, II, IV
(E) III, I, IV, II

108. I. Contradictory as it may sound, the more slowly a person reads, the less he absorbs.

II. This is probably because heavier concentration is required for rapid reading, and concentration enables a reader to grasp important ideas contained in the reading material.

III. The more rapidly he reads, the more he understands and retains.

IV. The two basic elements in reading interpretation are speed and comprehension.

Which of the following presents the best sequences of the sentences above to make a clear, sensible paragraph?

(A) I, II, III, IV
(B) I, III, II,IV
(C) IV, III, II, I
(D) IV, I, III, II
(E) IV, I, II, III

107. I. Along with the useful potential of genetic engineering comes the frightening prospect of its misuse.

II. Unscrupulous researchers might experiment with humans and create "Frankenstein's monsters."

III. If we choose to predetermine the heredity of humans and to "breed to order," who has the right to choose which shall be super-intelligent and which only marginally functional?

IV. And unanswered questions arise: When the ability to do so arrives, should we breed genetic "supermen" along with a lower species of human being to do distasteful work?

Which of the following presents the best sequence of the sentences above to make a clear, sensible paragraph?

(A) I, II, III, IV
(B) I, III, IV, II
(C) I, II, IV, III
(D) I, IV, II, III
(E) I, III, II, IV

109. I. Demonstrating citizens have greatest access to public streets and to public property that is regularly open to the public.

II. Obviously, the purpose of assembly and demonstration is to be seen and heard; therefore, locations with high visibility are most often targeted.

III. Subject to safety considerations, the more public the area, the greater the citizens' right to assemble and/or demonstrate.

IV. This latter category includes areas such as public parks and transportation facilities.

Which of the following presents the best sequence of the sentences above to make a clear, sensible paragraph?

(A) I, II, IV, III
(B) II, I, IV, III
(C) II, III, I, IV
(D) III, IV, I, II
(E) III, IV, II, I

110.

I. The manager should be particularly sensitive when personal issues are reached in the course of an interview.

II. They may ask for advice, but actually they want only a chance to express themselves.

III. Even when advice-giving is successful, there is the danger that the subordinate may become overly dependent on the superior officer and run to her whenever he has a minor problem.

IV. In situations like this, what most people want is a sympathetic, understanding listener rather than an advisor.

Which of the following presents the best sequence of the sentences above to make a clear, sensible paragraph?

(A) I, IV, II, III
(B) IV, I, II, III
(C) III, IV, II, I
(D) II, IV, III, I
(E) IV, II, III, I

END OF ENGLISH EXPRESSION QUESTIONS

IF ANY TIME REMAINS, CHECK OVER YOUR WORK ON THE
ENGLISH EXPRESSION QUESTIONS ONLY.

CORRECT ANSWERS FOR SECOND MODEL FOREIGN SERVICE OFFICER EXAM

Knowledge Questions

1. B	15. A	29. C	43. B	57. A
2. B	16. C	30. B	44. D	58. B
3. D	17. B	31. B	45. C	59. B
4. B	18. C	32. B	46. A	60. C
5. C	19. D	33. B	47. B	61. C
6. A	20. A	34. A	48. D	62. B
7. A	21. B	35. C	49. C	63. D
8. C	22. D	36. B	50. D	64. B
9. D	23. D	37. A	51. C	65. D
10. D	24. C	38. B	52. D	66. A
11. B	25. C	39. D	53. C	67. D
12. D	26. D	40. A	54. D	68. D
13. D	27. C	41. A	55. A	69. C
14. A	28. A	42. B	56. D	70. D

Key to Maps

Europe—*Questions 36 to 39*

1. Portugal
2. Spain
3. France
4. Switzerland
5. Italy
6. Yugoslavia
7. Albania
8. Greece
9. Turkey
10. Bulgaria
11. Romania
12. U.S.S.R.
13. Mallorca (Spain)
14. Sardinia (Italy)
15. Corsica (France)
16. Sicily (Italy)
17. Malta
18. Crete (Greece)
19. Cyprus (Turkey/ Greece)
20. Iceland
21. Ireland
22. England/ Scotland/Wales
23. Northern Ireland
24. Norway
25. Sweden
26. Finland
27. Denmark
28. German Democratic Republic (East Germany)
29. Czechoslovakia
30. Hungary

Middle East and the Indian Subcontinent—*Questions 58 to 60*

1. Turkey
2. Syria
3. Jordan
4. Israel
5. Lebanon
6. Iraq
7. Saudi Arabia
8. Iran
9. Afghanistan
10. Pakistan
11. Yemen
12. People's Democratic Republic of Yemen
13. Oman
14. Kuwait
15. United Arab Emirates
16. India
17. Sri Lanka
18. Bangladesh
19. Nepal
20. Bhutan

English Expression Questions

1. C	23. D	45. C	67. C	89. B
2. E	24. D	46. C	68. C	90. E
3. B	25. E	47. D	69. D	91. C
4. A	26. A	48. A	70. A	92. A
5. B	27. A	49. C	71. D	93. D
6. C	28. E	50. D	72. B	94. A
7. D	29. C	51. E	73. E	95. E
8. E	30. C	52. A	74. A	96. B
9. C		53. A	75. D	97. C
10. E	31. D	54. C	76. C	98. C
11. C	32. C	55. A	77. E	99. E
12. A	33. C	56. B	78. C	100. B
13. E	34. C	57. E	79. A	101. A
14. C	35. A	58. D	80. D	102. D
15. B	36. A	59. A	81. C	103. D
16. B	37. D	60. B	82. B	104. C
17. B	38. C	61. E	83. D	105. B
18. D	39. B	62. C	84. B	106. E
19. E	40. D	63. A	85. A	107. C
20. C	41. C	64. B	86. A	108. D
21. D	42. E	65. A	87. C	109. B
22. D	43. D	66. D	88. B	110. A
	44. B			

English Expression Questions: Correctly Stated Sentences

1. **(C)** Granting this to be true, what would you *infer* from the statement that he has made?

2. **(E)** This sentence is correct.

3. **(B)** He had a large *number* of friends until he lost all his money.

4. **(A)** *Because* she was a newcomer to our organization, Rose was shy.

5. **(B)** The florist asked three of us, Dan, Edward and *me*, to carry the plants down to the loading dock.

6. **(C)** My father, along with hundreds of other workers, *has* been on strike since New Year's Day.

7. **(D)** Jack likes all sports: tennis, basketball, football, *etc.*

8. **(E)** This sentence is correct.

9. **(C)** Neither John nor his children *are* likely to attend the ceremonies.

10. **(E)** This sentence is correct.

11. **(C)** The constant rise of prices and wages *brings* about inflation.

12. **(A)** That was the *same* damaged article that was returned to the store last month.

13. **(E)** This sentence is correct.

14. **(C)** It was not quite clear whether it was his friend or *he* who had requested the favor.

15. **(B)** After he had paid the fee and *had seen* the pictures, he was quite satisfied.

16. **(B)** Further acquaintance with the memoirs of Elizabeth Barrett Browning and Robert Browning *enables* us to appreciate the depth of influence that two people of talent can have on one another.

17. **(B)** Because he has always been popular and *wealthy,* he thoroughly enjoyed his college years.

18. **(D)** Having studied your report carefully, I am convinced that neither of your solutions *is* correct.

19. **(E)** This sentence is correct.

20. **(C)** In spite of his youth, no faster runner than *he* will be found on our Olympic team.

21. **(D)** Because of the poor lighting, they mistakenly supposed the intruder to be *me*.

22. **(D)** None of the diplomats at the conference was able either to comprehend or *to* solve the problem.

23. **(D)** It was agreed by a majority of the signers of the compact that truth as well as justice was to be *their* rule of life.

24. **(D)** Everybody was up early on Monday because our local store was having *its* annual sale.

25. **(E)** This sentence is correct.

26. **(A)** What *effect* the law will have on our drivers and how it will affect our lives remain to be seen.

27. **(A)** If I *were* you, I should be careful of who my friends are.

28. **(E)** This sentence is correct.

29. **(C)** Although his story had aspects of truth about it, I *could hardly* believe what he said. Or, Although his story had aspects of truth about it, I *couldn't* believe what he said.

30. **(C)** I would have attended your wedding gladly if you *had invited* me by mail or by phone.

31. **(D)** I don't understand your fondness for them; I can't stand *either* of them.

32. **(C)** A torrential downpour, in addition to long stretches of road construction that made it necessary to slow down to fifteen miles an hour, *has* so delayed us that we shall not be able to be on hand for the ceremony.

33. **(C)** The professor, along with a committee of honor students, *has* compiled a reading list.

34. **(C)** It was he, not I, who became *nauseated* because of the boat's motion.

35. **(A)** Although Richard graduated *from* high school with honors, he failed three subjects as a college freshman.

36. **(A)** At first Shakespeare's plays were performed more for the roles they provided the actors than for the truth of their characterizations or the beauty of their verse.

37. **(D)** Desiring to insure the continuity of their knowledge, the *chiefs transmit* magical lore to their descendants.

38. **(C)** Both diplomats have this point in common: their forte lies not so much in administrative routine or special activities *as in* securing the greatest advantage to their country at the conference table.

39. **(B)** If the parent *had shown* more interest, her daughter would be in college today.

40. **(D)** Having eaten a hearty luncheon, the judge was ready to *consider* the circumstances *seriously.*

41. **(C)** Crossing the bridge, *we caught* a glimpse of the islands.

42. **(E)** This book has been *lying* here for weeks.

43. **(D)** When the officer *returns,* I'll tell him you called.

44. **(B)** After he was graduated *from* school, he entered the army.

45. **(C)** I think they, as a rule, are much more conniving than *we.*

46. **(C)** Sitting around the fire, *each of us told* mystery stories.

47. **(D)** The loud noise of the subway trains and the trolley cars *frightens* country people.

48. **(A)** Inspecting the final report, the director could find no fault with the committee's recommendations.

49. **(C)** *Instead of going home,* he went to a movie.

50. **(D)** *I could not help feel* that her reasons for coming here were not honest.

51. **(E)** She *never has done* and she *never will do* any work. Even better—She *never has done any work* and she *never will.*

52. **(A)** He is not as talented as his wife.

53. **(A)** Did you see James's hat?

54. **(C)** Security Officers perform investigative and protective services in the United States and overseas; are responsible for the security of U.S. facilities, operations, and personnel abroad; and combat *worldwide* criminal, intelligence, and terrorist activities which might threaten American lives and property.

55. **(A)** The congressman attached an amendment to an appropriations bill providing that a condition of any agreement between the United States and Mexico would be that "neither slavery nor involuntary servitude shall ever exist" in any part of the territory to be acquired from Mexico.

56. **(B)** Each day in the four months *that have passed* since his dismissal, Alan has looked for work.

57. **(E)** The reason Frank is going to Arizona is that *he needs a dry climate.*

58. **(D)** When noon arrives, *we may have shot* five rabbits.

59. **(A)** I know a bank *whereon* the wild thyme grows.

60. **(B)** Oliver Wendell Holmes *decided to become a writer since* his father was a successful author.

61. **(E)** Whomever the gods wish to destroy, *they first make mad.*

62. **(C)** The language of Faulkner's novels *is somewhat like that of Proust's.*

63. **(A)** Try to be patient since *we can assist but one of you* at a time.

64. **(B)** By tomorrow *the book will have lain* on the shelf two weeks.

65. **(A)** Asia *is as valuable as and is more fully developed* than Africa.

66. **(D)** Neither the diplomats *nor our President was to blame* for the fiasco.

67. **(C)** Instead of *your ignoring the rules,* it would be advisable for you to consider all aspects.

68. **(C)** If you *had been prompt,* you might have arrived in time for the first act.

69. **(D)** The recurrence of identical sounds *helps to awaken the emotions.*

70. **(A)** Running in the rain, *Jerry tripped on a stick.*

71. **(D)** He wrote several kinds of plays*: comedies,* histories, and tragedies.

72. **(B)** The speed limit was reduced to fifty-five miles per hour on open highways in America *in order to save* a significant amount of gasoline.

73. **(E)** The fuel for such a lengthy trip has not yet been *compounded; therefore,* interstellar travel is considered improbable in the near future.

74. **(A)** Publishing first in paperback is beginning to make economic sense *because* hardcover novels have declined so in popularity.

75. **(D)** The attempts by the Western world to protect and stimulate domestic industries prior to and during the Depression by erecting high protective tariff barriers *proved futile.*

76. **(C)** During my forty years in China I learned the art of spiritual *peace from many friends,* who, though illiterate, were wise and sophisticated.

77. **(E)** Living in a cave with only stone implements at his disposal, *man, in both his mind* and his actions, was grooved into simple channels.

78. **(C)** Sure that the students alone were to blame for the discipline problems in the high school, the school board *retained* the principal.

79. **(A)** Because our spiritual and mental *inheritance is partly Greek, Greece* has a claim upon our attention.

80. **(D)** *Camus' ideas* belong in the broad stream of contemporary thought called Existentialism.

81. **(C)** As soon as the film *ended, the sobbing* crowd arose.

82. **(B)** We recommend that you buy that red dress over there which is, *nevertheless,* a bit shopworn.

83. **(D)** The actions of the legislature *were hardly affected* by the results of the poll.

84. **(B)** No precedent *could be found* for the judge's outrageous ruling in this case.

85. **(A)** An experienced debater can quickly and *easily detect such* fallacious reasoning.

86. **(A)** I am completely *exhausted; please* turn down the record player.

87. **(C)** It is *not known why some individuals* choose one way of adjusting to their difficulties and others choose another way.

88. **(B)** Nations having ambitions in the New World *had always had the goal of controlling the Mississippi.*

89. **(B)** Technical terminology can lose contact *with reality in* a very simple way.

90. **(E)** Today Venice seems to provide artists with such obvious subjects *to paint; we are* apt to forget that it was not always so.

ANSWER SHEET FOR THIRD MODEL FOREIGN SERVICE OFFICER EXAM

Knowledge Questions

1 Ⓐ Ⓑ Ⓒ Ⓓ   15 Ⓐ Ⓑ Ⓒ Ⓓ   29 Ⓐ Ⓑ Ⓒ Ⓓ   43 Ⓐ Ⓑ Ⓒ Ⓓ   57 Ⓐ Ⓑ Ⓒ Ⓓ

2 Ⓐ Ⓑ Ⓒ Ⓓ   16 Ⓐ Ⓑ Ⓒ Ⓓ   30 Ⓐ Ⓑ Ⓒ Ⓓ   44 Ⓐ Ⓑ Ⓒ Ⓓ   58 Ⓐ Ⓑ Ⓒ Ⓓ

3 Ⓐ Ⓑ Ⓒ Ⓓ   17 Ⓐ Ⓑ Ⓒ Ⓓ   31 Ⓐ Ⓑ Ⓒ Ⓓ   45 Ⓐ Ⓑ Ⓒ Ⓓ   59 Ⓐ Ⓑ Ⓒ Ⓓ

4 Ⓐ Ⓑ Ⓒ Ⓓ   18 Ⓐ Ⓑ Ⓒ Ⓓ   32 Ⓐ Ⓑ Ⓒ Ⓓ   46 Ⓐ Ⓑ Ⓒ Ⓓ   60 Ⓐ Ⓑ Ⓒ Ⓓ

5 Ⓐ Ⓑ Ⓒ Ⓓ   19 Ⓐ Ⓑ Ⓒ Ⓓ   33 Ⓐ Ⓑ Ⓒ Ⓓ   47 Ⓐ Ⓑ Ⓒ Ⓓ   61 Ⓐ Ⓑ Ⓒ Ⓓ

6 Ⓐ Ⓑ Ⓒ Ⓓ   20 Ⓐ Ⓑ Ⓒ Ⓓ   34 Ⓐ Ⓑ Ⓒ Ⓓ   48 Ⓐ Ⓑ Ⓒ Ⓓ   62 Ⓐ Ⓑ Ⓒ Ⓓ

7 Ⓐ Ⓑ Ⓒ Ⓓ   21 Ⓐ Ⓑ Ⓒ Ⓓ   35 Ⓐ Ⓑ Ⓒ Ⓓ   49 Ⓐ Ⓑ Ⓒ Ⓓ   63 Ⓐ Ⓑ Ⓒ Ⓓ

8 Ⓐ Ⓑ Ⓒ Ⓓ   22 Ⓐ Ⓑ Ⓒ Ⓓ   36 Ⓐ Ⓑ Ⓒ Ⓓ   50 Ⓐ Ⓑ Ⓒ Ⓓ   64 Ⓐ Ⓑ Ⓒ Ⓓ

9 Ⓐ Ⓑ Ⓒ Ⓓ   23 Ⓐ Ⓑ Ⓒ Ⓓ   37 Ⓐ Ⓑ Ⓒ Ⓓ   51 Ⓐ Ⓑ Ⓒ Ⓓ   65 Ⓐ Ⓑ Ⓒ Ⓓ

10 Ⓐ Ⓑ Ⓒ Ⓓ   24 Ⓐ Ⓑ Ⓒ Ⓓ   38 Ⓐ Ⓑ Ⓒ Ⓓ   52 Ⓐ Ⓑ Ⓒ Ⓓ   66 Ⓐ Ⓑ Ⓒ Ⓓ

11 Ⓐ Ⓑ Ⓒ Ⓓ   25 Ⓐ Ⓑ Ⓒ Ⓓ   39 Ⓐ Ⓑ Ⓒ Ⓓ   53 Ⓐ Ⓑ Ⓒ Ⓓ   67 Ⓐ Ⓑ Ⓒ Ⓓ

12 Ⓐ Ⓑ Ⓒ Ⓓ   26 Ⓐ Ⓑ Ⓒ Ⓓ   40 Ⓐ Ⓑ Ⓒ Ⓓ   54 Ⓐ Ⓑ Ⓒ Ⓓ   68 Ⓐ Ⓑ Ⓒ Ⓓ

13 Ⓐ Ⓑ Ⓒ Ⓓ   27 Ⓐ Ⓑ Ⓒ Ⓓ   41 Ⓐ Ⓑ Ⓒ Ⓓ   55 Ⓐ Ⓑ Ⓒ Ⓓ   69 Ⓐ Ⓑ Ⓒ Ⓓ

14 Ⓐ Ⓑ Ⓒ Ⓓ   28 Ⓐ Ⓑ Ⓒ Ⓓ   42 Ⓐ Ⓑ Ⓒ Ⓓ   56 Ⓐ Ⓑ Ⓒ Ⓓ   70 Ⓐ Ⓑ Ⓒ Ⓓ

TEAR HERE

English Expression Questions

1 Ⓐ Ⓑ Ⓒ Ⓓ Ⓔ   23 Ⓐ Ⓑ Ⓒ Ⓓ Ⓔ   45 Ⓐ Ⓑ Ⓒ Ⓓ Ⓔ   67 Ⓐ Ⓑ Ⓒ Ⓓ Ⓔ   89 Ⓐ Ⓑ Ⓒ Ⓓ Ⓔ

2 Ⓐ Ⓑ Ⓒ Ⓓ Ⓔ   24 Ⓐ Ⓑ Ⓒ Ⓓ Ⓔ   46 Ⓐ Ⓑ Ⓒ Ⓓ Ⓔ   68 Ⓐ Ⓑ Ⓒ Ⓓ Ⓔ   90 Ⓐ Ⓑ Ⓒ Ⓓ Ⓔ

3 Ⓐ Ⓑ Ⓒ Ⓓ Ⓔ   25 Ⓐ Ⓑ Ⓒ Ⓓ Ⓔ   47 Ⓐ Ⓑ Ⓒ Ⓓ Ⓔ   69 Ⓐ Ⓑ Ⓒ Ⓓ Ⓔ   91 Ⓐ Ⓑ Ⓒ Ⓓ Ⓔ

4 Ⓐ Ⓑ Ⓒ Ⓓ Ⓔ   26 Ⓐ Ⓑ Ⓒ Ⓓ Ⓔ   48 Ⓐ Ⓑ Ⓒ Ⓓ Ⓔ   70 Ⓐ Ⓑ Ⓒ Ⓓ Ⓔ   92 Ⓐ Ⓑ Ⓒ Ⓓ Ⓔ

5 Ⓐ Ⓑ Ⓒ Ⓓ Ⓔ   27 Ⓐ Ⓑ Ⓒ Ⓓ Ⓔ   49 Ⓐ Ⓑ Ⓒ Ⓓ Ⓔ   71 Ⓐ Ⓑ Ⓒ Ⓓ Ⓔ   93 Ⓐ Ⓑ Ⓒ Ⓓ Ⓔ

6 Ⓐ Ⓑ Ⓒ Ⓓ Ⓔ   28 Ⓐ Ⓑ Ⓒ Ⓓ Ⓔ   50 Ⓐ Ⓑ Ⓒ Ⓓ Ⓔ   72 Ⓐ Ⓑ Ⓒ Ⓓ Ⓔ   94 Ⓐ Ⓑ Ⓒ Ⓓ Ⓔ

7 Ⓐ Ⓑ Ⓒ Ⓓ Ⓔ   29 Ⓐ Ⓑ Ⓒ Ⓓ Ⓔ   51 Ⓐ Ⓑ Ⓒ Ⓓ Ⓔ   73 Ⓐ Ⓑ Ⓒ Ⓓ Ⓔ   95 Ⓐ Ⓑ Ⓒ Ⓓ Ⓔ

8 Ⓐ Ⓑ Ⓒ Ⓓ Ⓔ   30 Ⓐ Ⓑ Ⓒ Ⓓ Ⓔ   52 Ⓐ Ⓑ Ⓒ Ⓓ Ⓔ   74 Ⓐ Ⓑ Ⓒ Ⓓ Ⓔ   96 Ⓐ Ⓑ Ⓒ Ⓓ Ⓔ

9 Ⓐ Ⓑ Ⓒ Ⓓ Ⓔ   31 Ⓐ Ⓑ Ⓒ Ⓓ Ⓔ   53 Ⓐ Ⓑ Ⓒ Ⓓ Ⓔ   75 Ⓐ Ⓑ Ⓒ Ⓓ Ⓔ   97 Ⓐ Ⓑ Ⓒ Ⓓ Ⓔ

10 Ⓐ Ⓑ Ⓒ Ⓓ Ⓔ   32 Ⓐ Ⓑ Ⓒ Ⓓ Ⓔ   54 Ⓐ Ⓑ Ⓒ Ⓓ Ⓔ   76 Ⓐ Ⓑ Ⓒ Ⓓ Ⓔ   98 Ⓐ Ⓑ Ⓒ Ⓓ Ⓔ

11 Ⓐ Ⓑ Ⓒ Ⓓ Ⓔ   33 Ⓐ Ⓑ Ⓒ Ⓓ Ⓔ   55 Ⓐ Ⓑ Ⓒ Ⓓ Ⓔ   77 Ⓐ Ⓑ Ⓒ Ⓓ Ⓔ   99 Ⓐ Ⓑ Ⓒ Ⓓ Ⓔ

12 Ⓐ Ⓑ Ⓒ Ⓓ Ⓔ   34 Ⓐ Ⓑ Ⓒ Ⓓ Ⓔ   56 Ⓐ Ⓑ Ⓒ Ⓓ Ⓔ   78 Ⓐ Ⓑ Ⓒ Ⓓ Ⓔ   100 Ⓐ Ⓑ Ⓒ Ⓓ Ⓔ

13 Ⓐ Ⓑ Ⓒ Ⓓ Ⓔ   35 Ⓐ Ⓑ Ⓒ Ⓓ Ⓔ   57 Ⓐ Ⓑ Ⓒ Ⓓ Ⓔ   79 Ⓐ Ⓑ Ⓒ Ⓓ Ⓔ   101 Ⓐ Ⓑ Ⓒ Ⓓ Ⓔ

14 Ⓐ Ⓑ Ⓒ Ⓓ Ⓔ   36 Ⓐ Ⓑ Ⓒ Ⓓ Ⓔ   58 Ⓐ Ⓑ Ⓒ Ⓓ Ⓔ   80 Ⓐ Ⓑ Ⓒ Ⓓ Ⓔ   102 Ⓐ Ⓑ Ⓒ Ⓓ Ⓔ

15 Ⓐ Ⓑ Ⓒ Ⓓ Ⓔ   37 Ⓐ Ⓑ Ⓒ Ⓓ Ⓔ   59 Ⓐ Ⓑ Ⓒ Ⓓ Ⓔ   81 Ⓐ Ⓑ Ⓒ Ⓓ Ⓔ   103 Ⓐ Ⓑ Ⓒ Ⓓ Ⓔ

16 Ⓐ Ⓑ Ⓒ Ⓓ Ⓔ   38 Ⓐ Ⓑ Ⓒ Ⓓ Ⓔ   60 Ⓐ Ⓑ Ⓒ Ⓓ Ⓔ   82 Ⓐ Ⓑ Ⓒ Ⓓ Ⓔ   104 Ⓐ Ⓑ Ⓒ Ⓓ Ⓔ

17 Ⓐ Ⓑ Ⓒ Ⓓ Ⓔ   39 Ⓐ Ⓑ Ⓒ Ⓓ Ⓔ   61 Ⓐ Ⓑ Ⓒ Ⓓ Ⓔ   83 Ⓐ Ⓑ Ⓒ Ⓓ Ⓔ   105 Ⓐ Ⓑ Ⓒ Ⓓ Ⓔ

18 Ⓐ Ⓑ Ⓒ Ⓓ Ⓔ   40 Ⓐ Ⓑ Ⓒ Ⓓ Ⓔ   62 Ⓐ Ⓑ Ⓒ Ⓓ Ⓔ   84 Ⓐ Ⓑ Ⓒ Ⓓ Ⓔ   106 Ⓐ Ⓑ Ⓒ Ⓓ Ⓔ

19 Ⓐ Ⓑ Ⓒ Ⓓ Ⓔ   41 Ⓐ Ⓑ Ⓒ Ⓓ Ⓔ   63 Ⓐ Ⓑ Ⓒ Ⓓ Ⓔ   85 Ⓐ Ⓑ Ⓒ Ⓓ Ⓔ   107 Ⓐ Ⓑ Ⓒ Ⓓ Ⓔ

20 Ⓐ Ⓑ Ⓒ Ⓓ Ⓔ   42 Ⓐ Ⓑ Ⓒ Ⓓ Ⓔ   64 Ⓐ Ⓑ Ⓒ Ⓓ Ⓔ   86 Ⓐ Ⓑ Ⓒ Ⓓ Ⓔ   108 Ⓐ Ⓑ Ⓒ Ⓓ Ⓔ

21 Ⓐ Ⓑ Ⓒ Ⓓ Ⓔ   43 Ⓐ Ⓑ Ⓒ Ⓓ Ⓔ   65 Ⓐ Ⓑ Ⓒ Ⓓ Ⓔ   87 Ⓐ Ⓑ Ⓒ Ⓓ Ⓔ   109 Ⓐ Ⓑ Ⓒ Ⓓ Ⓔ

22 Ⓐ Ⓑ Ⓒ Ⓓ Ⓔ   44 Ⓐ Ⓑ Ⓒ Ⓓ Ⓔ   66 Ⓐ Ⓑ Ⓒ Ⓓ Ⓔ   88 Ⓐ Ⓑ Ⓒ Ⓓ Ⓔ   110 Ⓐ Ⓑ Ⓒ Ⓓ Ⓔ

TEAR HERE

THIRD MODEL
FOREIGN SERVICE OFFICER EXAM

KNOWLEDGE QUESTIONS

70 questions—2 hours

1. Congress has approved the opening of a United States mission in the country of Bangurm. An administrative officer in the State Department assigned to compare the costs of buying, leasing, or building facilities for this mission should consider which of the following?
   I. Linear break-even analysis
   II. Present-worth comparison
   III. Depreciation
   IV. Program Evaluation and Review Technique
   (A) I only
   (B) II and III only
   (C) II, III, and IV only
   (D) I, II, III, and IV

2. The Atlantic Charter was reminiscent of Wilson's Fourteen Points, but differed from the latter in that it
   (A) did not advocate self-determination of peoples
   (B) omitted reference to disarmament
   (C) did not emphasize economic advancement
   (D) was stated in general rather than specific terms

3. A latent function of a primitive rain dance is to
   (A) aid the rainfall
   (B) provide a prelude to puberty rites
   (C) solidify the group
   (D) provide a *rite de passage*

4. Which one of the following resulted from the Suez Affair of 1956?
   (A) President Nasser emerged on the gaining side even though Egypt suffered military defeat.
   (B) The Great Powers sent contingents of police forces to maintain peace along the Gaza strip.
   (C) The Egyptian government insisted on clearing the Suez Canal by itself to demonstrate its ability to manage the Canal.
   (D) Egypt ceded a piece of territory to Israel.

5. The largest item, after national defense, in the current budget of the federal government is for
   (A) conservation and development of natural resources
   (B) interest on the national debt
   (C) veterans' services
   (D) international assistance and foreign affairs

6. During the entire period from 1800 to 1850, the greatest number of immigrants to the United States came from
   (A) Germany
   (B) England
   (C) Scandinavia
   (D) Ireland

7. Studies of social class in the United States show that the overwhelming majority of Americans
   (A) refer to themselves as working-class people
   (B) conceptualize themselves as middle-class
   (C) believe that there are no social classes in the United States
   (D) resent the dominance of middle-class values

8. In which was the second event a result of the first?
 (A) Outbreak of the Napoleonic Wars—enactment of the Embargo Act.
 (B) Passage of the Missouri Compromise—*Alabama* claims.
 (C) Tariff of 1828—calling of the Hartford Convention.
 (D) Homestead Act—establishment of "pet banks."

9. Under the treaty-making power, it is possible for
 (A) the national government to abridge rights specifically guaranteed by the Constitution
 (B) Congress to abrogate the application of the provisions of a treaty within the United States
 (C) a state to disregard self-executing treaties
 (D) Congress to act only on subjects within the lawmaking power granted by the Constitution

10. When the German colonies in central Africa were mandated to Great Britain and France following the First World War, the mandatories assumed all of the following obligations EXCEPT to
 (A) deny themselves special economic advantages
 (B) prepare the colonies for immediate self-government
 (C) guarantee freedom of conscience and religion
 (D) prevent the establishment of military bases

11. Tariffs are imposed to protect a producer who, perhaps for reasons which are not in any way that producer's own fault, is at a disadvantage in the larger economy. While the tariffs are in existence, the larger economy suffers because all the units of a given good are not being produced in a way which maximizes the quality of the product and minimizes the cost of production. In imposing the tariffs, one hopes, however, to promote the development of the protected constituency. When the protected constituency is a geographic region, that development includes social and political goals as well as economic ones. Ideally, with the assistance of temporary protection, the protected producer will eventually be able to forego the protection, meld with the larger economy as a healthy producer (or, sometimes, also as a healthy social and political actor), and carry the production of the larger economy to new heights.

The short-term goals of a tariff include
 I. bolstering of the general economy
 II. maximizing the quality of the product
 III. punishment of protected producers
 IV. development of a weak producer
 (A) I and II only
 (B) II, III, and IV only
 (C) IV only
 (D) none of these

12. All modern governments have developed specific procedures to ensure accountability for the receipt and expenditure of public funds. The steps in one such procedure are given below, out of their logical order. Select the option which best presents these stages in their logical sequence.
 (1) Disbursing officers provide for the payment of cash or check to satisfy the liability.
 (2) The central financial authority (treasury) places money at the disposal of disbursing officers.
 (3) The heads of agencies extend to designated officials within the agency the authorization to incur obligations. Designated officials award contracts for goods and services and incur obligations for the payment of salaries.
 (4) The legislature authorizes the chief executive to make expenditure authority available to administrative agencies. The executive authority responsible for the execution of the budget, in accordance with legislative action, extends to the agencies authorization to incur obligations.
 (5) Fiscal officers within agencies prepare and certify vouchers to show that obligations are due and payable by disbursing officers. Orders for payment are prepared by fiscal officers and submitted to disbursing officers.
 (A) 2, 5, 4, 1, 3
 (B) 3, 2, 5, 1, 4
 (C) 4, 3, 2, 5, 1
 (D) 5, 1, 3, 4, 2

13. A feature common to the governments of Britain and of the United States is
    (A) a federal system
    (B) local self-government
    (C) judicial review of laws
    (D) separation of legislative and executive powers

14. American dance companies with both classical and contemporary works in their repertoires incude all of the following EXCEPT the
    (A) New York City Ballet
    (B) American Ballet Theater
    (C) Alwin Nikolais Dance Company
    (D) City Center Joffrey Ballet

15. The use of the term *appeasement* in international affairs became well known as a result of the
    (A) Munich Pact
    (B) Fourteen Points
    (C) Stimson Doctrine
    (D) Statute of Westminster

16. Which one of the following events is *incorrectly* paired with a foreign policy action of the United States?
    (A) Communist threat to Western Europe—Formation of North Atlantic Treaty Organization (NATO)
    (B) Communist threat to Greece and Turkey—Issuance of the Truman Doctrine
    (C) war-shattered economies of Europe—Issuance of the Eisenhower Doctrine
    (D) Communist threat in Asia—Formation of South East Asia Treaty Organization (SEATO)

17. Prior to the 19th century, state formation in the interior of East Africa was stimulated by all of the following EXCEPT
    (A) the growth of long-distance trade
    (B) the development of an economy based on fixed cultivation
    (C) a need to control conquered territory
    (D) introduction of European forms of political organization

18. The "two-step flow theory" of communications states that
    (A) communication moves from the media to opinion leaders to the masses
    (B) attitudinal change relates first to educational level and next to ego involvement
    (C) governments tend to exercise media control first by licensing and then by strict regulation
    (D) communication moves from the media to the masses and from the masses to the media

Question 19 is based upon the graph below:

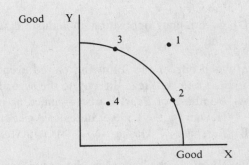

19. Which of the following statements is correct concerning the production-possibilities frontier for the economy shown above?
    (A) Point 1 is the maximum output at full employment.
    (B) The economy is better off at point 3 than at point 2.
    (C) The economy is better off at point 2 than at point 3.
    (D) Production at point 4 involves substantial unemployment.

20. Historically, patterns of population change during the process of industrialization generally have shown that
    (A) the birth rate drops markedly and is followed by decreases in the death rate
    (B) the birth and death rates show marked and simultaneous reductions
    (C) the death rate falls initially and is followed by reductions in the birth rate
    (D) both birth and death rates remain fairly constant until very high levels of material prosperity are achieved

21. During the last half of the 19th century, an important aim of Japan in modernizing itself was to
(A) improve the living conditions of the peasants
(B) remove Western European nations from China
(C) resist threats of foreign domination
(D) increase the power of the feudal lords

22. Which handicap to industrialization is found most generally in the underdeveloped countries?
(A) industrial income so low that capital cannot be accumulated
(B) inadequate supply of labor
(C) inadequate amount of raw materials for industry
(D) government opposition to industrialization

23. In which one of the following paired events did the first event lead directly to the second?
(A) Bombing of Pearl Harbor—annexing of Hawaii by the United States of America
(B) Purchase of Alaska—cold war with Russia
(C) Failure of the League of Nations—World War I
(D) Assassination of President Garfield—passage of the Pendleton Civil Service Act

Questions 24 to 26 are based on the following map:

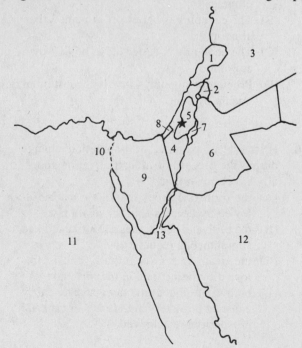

24. The starred city is
I. holy to Muslims, Jews, and Christians
II. administered by an international committee
III. a bargaining chip in all manner of Middle East negotiations
IV. divided into sectors which are rigidly restricted to members of specific groups
(A) I only
(B) I and II only
(C) II, III, and IV only
(D) I, III, and IV only

25. Area number 7 is
(A) a territory over which 4, 5, and 6 are constantly at war
(B) the only neutral country in the Middle East
(C) the source of waters which irrigate lands to its south
(D) a rich source of salt and minerals

26. The entire area represented by this map is of importance to United States foreign policy because of
I. its militarily strategic location
II. the natural resources it possesses or controls
III. the historic/religious significance of the area
IV. the possibility of Russian influence
(A) I and II only
(B) I, II, and III only
(C) II, III, and IV only
(D) I, II, and IV only

27. An American novel which greatly influenced lifestyles in the United States and much of Europe in the late 1950s was
(A) Aleister Crowley's *Liber Trigrammaton*
(B) Jack Kerouac's *On the Road*
(C) Vladimir Nabokov's *Lolita*
(D) Aldous Huxley's *Brave New World*

28. In 1986 and 1987, Brazil's economy faltered severely, forcing Brazil to default on a number of large loans made by major United States banks to help Brazil during the time of high oil costs. This was not the first time that Brazil had had economic difficulties. In 1928 Brazil's economy collapsed because of
(A) floods
(B) overproduction of coffee
(C) the costs of a typhus epidemic
(D) international depression

29. The Treaties of Rome in March 1957 produced a number of pacts serving various purposes. Among these were the
    I. European Maritime Convention
    II. Inter-European Agreement on Guest Labor
    III. European Economic Community
    IV. European Atomic Energy Community
    (A) I and III only
    (B) II and IV only
    (C) III and IV only
    (D) II, III, and IV only

30. The writings of John Maynard Keynes have been influential in justification of
    (A) lower interest and availability of money
    (B) German reparation payments to England
    (C) high interest rates
    (D) deficit financing

31. With the general abandonment of some of the basic requirements of the traditional gold standard, the par value for each of the monetary units of the world
    (A) no longer exists
    (B) is adjusted unilaterally by countries in the light of their balance of payments position
    (C) is adjusted through the International Monetary Fund
    (D) is regulated by regional agreements such as the European Payments Union

32. Which of the following can be best classified as nations marked by low birth rates and low death rates?
    (A) Communist China, India, the United Arab Republic
    (B) The United States, Brazil, Indonesia
    (C) Great Britain, France, Austria
    (D) Ghana, Mexico, Spain

33. With respect to which of the following is there the greatest similarity between the countries of the Middle East and those of Latin America?
    (A) The traditional lack of a middle class
    (B) The lack of economic viability
    (C) Dependence on agricultural products for export earnings
    (D) Type of government organization

34. "He set out to fulfill the American dream of a public school system that was the chief training ground for democracy. He advocated a curriculum that had meaning for an urban age. He taught, moreover, that curriculum and subject matter should be adapted to the needs and capabilities of children."
    Which of the following most strongly advocated the principles stated above?
    (A) Horace Mann
    (B) John Dewey
    (C) Henry Thoreau
    (D) Henry James

35. Which one of the following is generally characteristic of modern underdeveloped countries?
    (A) Rising nationalism, population problems, middle-class philosophy
    (B) Low savings rate, inequality of wealth, need for land reform
    (C) Poor endowment of natural resources, failure of the wealthy to invest in manufacturing, security of foreign investments
    (D) Desire for Western material goods, large role of government investment, full utilization of manpower

36. The right to use the airways is controlled by the government in which of the following countries?
    I. The former Soviet Union
    II. The United States
    III. Great Britain
    IV. Lebanon
    (A) I and IV only
    (B) II and III only
    (C) I, II, and III only
    (D) I, II, III, and IV

37. The President's power to remove an executive officer
    (A) is unlimited
    (B) is limited by the Senate
    (C) can be limited by an act of Congress
    (D) is defined by the Constitution

38. The reply was to the effect that the ''Creative Power,'' when he made the earth, made no marks, no lines of division or separation upon it, and that it should be allowed to remain as then made. The earth was his mother. He was made of earth and grew up on its bosom. The earth, as his mother and nurse, was sacred to his affections, too sacred to be valued by or sold for silver or gold. He could not consent to sever his affections from the land that bore him. He was content to live upon such fruits as the ''Creative Power'' placed within and upon it, and unwilling to barter these and his free habits away for the new modes of life proposed by us.

This reply was most likely made by

(A) a Massachusetts Puritan to the English Privy Council
(B) an American Indian to a U.S. government commission
(C) a Mormon leader to the governor of the Utah Territory
(D) a Mexican official to American settlers in Texas

39. The ''Uniting for Peace'' resolution adopted by the General Assembly of the United Nations in 1950

(A) curbed the veto power in the Security Council
(B) charged the General Assembly with primary responsibility for preserving peace
(C) permitted the General Assembly to consider a threat to peace after a veto in the Security Council
(D) charged the Secretary-General with special responsibility for preserving peace

40. Each of the following leaders is correctly paired with the country he or she once led EXCEPT

(A) Haile Selassie—Ethiopia
(B) Golda Meir—Israel
(C) Shah Pahlevi—Hashemite Kingdom of Jordan
(D) Eamon De Valera—Ireland

41. Worldwide hostage taking has become a major problem during the twentieth century. The most important reason for not negotiating with terrorists is

(A) to avoid granting legitimacy to their movements
(B) the cost of ransom may become staggering
(C) you can't trust terrorists to negotiate in good faith
(D) negotiation and compromise sets a precedent which encourages future hostage-taking for gain

42. John K. Galbraith's concept of *countervailing power* leads to the conclusion that

(A) more government action and regulation is necessary to restore competition
(B) a spontaneous growth of economic forces has, in effect, curbed the power of oligopoly
(C) oligopoly will, in due time, replace competition
(D) competition is doomed in any highly advanced industrial country

43. A comparison of the general situation in Europe at the opening of the 20th century with that at the opening of the 18th century would show the greatest difference with respect to the

(A) character of the social class structure
(B) practice of balance-of-power diplomacy
(C) interest in imperialism
(D) role of technology in the economy

Questions 44 and 45 are based on the following paragraph:

In-basket tests are often used to assess managerial potential. The exercise consists of a set of papers that would be likely to be found in the in-basket of an administrator or manager at any given time and requires the individuals participating in the examination to indicate how they would dispose of each item found in the in-basket. In order to handle the in-basket effectively, participants must successfully manage their time, refer and assign some work to subordinates, juggle potentially conflicting appointments and meetings, and arrange for follow-up of problems generated by the items in the in-basket. In other words, the in-basket test is attempting to evaluate the participants' abilities to organize their work, set priorities, delegate, control, and make decisions.

44. To succeed in an in-basket test, an administrator must
    (A) be able to read very quickly
    (B) have a great deal of technical knowledge
    (C) know when to delegate work
    (D) arrange a lot of appointments and meetings

45. All of the following abilities are indications of managerial potential EXCEPT the ability to
    (A) organize and control
    (B) manage time
    (C) conform to social norms
    (D) make appropriate decisions

46. In this world of high-speed travel, electronic transfer of money, and instant communications, events in one country can have a profound effect on events in many other countries. If, in the Tokyo market, the dollar drops sharply against the Japanese yen,
    (A) the price of gold will rise in London
    (B) the dollar will strengthen against the German mark
    (C) trading will cease on the New York stock exchange
    (D) American tourism in Japan will increase radically

47. The concept of the economic man in the history of economic thought relates to an individual who
    (A) seeks to further his economic self-interest above anything else
    (B) seeks to create a balance and equilibrium among the factors of consumption, production, distribution, and exchange
    (C) seeks to interpret politics mainly in the light of economic factors
    (D) seeks to make the superiority of capitalism over socialism a reality

48. The signatories to the Helsinki Accords, including the United States, Canada, and thirty-three European nations, agreed to all of the following EXCEPT
    (A) broadening detente
    (B) freezing national borders
    (C) restricting nuclear testing in the atmosphere
    (D) respecting human freedoms

49. In his handling of the Cuban missile crisis in 1962, President Kennedy chose to gamble by demanding the removal of Soviet missiles from Cuba without any reciprocal dismantling of missile sites by the United States. The Soviet missiles left Cuba, but our missiles remained in
    (A) Puerto Rico
    (B) Turkey
    (C) Algeria
    (D) Formosa

50. President Kennedy did, however, strike one bargain with Khrushchev when he demanded that Russian missiles be removed from Cuba. Kennedy promised Khrushchev
    (A) that the United States would give most favored nation status to the U.S.S.R.
    (B) that the United States would one day turn over control of the canal to Panama
    (C) that the United States would come to Cuba's defense if Cuba were attacked, since removal of the missiles left Cuba defenseless
    (D) that the United States would never invade Cuba

51. Which of the following descriptions is most consistent with ''a favorable balance of trade''?
    (A) Goods and services available for domestic use exceed the value of domestic production
    (B) Domestic holdings of gold increase
    (C) Domestic exports of merchandise exceed imports of merchandise
    (D) Net foreign investment is negative

52. The field of international relations has a language all its own. The foreign service officer must be familiar with the meanings and nuances of meaning of the words which are bandied about daily. Which of the following best describes the relationship between *entente* and *detente*?
    (A) They are synonyms
    (B) *Entente* is basically a positive word, while *detente* has a negative connotation
    (C) *Detente* might well be a point along a continuum towards *entente*
    (D) The words are totally unrelated

53. The term "laws of war" on its surface appears to be an oxymoron. One's first impression is that war is lawless. Actually, the laws of war as they apply to nonhostile contacts between the warring parties are generally observed and are quite effective. Nonhostile contacts include such activities as
(A) flags of truce, armistices, and safe passage
(B) bomb shelters, demilitarized zones, and armistices
(C) espionage, peace treaties, and first aid stations
(D) respect for the dead, flags of truce, and mine sweeping

54. Film is a powerful art form. It may be used to educate, to entertain, to make moral statements, and to make political statements. Under the guarantees of free speech, the statement made by a film might not always be for the common good, as witness the film below, which openly praises the Ku Klux Klan and implicitly condemns miscegenation. This film is
(A) Arthur Penn's *Bonnie and Clyde*
(B) Jean Renoir's *The Rules of the Game*
(C) Man Ray's *Return to Reason*
(D) D. W. Griffith's *The Birth of a Nation*

55. Which one of the following was NOT provided for in the Treaty of Rome (1957), which established the European Economic Community?
(A) Common action will be taken to improve living and working conditions for employees
(B) Monetary policies of the members are to be coordinated
(C) The colonies and associated territories of the members are to be excluded from the Common Market
(D) Trade barriers are to be gradually eliminated among the six members over a period of years

Questions 56 to 58 are based on the map below:

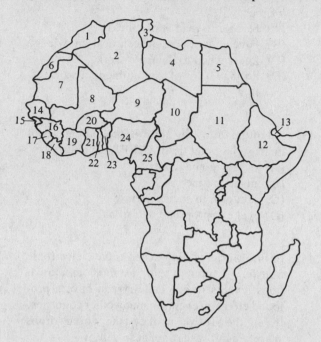

56. While much of Africa is rich in natural resources and a large part of the continent is fertile and productive, the economic situation of the continent, as a whole, is very bleak. Large areas of the continent are arid, and every ten years or so, there is a prolonged drought which creates severe famine and widespread starvation. Corruption, exploitation, and poor transportation and distribution all contribute to economic problems. In an attempt to better the lot of his people by channeling funds from his military defense budget to his economic development budget, the leader of one country made an innovative and courageous peace overture to an enemy of long standing. This ruler came from
(A) 1
(B) 5
(C) 12
(D) 20

57. The influence of Italy on the African continent has been minimal, but in a show of his "superior military power" Mussolini invaded and easily conquered a weak, unprepared African country. That country was
(A) 5
(B) 11
(C) 12
(D) 13

58. When one thinks of oil one thinks of the Middle East, but some African nations are oil-producing and some belong to OPEC. Among the OPEC nations are
    (A) 2 and 3
    (B) 4 and 5
    (C) 5 and 11
    (D) 4 and 24

59. The doctrine of purchasing-power-parity indicates that the balance of payments disequilibrium which is due to inflation may be corrected by
    (A) depreciation of the foreign exchange rate by a percentage equal to the price rise
    (B) appreciation of the foreign exchange rate by the same percentage as the price rise
    (C) an increase in the money supply by the same amount as prices
    (D) increased taxes so as to reduce purchasing power

60. In the middle of the night, five people—a mother, father, their adult son, and two young teenage daughters—approach the American embassy in a foreign country and beg for asylum. They claim that they are being harrassed because of their religious beliefs, that their home is regularly searched and pillaged, that they are unable to earn a living, and that the daughters have been molested by official police and by soldiers. Under further questioning, they admit that the son is facing a number of criminal charges, but they insist that these are trumped-up charges and that the son has been framed. They fear for his safety and, indeed, for his life. They are quite certain that they were observed as they approached the embassy.

    If the family is permitted temporary residence in the legation until long-range plans for their safety are completed, they will be following a precedent typified by
    (A) Archbishop Stepinac in our legation in Yugoslavia
    (B) Cardinal Mindzenty in our legation in Budapest
    (C) Cardinal Wyszynski in our legation in Warsaw
    (D) Archbishop Iacovos in our legation in Athens

61. According to Julius Nyerere, former President of Tanzania, a two-party system is justified only when parties differ on a fundamental issue—when one group fights to remove a grievous wrong from society that hurts all of society. In any other situation, a two-party system merely reduces politics to the level of a football match, as both sides agree on the general goals of society but haggle over which group or class will get a greater share of the nation's wealth or power, thereby hindering their effort to increase the prosperity and well-being of the nation.

    While Nyerere's assessment might hold true in his country, the two-party system served a real social purpose in the United States right after the turn of the century. Rivalries between the parties provided for
    (A) an arena in which to settle arguments by debate rather than by violence
    (B) extensive social services to new immigrants in hopes of cultivating their support once they became citizens
    (C) clubhouses which kept men off the street at night
    (D) efforts to eliminate sweatshops and to improve working conditions

62. All of the following statements about the Afrikaners in South Africa are correct EXCEPT
    (A) They constitute 60% of the white population.
    (B) They are the modern-day successors to the Boers.
    (C) Their National Party controls the government.
    (D) They live in their own homeland.

63. The common conception—or misconception—of the Native American is that of the painted savage or fierce warrior. Secondarily Native Americans are thought of as fine artisans and artists and as skillful woodsmen. In truth, Native Americans—as typified by Standing Bear, Red Cloud, and John Logan, among others, are especially to be admired for their skill and success as
    (A) songwriters
    (B) physicians
    (C) calligraphers
    (D) orators

64. Under Title VII of the Civil Rights Act and the Equal Employment Opportunity Act persons of certain race and national origin categories are singled out for special consideration. For Affirmative Action programs giving preference to members of certain minority groups, American Indians and Alaskan natives qualify ONLY if
(A) they have lived at least 70% of their lives on reservations
(B) they have left the reservation
(C) they maintain cultural identification through tribal affiliation or community recognition
(D) they have made an honest attempt at assimilation

65. The rationale for the above rule is that Affirmative Action is meant to
(A) hasten assimilation of ethnic minorities
(B) help specific disadvantaged individuals to acquire advanced training which they could not otherwise afford
(C) atone for past discrimination by promoting minority workers more quickly through the ranks
(D) assist representative members of a racial group which has deficiencies of background created by prior discrimination, thereby helping to move the group into the economic mainstream

66. The Constitution of the United States is a very short document and is specific on very few subjects; however, it does state "The Congress shall have Power To Promote the Progress of Science and useful Arts, by securing for limited Times to Authors and Inventors the exclusive Right to their respective Writings and Discoveries." By guaranteeing the protection of patents and copyrights the Constitution establishes that
(A) there will be free enterprise in the United States
(B) Congress will closely regulate granting of patents and copyrights
(C) scientists and authors will have freedom of speech
(D) authors and inventors are a superior class of citizen

67. If the end result was arms reduction and reversal of nuclear proliferation along with national security, the impetus which brought the Soviet Union and the United States to the bargaining table and led to the agreement was immaterial. The chief reason that the Soviet Union proposed such talks and agreements was
(A) the pressure of international criticism that the nuclear arms race was irresponsible
(B) budgetary pressures and economic reality
(C) fear of "nuclear winter"
(D) fear that the deployment of "Star Wars" would leave the Soviet Union vulnerable

68. The subject matter and emphases of the musical shows "The Red Mill" and "Stop the World I Want to Get Off" would make them good openers for lively discussion at a convention of
(A) psychiatrists
(B) feminists
(C) prohibitionists
(D) socialists

69. An impressive statistic coming from many Communist LDCs is the low infant mortality rate, not just a reduced mortality rate from the precommunist era but truly a low rate and often a rate considerably lower than that in highly developed, capitalistic nations. The most likely explanation of this phenomenon is that
(A) Communist countries have a controlled press and may manipulate figures to impress the world
(B) in capitalist countries there is competition for public health dollars, so the rate of infant mortality is exaggerated in local reporting in order to get greater funding for research and services
(C) health care is visible and is always appreciated, so Communist regimes invest in it disproportionately as a means of satisfying their own citizens and displaying their humanity to the world
(D) The LDCs being less industrialized have less pollution, less stress, and healthier lifestyles

70. Every major unit of government has interests which may not entirely correspond with those of the State Department. In a large embassy, this state of affairs leads to

(A) an administrative challenge in coordinating these varying interests in light of space, personnel, and equipment allotments

(B) frequent shake-ups of high-ranking personnel in the political, economic, and cultural sections

(C) a fragmented portrayal of the American position to the government of the host country

(D) a strict hierarchical structure within the embassy

END OF KNOWLEDGE QUESTIONS

IF YOU FINISH BEFORE TIME IS UP, CHECK OVER YOUR
ANSWERS ON THIS PART ONLY. DO NOT CONTINUE UNTIL
THE SIGNAL IS GIVEN.
THERE WILL BE A TEN MINUTE BREAK BETWEEN PARTS.

ENGLISH EXPRESSION

110 questions—60 minutes

Directions: Some of the following sentences contain problems in grammar, usage, diction (choice of words), and idiom. Some sentences are correct. No sentence contains more than one error.

You will find that the error, if there is one, is underlined and lettered. Assume that all other elements of the sentence are correct and cannot be changed. In choosing answers, follow the requirements of standard written English.

If there is an error, select the one underlined part that must be changed in order to make the sentence correct and blacken the corresponding space on the answer sheet. If there is no error, mark answer space E.

1. He had a chance to <u>invest wisely</u>, to estab-
   A

   lish <u>his position</u>, and <u>displaying</u> his ability
   B C

   as an executive. <u>No error</u>
   D E

2. When one <u>prepares</u> systematically and dili-
   A

   gently for the examination, <u>you</u> can
   B

   be <u>confident</u> of <u>passing</u> it. <u>No error</u>
   C D E

3. Jones seems <u>slow</u> on the track, but you will
   A

   find few men <u>quicker</u> <u>than</u> <u>him</u> on the bas-
   B C D

   ketball court. <u>No error</u>
   E

4. We had <u>swam</u> <u>across</u> the lake <u>before</u> the sun
   A B C

   <u>rose</u>. <u>No error</u>
   D E

5. As Martha <u>dived</u> off the springboard, she
   A

   was <u>horrified</u> to see that the water
   B

   was <u>drained</u> from the pool the night
   C

   <u>before</u>. <u>No error</u>
   D E

6. <u>Their</u> are <u>still</u> people who say that it has
   A B

   never <u>really</u> been <u>proved</u> that the earth is
   C D

   round. <u>No error</u>
   E

7. John Kennedy <u>effected</u> many <u>executive</u>
   A B

   reforms during the <u>tragically</u> few years that
   C

   he served as <u>president</u>. <u>No error</u>
   D E

8. Mary was so <u>disinterested</u> in the <u>baseball</u>
   A B

   game <u>that</u> she yawned <u>unashamedly</u>.
   C D

   <u>No error</u>
   E

9. Today's *Times* has headlines about another
   A

   woman <u>who</u> has just <u>swam</u> the English
   B C

   <u>Channel</u>. <u>No error</u>
   D E

10. Clearly visible on the desk <u>were</u> <u>those letters</u>
    A B

    he claimed to <u>have mailed</u> yesterday. <u>No error</u>
    C D E

11. An inexperienced <u>liar</u>, Mary explained her
    A

    absence from work with an <u>incredulous</u> tale
    B

    <u>of daring</u> in which she played the <u>role of the</u>
    C D

    heroine. <u>No error</u>
    E

12. The <u>loud noise</u> of the cars and trucks
    A

    <u>aggravates</u> <u>those who</u> live <u>near the road</u>.
    B C D

    <u>No error</u>
    E

13. <u>Irregardless</u> of <u>what people say</u>, I must re-
    A B

    peat that these are the <u>facts concerning</u> the
    C

    requirements for the position. <u>No error</u>
    D E

14. There <u>is</u> no <u>objection to him</u> joining the
    A B

    party <u>if he is</u> willing to <u>fit in with</u> the plans
    C D

    of the group. <u>No error</u>
    E

15. Rather than go with John, he decided to
    <u>A</u>   <u>B</u>   <u>C</u>
    stay at home. No error
    <u>D</u>   <u>E</u>

16. You telling the truth in the face of such dire
    <u>A</u>   <u>B</u>
    consequences required great moral courage.
                    <u>C</u>   <u>D</u>
    No error
    <u>E</u>

17. The following description, together with the
                                <u>A</u>
    drawings, present a master plan for the
              <u>B</u>   <u>C</u>
    development of the airport. No error
    <u>D</u>   <u>E</u>

18. For conscience' sake he gave himself up,
        <u>A</u>   <u>B</u>
    though no suspicion had been directed
    <u>C</u>   <u>D</u>
    toward him. No error
                <u>E</u>

19. I am depending on the medicine being
         <u>A</u>   <u>B</u>
    delivered without delay. No error
    <u>C</u>   <u>D</u>   <u>E</u>

20. Placing his longbow on the grass beside him,
               <u>A</u>   <u>B</u>
    Robin Hood, who had had an exciting day,
                <u>C</u>
    laid down to rest. No error
    <u>D</u>   <u>E</u>

21. I was not at all surprised to hear of Jim
         <u>A</u>   <u>B</u>
    Dolan winning the election
          <u>C</u>
    for town councilman. No error
    <u>D</u>   <u>E</u>

22. She saw that there was nothing else she
                                    <u>A</u>
    could do; the room was clean like it had
        <u>B</u>   <u>C</u>
    never been before. No error
    <u>D</u>   <u>E</u>

23. The instructor was justly annoyed by him
                       <u>A</u>   <u>B</u>
    walking in late and disturbing the class.
           <u>C</u>   <u>D</u>
    No error
    <u>E</u>

24. Each of the nurses were scrupulously
                       <u>A</u>   <u>B</u>
    careful about personal cleanliness. No error
           <u>C</u>   <u>D</u>   <u>E</u>

25. I enjoy eating in good restaurants and to go
      <u>A</u>   <u>B</u>   <u>C</u>
    to the theater afterwards. No error
                   <u>D</u>   <u>E</u>

26. His sworn statement, together with the tes-
        <u>A</u>   <u>B</u>
    timony and statements from other wit-
                          <u>C</u>
    nesses, were made a part of the file.
           <u>D</u>
    No error
    <u>E</u>

27. Being able to trust his sources, it is
    <u>A</u>   <u>B</u> <u>C</u>
    indispensable for the investigative reporter.
    <u>D</u>
    No error
    <u>E</u>

28. No one among the staff was more
    <u>A</u>   <u>B</u>
    disgruntled than she when the assignment
    <u>C</u>   <u>D</u>
    was handed out. No error
                    <u>E</u>

29. The government, announcing a bill of rights
    for its citizens, promising them equal rights
        <u>A</u>   <u>B</u>
    under the law and due process in the courts.
    <u>C</u>   <u>D</u>
    No error
    <u>E</u>

30. Neither tears or protests effected the
                <u>A</u>   <u>B</u>
    least change in their parents' decision.
    <u>C</u>   <u>D</u>
    No error
    <u>E</u>

31. The victim's mother, besides herself
        <u>A</u>   <u>B</u>
    with grief, could give no coherent account
    <u>C</u>   <u>D</u>
    of the accident. No error
                    <u>E</u>

32. If he had had the forethought to arrange an
            <u>A</u>   <u>B</u>

appointment, his reception <u>would have been</u>
          C   D

more friendly. <u>No error</u>
            E

33. His education had filled him <u>with anger</u>
                                A

against those <u>whom</u> he <u>believed</u> had hurt or
             B   C

<u>humiliated</u> him. <u>No error</u>
   D   E

34. <u>Admirers</u> of American ballet have made the
    A

claim that <u>its</u> stars can dance <u>as well</u> or
          B   C

<u>better than</u> the best of the Russian artists.
    D

<u>No error</u>
  E

35. When you <u>go</u> to the library tomorrow,
         A

please <u>bring</u> this book to the
       B

<u>librarian that sits</u> behind the desk on the
         C

far right of the reference room. <u>No error</u>
        D   E

Directions: In each of the following sentences, some part of the sentence or the entire sentence is underlined. Beneath each sentence you will find five ways of phrasing the underlined part. The first of these repeats the original; the other four are different. If you think the original is better than any of the alternatives, choose answer A; otherwise choose one of the others. Select the best version and blacken the corresponding space on your answer sheet.

This is a test of correctness and effectiveness of expression. In choosing answers, follow the requirements of standard written English; that is, pay attention to grammar, choice of words, sentence construction, and punctuation. Choose the answer that produces the most effective sentence—clear and exact, without awkwardness or ambiguity. Do no make a choice that changes the meaning of the original sentence.

36. Marchand is more concerned with <u>demonstrating that racial prejudice exists than preventing it from doing harm, which explains</u> why his work is not always highly regarded.
  (A) Marchand is more concerned with demonstrating that racial prejudice exists than preventing it from doing harm, which explains

(B) Marchand is more concerned with demonstrating that racial prejudice exists than with preventing it from doing harm, and this explains

(C) Marchand is more concerned with demonstrating that racial prejudice exists than with preventing it from doing harm, an explanation of

(D) Marchand's greater concern for demonstrating that racial prejudice exists than preventing it from doing harm—this explains

(E) Marchand's greater concern for demonstrating that racial prejudice exists than for preventing it from doing harm explains

37. <u>Throughout this history of the American West there runs a steady commentary on the deception and mistreatment of the Indians.</u>

(A) Throughout this history of the American West there runs a steady commentary on the deception and mistreatment of the Indians.

(B) There is steady commentary provided on the deception and mistreatment of the Indians and it runs throughout this history of the American West.

(C) The deception and mistreatment of the Indians provide a steady comment that runs throughout this history of the American West.

(D) Comment on the deception and mistreatment of the Indians is steadily provided and runs throughout this history of the American West.

(E) Running throughout this history of the American West is a steady commentary that is provided on the deception and mistreatment of the Indians.

38. <u>If you would have considered</u> all the alternatives, you would have chosen another course.

(A) If you would have considered

(B) If you would've considered

(C) If you considered

(D) If you had considered

(E) If you have considered

39. The findings resulted from extensive international cooperation, it was impossible to select fairly a single recipient for the prize.
    (A) The findings resulted
    (B) Seeing as the findings resulted
    (C) Since the findings resulted
    (D) Although the findings resulted
    (E) The findings being resultant

40. The wild game hunter stalked the tiger slowly, cautiously, and in a silent manner.
    (A) and in a silent manner.
    (B) and silently.
    (C) and by acting silent.
    (D) and also used silence.
    (E) and in silence.

41. European film distributors originated the art of "dubbing"—the substitution of lip-synchronized translations in foreign languages for the original soundtrack voices.
    (A) —the substitution of lip-synchronized translations
    (B) ; the substitution of lip-synchronized translations
    (C) —the substitutions of translations synchronized by the lips
    (D) , the lip-synchronized substitution of translations
    (D) . The substitution of lip-synchronized translations

42. The crisis we face deals with a growing population and diminishing food supply.
    (A) The crisis we face deals with a
    (B) The crisis we must face up to deals with a
    (C) We face a crisis of
    (D) The crisis we face deal with a
    (E) We face a crisis that concerns a

43. Although it is contrary to popular belief, no dialect of English is inherently superior to any other.
    (A) Although it is contrary
    (B) Contrarily
    (C) Contrary
    (D) Although contrary
    (E) Although it is being contrary

44. The epidemic worsened because of overcrowded conditions and they were unsanitary.
    (A) of overcrowded conditions and they were unsanitary.
    (B) of overcrowded and unsanitary conditions.
    (C) of overcrowded conditions and unsanitary ones.
    (D) they were overcrowded and unsanitary conditions.
    (E) of there being overcrowded and unsanitary conditions.

45. To learn to speak a foreign language fluently it requires much practice and a certain lack of embarrassment.
    (A) it requires much practice
    (B) it has to be practiced a lot
    (C) it requires much practicing
    (D) much practice is required
    (E) requires much practice

46. The director of the agency had, more than once, disagreed publicly from administration policy.
    (A) disagreed publicly from administration
    (B) publicly disagreed from administration
    (C) disagreed publicly with administration
    (D) been publicly disagreeable to administration
    (E) disagreed publicly from administrative

47. Honor as well as profit are to be gained by this work.
    (A) Honor as well as profit are to be gained by this work.
    (B) Honor as well as profit is to be gained by this work.
    (C) Honor in addition to profit are to be gained by this work.
    (D) Honor, as well as profit, are to be gained by this work.
    (E) Honor and profit is to be gained by this work.

48. He was neither in favor of or opposed to the plan.
    (A) He was neither in favor of or opposed to the plan.
    (B) He was not in favor of or opposed to the plan.

(C) He was neither in favor of the plan or opposed to it.

(D) He was neither in favor of the plan or opposed to the plan.

(E) He was neither in favor of nor opposed to the plan.

49. I don't do well in those kinds of tests.
(A) I don't do well in those kinds of tests.
(B) I don't do well in those kind of tests.
(C) I don't do good in those kinds of tests.
(D) I don't do good in those kind of tests.
(E) I don't do good in tests like those.

50. We were amazed to see the amount of people waiting in line at Macy's.
(A) amount of people waiting in line at Macy's.
(B) number of people waiting in line at Macy's.
(C) amount of persons waiting in line at Macy's.
(D) amount of people waiting in line at Macys.
(E) amount of people waiting at Macy's in line.

51. The group called a rally to demonstrate how it was opposed to the proposed construction.
(A) to demonstrate how it was opposed to
(B) to demonstrate how it was in opposition to
(C) to demonstrate its opposition to
(D) to remonstrate its opposition to
(E) for a demonstration of its being opposed to

52. By 2 o'clock, the child will have lain in his bed for ten solid hours.
(A) will have lain
(B) will have lied
(C) will have laid
(D) will have lay
(E) will be laying

53. Because they were unaware of his interest in the building, they did not understand why he felt so bad about it's being condemned.
(A) why he felt so bad about it's
(B) why he felt so badly about it's
(C) why he felt so badly about its
(D) why he felt so bad about its
(E) the reason why he felt so bad about its

54. Support Communications Officers are assigned to overseas posts and to Washington, D.C., and often work on rotating shifts as well as performing call-in/stand-by duties involving a variety of activities.
(A) Washington, D.C., and often work
(B) Washington, D.C. and often work
(C) Washington, D.C., often working
(D) Washington, D.C., and they often work
(E) Washington, D.C., and work often

55. A "cliometrician" is an economist or economic historian who works with mathematical statistics to solve historical problems.
(A) an economist or economic historian who works with mathematical statistics to solve historical problems.
(B) an economist or economic historian which works with mathematical statistics to solve historical problems.
(C) an economist or economical historian who works with mathematical statistics to solve historical problems.
(D) an economist or economic historian who works with mathematics and statistics in the solution of historical problems.
(E) an economist or economic historian who works with mathematical statistics to solve historic problems.

Directions: In each of the following questions, you are given a complete sentence to be rephrased according to the directions which follow it. You should rephrase the sentence mentally to save time, although you make notes in your test book if you wish.

Below each sentence and its directions are listed words or phrases that may occur in your revised sentence. When you have thought out a good sentence, look in the choices A through E for the word or entire phrase that is included in your revised sentence and blacken the corresponding space on the answer sheet. The word or phrase you choose should be the most accurate and most nearly complete of all the choices given and should be part of a sentence that meets the requirements of standard written English.

Of course, a number of different sentences can be obtained if the sentence is revised according to the directions, and not all of these possibilities can be included in only five choices. If you should find that you have thought of a sentence that contains none of the words or phrases listed in the choices, you should attempt to rephrase the sentence again so that it includes a word or phrase that is listed.

Although the directions may at times require you to change the relationship between parts of the sentence or to make slight changes in meaning in other ways, *make only those changes that the directions require*: that is, keep the meaning the same, or as nearly the same as the directions permit. If you think that more than one good sentence can be made according to the directions, select the sentence that is most exact, effective, and natural in phrasing and construction.

56. Owing to her wealth, Sarah had many suitors.

    Begin with Many men courted.

    (A) so
    (B) while
    (C) although
    (D) because
    (E) and

57. It displeases the director when Richard and I arrive late for work.

    Begin with The director does not approve.

    (A) of me and Richard arriving
    (B) of Richard and me arriving
    (C) of Richard's and my arriving
    (D) when Richard and me arrive
    (E) about Richard and me arriving

58. She shows laziness which annoys me.

    Change shows laziness to is lazy.

    (A) which annoys me.
    (B) and this annoys me.
    (C) and this habit annoys me.
    (D) which is something that annoys me.
    (E) which is annoying.

59. There is a stain on my tie so can you remove it?

    Eliminate so.

    (A) , can you remove the stain?
    (B) , can you remove it?
    (C) ; can you remove it?
    (D) . Can you remove it?
    (E) . Can you remove the stain?

60. The storm, as it seems, will soon be upon us.

    Begin with It looks.

    (A) like the storm
    (B) like as if the storm

(C) as if the storm
(D) as though the storm
(E) like that the storm

61. Miss Talbot resisted the temptation to expand too quickly beyond the company's financial means, so BonTon grew slowly and steadily.

    Begin with BonTon grew slowly and steadily

    (A) in spite of
    (B) in light of
    (C) although
    (D) whenever
    (E) because of

62. She is one of those people of the type who complain all the time.

    Change of the type who to who.

    (A) is always complaining.
    (B) complain and complain and complain.
    (C) complain.
    (D) complain quite a bit.
    (E) complain unceasingly.

63. We buy only cherry plums since those are the kind we like best of all.

    Instead of beginning the clause with since those, begin it with since we.

    (A) are very fond of cherry plums.
    (B) like cherry plums most of all.
    (C) eat cherry plums frequently.
    (D) like that kind best.
    (E) just adore cherry plums.

64. That he was bitterly disappointed was clearly indicated by his tone.

    Begin with His tone.

    (A) clearly implied
    (B) clearly inferred
    (C) clearly remarked
    (D) implied a clear inference
    (E) clearly implied and inferred

65. At this time kick your feet in the water in the way that Gregory just did.

    Begin with Now.

    (A) like Gregory just done.
    (B) just like Gregory did.
    (C) like Gregory just did.
    (D) just as Gregory did.
    (E) as Gregory just did.

66. Carson's sells merchandise of equal quality while having a lower price.

    Change <u>while</u> to <u>and</u>.

    (A) prices its merchandise lower.
    (B) sells at a lower price.
    (C) is having a lower price.
    (D) has a lower price.
    (E) its prices are lower.

67. My mother is roasting chicken for dinner tonight so I don't want to miss dinner.

    Change <u>so</u> to <u>and</u>.

    (A) I don't want to miss the chicken.
    (B) I don't want to miss it.
    (C) I don't want to miss tonight.
    (D) I don't want to miss the dinner.
    (E) I don't want to miss the chicken and the dinner.

68. It is more rewarding to make friends than it is being antisocial.

    Begin with <u>Making friends</u>.

    (A) than to be antisocial
    (B) than being antisocial
    (C) than to be like an antisocial person
    (D) than it is to be antisocial
    (E) than antisocial

69. I called you last night and I called several times.

    Begin with <u>Last night</u>.

    (A) I have called you several times.
    (B) I kept calling you several times.
    (C) I called you several times.
    (D) I had called you several times.
    (E) several times did I call you.

70. Help was asked of Tom and me by the distraught traveler.

    Begin with <u>The distraught traveler</u>.

    (A) of Tom and me to help.
    (B) me and Tom to help.
    (C) Tom and I to help.
    (D) I and Tom to help.
    (E) help from Tom and me.

71. Was she really the one whom you saw last night?

    Begin with <u>Was it really</u>.

    (A) she which
    (B) she who
    (C) her who
    (D) her whom
    (E) she whom

72. Saying only that she was a friend of Mary's, she left without giving her name.

    Change <u>Saying only</u> to <u>She said</u>.

    (A) and didn't give her name.
    (B) , and left without giving her name.
    (C) , she left without giving her name.
    (D) and left without giving her name.
    (E) ; and left without giving her name.

73. Fugitive slaves in the North were counted as slaves rather than as free blacks, hence increasing the percentage of slaves in the total black population.

    Begin with <u>The percentage of slaves</u>.

    (A) and counted as
    (B) by the counting of
    (C) the count was made
    (D) because the way they counted
    (E) the count of

74. Jules Verne has been called the father of modern science fiction. In his tales of adventure and romance, he predicted many scientific achievements of the 20th century.

    Rewrite as one sentence beginning with <u>In his tales</u>.

    (A) ; he was called
    (B) which made him
    (C) leading to his being called
    (D) because he was called
    (E) calling him

75. A federal employee must restrict the expression of his political sympathies to the voting booth.

    Begin with <u>As a federal employee</u>.

    (A) restrictions on
    (B) and restricting
    (C) restrict and
    (D) have to restrict
    (E) have to be restricted

76. Owing to her political skill, Ms. French had many supporters.

   Begin with <u>Many people supported</u>.

   (A) so
   (B) while
   (C) although
   (D) because
   (E) and

77. The ambassador became ill after eating at the restaurant, but she did not sue the management.

   Omit <u>but she</u>.

   Your rewritten sentence will begin with which of the following?

   (A) Since the
   (B) Although she
   (C) When becoming
   (D) Even if becoming
   (E) After eating

78. Unless we have both wage and price controls, inflation cannot be stopped.

   Begin with <u>To stop inflation</u>.

   (A) is a necessity
   (B) there are needed
   (C) there has to be
   (D) must be had
   (E) must have

79. Extremely low wages are paid to migrant workers, and they must live and work under substandard conditions. Cesar Chavez sees the development of strong unions as the way to improve their lot.

   Write as one sentence, beginning with <u>Cesar Chavez has developed</u>.

   (A) to improve the conditions
   (B) along with the conditions
   (C) thereby improving the conditions
   (D) with improved conditions
   (E) wages; in addition, the conditions

80. The often expressed wish of the negotiators was that, if the cultural exchange program were initiated, that event would begin an era of increasingly cordial relations between the two countries.

   Delete <u>if</u>.

   (A) program's initiation
   (B) program being initiated
   (C) the initiation of
   (D) to be initiated
   (E) by the initiation of

81. There are times when the medical profession appears to be a mystical cabal and not a scientific field.

   Substitute <u>appears more</u> for <u>appears to be</u>.

   (A) than a scientific field
   (B) being a scientific field
   (C) rather than a mystical cabal
   (D) and less than scientific
   (E) and being mystical as well as

82. When we lived with our parents and depended on them for all our needs, life was much simpler and our daily routine more circumscribed.

   Begin with <u>Living with our parents</u>.

   (A) when we depended on them
   (B) and having depended on them
   (C) depending on them
   (D) since we depended on them
   (E) having to depend on them

83. It delights my students when the principal of the school and I disagree on an issue.

   Begin with <u>My students approve</u>.

   (A) of the principal of the school and me disagreeing
   (B) of the school principal's and my disagreeing
   (C) of the school principal and I disagreeing
   (D) when the principal of the school and me disagree
   (E) of I and the principal of the school disagreeing

84. It was very kind of you to arrange for the meeting to be postponed, but now it will be impossible to reschedule his appearance.

Begin with <u>Although.</u>

(A) postponed. But
(B) postponed, but
(C) impossible for rescheduling
(D) postponed, now
(E) impossible to postpone

85. The agent recommended planting a stand of alfalfa to restore nitrogen to the farmer's acreage.

Begin with <u>Following the agent's recommendation.</u>

(A) planting a stand
(B) alfalfa restored
(C) acreage is planted
(D) nitrogen restored
(E) planted a stand

86. Every normal human being learns at least one language in childhood, which he continues to use throughout life.

Begin with <u>At least one language.</u>

(A) throughout life by learning
(B) throughout living and learning by
(C) throughout life had been learned of
(D) throughout life is learned
(E) throughout life is learned about

87. It was abundantly clear to Sir Winston Churchill that the long-term aims of the three principal allies were very different.

Begin with <u>The long-term aims.</u>

(A) different, it was
(B) differently so it was a fact
(C) different (a fact that was
(D) different; a fact that
(E) different and so it was

88. A pilot leaving London will arrive in New York at the hour, by the clock, at which he departed.

Start with <u>Flying from London.</u>

(A) at the hour of departure
(B) to New York, a plane landed
(C) a plane shall be arriving
(D) a pilot is arriving in New York
(E) to New York, a pilot will arrive

89. The enemy's air bombardment began and continued for five successive days.

Begin with <u>For five successive days.</u>

(A) enemy's bombarded us
(B) had been bombarded by us
(C) we were bombarded from
(D) we bombarded the enemy
(E) we had bombarded from

90. T. S. Eliot was a highly developed scholar and a magnificent poet.

Begin with <u>T. S. Eliot was not only.</u>

(A) scholar, but wrote a
(B) scholar as well as
(C) scholar, a magnificent
(D) leader and also
(E) scholar but also

Directions: In each of the following questions you are given four sentences and a question that asks for the best sequence to make a clear, sensible paragraph. Choose the correct option that reflects the ordering of the sentences that represents the best order for a clear, sensible paragraph.

91. I. The state that best epitomizes this ideal and hopefully foreshadows the United States of the future is Hawaii.

II. Such a person should be told that there are many successful multi-ethnic communities in which people of diverse backgrounds and cultures live and work together in harmony.

III. Just as events in Third World nations may be distorted in the American press, so also events in the United States may be selectively reported and sensationalized in the foreign press.

IV. Hence, a foreigner with any hostility towards the United States is apt to seize upon the status of American race relations.

Which of the following presents the best sequence of the sentences above to make a clear, sensible paragraph?

(A) III, IV, II, I
(B) IV, II, I, III
(C) III, II, I, IV
(D) I, III, IV, II
(E) I, IV, III, II

92.   I. Most of the migrants came with the intention of working for a few years and then going back to their home countries.

II. Whether called ''guest worker,'' ''migrant,'' ''temporary labor,'' or ''immigrant,'' the foreign laborer consistently appeared on the scene in the industrialized nations of Northern and Western Europe, shocking nations that had been culturally and racially homogeneous for centuries.

III. One of the greatest changes in Western Europe after World War II was the arrival of the immigrant worker.

IV. However, many of these ''migrants'' have ended up staying in the West, and there is not a country in Europe where they do not suffer from some degree of prejudice and discrimination.

Which of the following presents the best sequence of the sentences above to make a clear, sensible paragraph?

(A) III, I, II, IV
(B) III, II, I, IV
(C) II, I, IV, III
(D) II, III, I, IV
(E) I, II, IV, III

93.   I. This implies a duty to accept the verdict of the courts if we challenge the law and our challenge is not vindicated.

II. To be morally justified in such a stance, one must be prepared to submit to legal prosecution for violation of the law and accept the punishment if his attack is unsuccessful.

III. He should even demand that the law be enforced and then be willing to acquiesce in the ultimate judgment of the courts.

IV. The assumption that a law is a valid target of civil disobedience is filled with moral and legal responsibility that cannot be taken lightly.

Which of the following presents the best sequence of the sentences above to make a clear, sensible paragraph?

(A) II, I, III, IV
(B) III, II, I, IV
(C) III, I, IV, II
(D) IV, II, III, I
(E) IV, III, II, I

94.   I. Life and its perpetuation was what the animal world seemed to be about—indeed, the only thing it seemed to be about—and until Darwin, there was no one, large, encompassing idea under which the great variety of animal life could be gathered and related.

II. Zoology then set upon a sometimes fantastic journey from the mythical, moralizing bestiaries of medieval times through the rigid classifying methods of the eighteenth century and the charm and naiveté of its popular natural history phase to the broader, sounder science of more modern times.

III. Despite these scientific ups and downs and the vagaries and trends of scientific fashion, the core phenomenon of zoology has remained constant throughout—the phenomenon of life.

IV. As they did with nearly all the sciences, the Greeks set zoology off on the right road, but with their decline, the scientific pathways became overgrown and were finally lost.

Which of the following presents the best sequence of the sentences above to make a clear, sensible paragraph?

(A) I, II, III, IV
(B) I, II, IV, III
(C) III, I, II, IV
(D) IV, III, I, II
(E) IV, II, III, I

95.   I. The first is that, in any enforcement action, the great powers must necessarily bear the predominant burden.

II. The second is that the organization must depend for its strength upon the essential solidarity of the great powers.

III. Open as it is, on theoretical democratic grounds, to serious objection, the system of economic sanctions provided for the Covenant of the League of Nations rests on two basic assumptions.

IV. If this solidarity fails, then the security of enforcement arrangements will surely fail.

Which of the following presents the best sequence of the sentences above to make a clear, sensible paragraph?

(A) I, II, III, IV
(B) I, II, IV, III
(C) III, I, II, IV
(D) III, IV, I, II
(E) IV, I, II, III

96. I. The former arrangement was called the contract system, while the latter came to be known as the piece-price system.

II. Prisoners were typically either leased to private companies who set up shop in the prison or used by prison officials to produce finished goods for a manufacturer who supplied the raw materials to the prison.

III. When the United States replaced corporal punishment with confinement as the primary punishment for criminals in the early 19th century, the private sector was the most frequent employer of convict labor.

IV. Private enterprise is no stranger to the American prison.

Which of the following presents the best sequence of the sentences above to make a clear, sensible paragraph?

(A) I, II, III, IV
(B) III, II, I, IV
(C) II, I, III, IV
(D) IV, II, I, III
(E) IV, III, II, I

97. I. The Communists' preoccupation with economic growth and their whole attitude toward economic progress have been shaped by Marx's theory of long-run development of human society.

II. This theory places economic development at the center of the entire social philosophy, and it is impossible to study the Marxists' political, social, and economic views without referring to it.

III. Without the knowledge of this theory, it is difficult to understand the Communists' dogmatic belief in the superiority of their system, whatever the observable facts are, and their faith in the final victory over capitalism.

IV. Economic development has to lead, sooner or later, to socialism and communism, and it is necessary to build socialism and, later, communism to make future economic growth possible.

Which of the following presents the best sequence of the sentences above to make a clear, sensible paragraph?

(A) I, II, III, IV
(B) II, III, I, IV
(C) III, IV, I, II
(D) IV, III, I, II
(E) IV, III, II, I

98. I. They had a press.

II. The founding fathers knew precisely what they were dealing with.

III. Indeed, the founding fathers were themselves often at the point end of the press sword.

IV. And the press of their time was not only guilty of bad taste and inaccuracy; it was partisan, reckless, sometimes vicious.

Which of the following presents the best sequence of the sentences above to make a clear, sensible paragraph?

(A) III, IV, I, II
(B) I, III, II, IV
(C) II, I, III, IV
(D) I, II, III, IV
(E) III, I, II, IV

99. I. Organizing, which creates the conditions that must be present before the execution of the plan can be undertaken successfully, cannot be done intelligently without knowledge of the organizational objectives.

II. Management, which is the function of executive leadership, has as its principal phases the planning, organizing, and controlling of the activities of subordinate groups in the accomplishment of organizational objectives.

III. Planning specifies the kind and extent of the factors, forces, and effects, and the relationships among them, that will be required for satisfactory accomplishment.

IV. Control, which has to do with the constraint and regulation of activities entering into the execution of the plan, must be exercised in accordance with the characteristics and requirements of the activities demanded by the plan.

Which of the following presents the best sequence of the sentences above to make a clear, sensible paragraph?

(A) I, II, III, IV
(B) I, IV, III, II
(C) II, I, III, IV
(D) II, III, I, IV
(E) III, I, IV, II

100. I. Even the most objectively conceived critical elucidation is bound to contain signs of a judgment.

II. Yet the task of elucidation is not easily separable from another important function of criticism, evaluation.

III. The first task of the critic is to see the work of art and describe its qualities and attributes as clearly as possible.

IV. This is the task of elucidation, and it is fundamental to all criticism worthy of the name.

Which of the following presents the best sequence of the sentences above to make a clear, sensible paragraph?

(A) I, II, IV, III
(B) III, IV, II, I
(C) III, II, I, IV
(D) IV, I, III, II
(E) IV, III, II, I

101. I. Women were trained in "women's work"—housework or fieldwork according to the nature of the society.

II. Along with their training in defense of the community and support for their families, men were instructed in the structure of that community and were trained to sit on its councils.

III. Men were taught the history and folklore of their nations, the religious beliefs and practices, and the healing arts.

IV. From the very earliest times, boys and young men have been educated in the ways of their people.

Which of the following presents the best sequence of the sentences above to make a clear, sensible paragraph?

(A) I, II, III, IV
(B) II, III, IV, I
(C) III, II, IV, I
(D) IV, II, III, I
(E) IV, III, II, I

102. I. It seems that in instances in which the predictions may have life-and-death consequences, the meteorologists serve us well; but we had best not count on the weather for our picnic tomorrow.

II. Countless lives have been saved by the weather service's timely warning of the approach of severe weather.

III. To the meteorologists' credit, scientific weather forecasting can claim many successes.

IV. If we will allow for a margin of error either in days or in miles, the rate of accuracy rises dramatically.

Which of the following presents the best sequence of the sentences above to make a clear, sensible paragraph?

(A) II, III, I, IV
(B) I, III, II, IV
(C) III, II, IV, I
(D) IV, II, III, I
(E) IV, III, II, I

103. I. No one questions it in calm days, because it is not needed.

II. And the reverse is true also; only when free utterance is suppressed is it needed, and when it is needed, it is most vital to justice.

III. I reply with the sad truth that only in time of stress is freedom of utterance in danger.

IV. You say that freedom of utterance is not for time of stress.

Which of the following presents the best sequence of the sentences above to make a clear, sensible paragraph?

(A) I, II, IV, III
(B) III, I, II, IV
(C) IV, I, II, III
(D) IV, III, I, II
(E) IV, I, II, III

104.
 I. The American university is a direct descendant of the ancient universities in Europe.

 II. These are the oldest institutions, aside from the church itself, in Western civilization.

 III. But the tradition of learning and of scholarly inquiry has lived on.

 IV. They have survived many periods of trouble, of revolution, and of persecution.

Which of the following presents the best sequence of the sentences above to make a clear, sensible paragraph?

(A) I, II, IV, III
(B) I, IV, III, II
(C) II, I, IV, III
(D) II, IV, III, I
(E) III, II, I, IV

105.
 I. In most regions of the world, recorded history is short relative to the time between the largest earthquakes.

 II. Historical records as such rarely constitute an adequate or, more important, reliable basis for estimating earthquake potential.

 III. It may alternatively be due to the short length of available records relative to the long repeat time for large earthquakes.

 IV. Thus, the fact that there have been no historic earthquakes larger than a given size does not make us confident that they will also be absent in the future.

Which of the following presents the best sequence of the sentences above to make a clear, sensible paragraph?

(A) I, IV, III, II
(B) II, I, III, IV
(C) II, I, IV, III
(D) I, II, III, IV
(E) I, III, IV, II

106.
 I. Third World development plans have been largely based on energy-intensive industries (such as steel, metals, and paper), energy-intensive agriculture (using petroleum-based fertilizers as well as harvesting combines), and increased transportation.

 II. High energy prices have created many problems for the Non-Oil-Producing Less Developed Countries (NOLDCs) and, in turn, for the rest of the world.

 III. As these programs are cut back, the NOLDCs have even less money from foreign exchange to pay for imported food and oil.

 IV. High oil prices have caused cutbacks in these programs.

Which of the following presents the best sequence of the sentences above to make a clear, sensible paragraph?

(A) I, II, IV, III
(B) I, II, III, IV
(C) II, III, I, IV
(D) II, I, IV, III
(E) IV, II, I, III

107.
 I. In all cases, supervisors on all levels must be alert to discover the needs of their employees for training.

 II. Such conditions can be observed without any formal analysis in most cases.

 III. Many conditions can signal training needs: poor work performance, poor service, low employee morale, etc.

 IV. The need for training can be brought more sharply into focus, however, if time is spent on a survey of the problems.

Which of the following presents the best sequence of the sentences above to make a clear, sensible paragraph?

(A) I, IV, II, III
(B) II, III, IV, I
(C) III, II, IV, I
(D) IV, I, III, II
(E) III, IV, I, II

108.
 I. Recent scientific discoveries are throwing new light on the basic nature of viruses and the possible nature of cancer, genes, and even life itself.

 II. Too often one works and thinks within too narrow a range and hence fails to recognize the significance of certain facts for other areas.

 III. These discoveries are providing evidence for relationships among these four subjects that indicate that one may be dependent upon another to an extent not fully appreciated heretofore.

IV. Sometimes the important new ideas and subsequent fundamental discoveries come from the borderline areas between two well-established fields of investigation.

Which of the following presents the best sequence of the sentences above to make a clear, sensible paragraph?

(A) I, III, II, IV
(B) II, III, I, IV
(C) III, IV, I, II
(D) IV, III, II, I
(E) IV, II, III, I

109.   I. As a unit, these ten amendments are referred to as the Bill of Rights.

II. Although it spelled out the law of the land, it truly did not provide sufficient protection for individuals against the power and might of the newly formed federal republic.

III. This lack of protection for individuals led to the first ten amendments to the Constitution.

IV. When the United States Constitution was originally written, the framers realized that the Constitution by itself left something to be desired.

Which of the following presents the best sequence of the sentences above to make a clear, sensible paragraph?

(A) I, III, II, IV
(B) II, IV, III, I
(C) IV, III, II, I
(D) IV, II, I, III
(E) IV, II, III, I

110.   I. There were several social and economic objectives behind the promotion of Small Scale Rural Industrialization (SSRI) during the "high Maoist" period, many of which were held during the Great Leap as well.

II. The enterprises could use scattered raw materials which would be inefficient to gather together for use in distant large-scale plants.

III. Practically all of these objectives were, in one way or another, rooted in the enterprises' "local character."

IV. Similarly, the industries could efficiently mobilize underutilized labor resources in the countryside.

Which of the following presents the best sequence of the sentences above to make a clear, sensible paragraph?

(A) I, II, III, IV
(B) I, III, II, IV
(C) II, III, I, IV
(D) III, II, IV, I
(E) III, IV, I, II

END OF ENGLISH EXPRESSION QUESTIONS

IF TIME REMAINS, CHECK OVER YOUR WORK ON THE
ENGLISH EXPRESSION QUESTIONS ONLY.

CORRECT ANSWERS FOR THIRD MODEL FOREIGN SERVICE OFFICER EXAM

Knowledge Questions

1. B	15. A	29. C	43. D	57. C
2. D	16. C	30. D	44. C	58. D
3. C	17. D	31. A	45. C	59. B
4. C	18. A	32. C	46. A	60. B
5. B	19. D	33. A	47. A	61. B
6. A	20. C	34. B	48. C	62. D
7. B	21. C	35. B	49. B	63. D
8. A	22. A	36. D	50. D	64. C
9. D	23. D	37. C	51. C	65. D
10. B	24. A	38. B	52. C	66. A
11. C	25. D	39. C	53. A	67. B
12. C	26. D	40. C	54. D	68. B
13. B	27. B	41. D	55. C	69. C
14. C	28. B	42. B	56. B	70. A

Key to Maps

Israel and Its Neighbors—*Questions 24 to 26*

1. Lebanon
2. Golan Heights/ Syria
3. Syria
4. Israel
5. West Bank/ Judea and Samaria
6. Jordan
7. Dead Sea
8. Gaza Strip
9. Sinai Peninsula/Egypt
10. Suez Canal
11. Egypt
12. Saudi Arabia
13. Gulf of Aqaba

Northern Africa—*Questions 56 to 58*

1. Morocco
2. Algeria
3. Tunisia
4. Libya
5. Egypt
6. Western Sahara
7. Mauritania
8. Mali
9. Niger
10. Chad
11. Sudan
12. Ethiopia
13. Djibouti
14. Senegal
15. Guinea-Bissau
16. Guinea
17. Sierra Leone
18. Liberia
19. Ivory Coast
20. Birkana Faso
21. Ghana
22. Togo
23. Benin
24. Nigeria
25. Cameroon

English Expression Questions

1. C	23. B	45. E	67. B	89. C
2. B	24. A	46. C	68. B	90. E
3. D	25. C	47. B	69. C	91. A
4. A	26. D	48. E	70. E	92. B
5. C	27. C	49. A	71. E	93. D
6. A	28. E	50. B	72. D	94. E
7. E	29. B	51. C	73. B	95. C
8. A	30. A	52. A	74. C	96. E
9. C	31. B	53. D	75. D	97. A
10. E	32. E	54. C	76. D	98. C
11. B	33. B	55. A	77. B	99. D
12. B	34. C	56. D	78. E	100. B
13. A	35. B	57. C	79. A	101. E
14. B	36. E	58. B	80. C	102. C
15. E	37. A	59. E	81. A	103. D
16. A	38. D	60. C	82. C	104. A
17. B	39. D	61. E	83. B	105. C
18. E	40. B	62. A	84. D	106. D
19. B	41. A	63. D	85. E	107. C
20. D	42. C	64. A	86. D	108. A
21. C	43. C	65. E	87. C	109. E
22. C	44. B	66. D	88. E	110. B

English Expression Questions: Correctly Stated Sentences

1. **(C)** He had a chance to invest wisely, to establish his position, and *to display* his ability as an executive.

2. **(B)** When one prepares systematically and diligently for the examination, *one* can be confident of passing it.

3. **(D)** Jones seems slow on the track, but you will find few men quicker than *he* on the basketball court.

4. **(A)** We had *swum* across the lake before the sun rose.

5. **(C)** As Martha dived off the springboard, she was horrified to see that the water *had been drained* from the pool the night before.

6. **(A)** *There* are still people who say that it has never really been proved that the earth is round.

7. **(E)** This sentence is correct.

8. **(A)** Mary was so *uninterested* in the baseball game that she yawned unashamedly.

9. **(C)** Today's *Times* has headlines about another woman who has just *swum* the English Channel.

10. **(E)** This sentence is correct.

11. **(B)** An inexperienced liar, Mary explained her absence from work with an *incredible* tale of daring in which she played the role of the heroine.

12. **(B)** The loud noise of the cars and trucks *annoys* those who live near the road.

13. **(A)** *Regardless* of what people say, I must repeat that these are the facts concerning the requirements for the position.

14. **(B)** There is no objection to *his* joining the party if he is willing to fit in with the plans of the group.

15. **(E)** This sentence is correct.

16. **(A)** *Your* telling the truth in the face of such dire consequences required great moral courage.

17. **(B)** The following description, together with the drawings, *presents* a master plan for the development of the airport.

18. **(E)** This sentence is correct.

19. **(B)** I am depending on the *medicine's* being delivered without delay.

20. **(D)** Placing his longbow on the grass beside him, Robin Hood, who had had an exciting day, *lay* down to rest.

21. **(C)** I was not at all surprised to hear of Jim *Dolan's* winning the election for town councilman.

22. **(C)** She saw that there was nothing else she could do; the room was clean *as* it had never been before.

23. **(B)** The instructor was justly annoyed by *his* walking in late and disturbing the class.

24. **(A)** Each of the nurses *was* scrupulously careful about personal cleanliness.

25. **(C)** I enjoy eating in good restaurants and *going* to the theater afterwards.

26. **(D)** His sworn statement, together with the testimony and statements from other witnesses, *was* made a part of the file.

27. **(C)** Being able to trust his sources *is* indispensable for the investigative reporter.

28. **(E)** This sentence is correct.

29. **(B)** The government, announcing a bill of rights for its citizens, *promised* them equal rights under the law and due process in the courts.

30. **(A)** Neither tears *nor* protests effected the least change in their parents' decision.

31. **(B)** The victim's mother, *beside* herself with grief, could give no coherent account of the accident.

32. **(E)** This sentence is correct.

33. **(B)** His education had filled him with anger against those *who* he believed had hurt or humiliated him.

34. **(C)** Admirers of American ballet have made the claim that its stars can dance as well *as* or better than the best of the Russian artists.

35. **(B)** When you go to the library tomorrow, please *take* this book to the librarian that sits behind the desk on the far right of the reference room.

36. **(E)** *Marchand's greater concern* for demonstrating that racial prejudice exists than for preventing it from doing harm *explains* why his work is not always highly regarded.

37. **(A)** Throughout this history of the American West there runs a steady commentary on the deception and mistreatment of the Indians.

38. **(D)** If you *had considered* all the alternatives, you would have chosen another course.

39. **(D)** *Although the findings resulted* from extensive international cooperation, it was impossible to select fairly a single recipient for the prize.

40. **(B)** The wild game hunter stalked the tiger slowly, cautiously, and *silently*.

41. **(A)** European film distributors originated the art of "dubbing"—the substitution of lip-synchronized translations in foreign languages for the original soundtrack voices.

42. **(C)** *We face a crisis* of growing population and diminishing food supply.

43. **(C)** *Contrary* to popular belief, no dialect of English is inherently superior to any other.

44. **(B)** The epidemic worsened because *of overcrowded and unsanitary conditions*.

45. **(E)** To learn to speak a foreign language fluently *requires much practice*.

46. **(C)** The director of the agency had, more than once, *disagreed publicly with administration* policy.

47. **(B)** Honor as well as profit *is* to be gained by this work.

48. **(E)** He was *neither* in favor of *nor* opposed to the plan.

49. **(A)** I don't do well in those kinds of tests.

50. **(B)** We were amazed to see the *number* of people waiting in line at Macy's.

51. **(C)** The group called a rally *to demonstrate its opposition to* the proposed construction.

52. **(A)** By 2 o'clock, the child will have lain in his bed for ten solid hours.

53. **(D)** Because they were unaware of his interest in the building, they did not understand why he felt so *bad* about *its* being condemned.

54. **(C)** Support Communications Officers are assigned to overseas posts and to Washington, D.C., *often working* on rotating shifts as well as performing call-in/stand-by duties involving a variety of activities.

55. **(A)** A "cliometrician" is an economist or economic historian who works with mathematical statistics to solve historical problems.

56. **(D)** Many men courted Sarah *because* of her wealth.

57. **(C)** The director does not approve of *Richard's and my* arriving late for work.

58. **(B)** She is lazy *and this* annoys me.

59. **(E)** There is a stain on my *tie. Can* you remove the stain?

60. **(C)** It *looks as if the storm* will soon be upon us.

61. **(E)** BonTon grew slowly and steadily *because of* Miss Talbot's resistance of the temptation to expand too quickly beyond the company's financial means.

62. **(A)** She is one of those people *who is always complaining.*

63. **(D)** We buy only cherry plums since we *like that kind best.*

64. **(A)** His tone *clearly implied* that he was bitterly disappointed.

65. **(E)** Now kick your feet in the water *as Gregory just did.*

66. **(D)** Carson's sells merchandise of equal quality and *has a lower price.*

67. **(B)** My mother is roasting a chicken for dinner, *and I don't want to miss it.*

68. **(B)** Making friends is more rewarding *than being antisocial.*

69. **(C)** Last night *I called you* several times.

70. **(E)** The distraught traveler asked for *help from Tom and me.*

71. **(E)** Was it really *she whom* you saw last night?

72. **(D)** She said only that she was a friend of Mary's *and left without* giving her name.

73. **(B)** The percentage of slaves in the total black population was increased *by the counting of* fugitive slaves in the North as slaves rather than as free blacks.

74. **(C)** In his tales of adventure and romance, Jules Verne predicted many scientific achievements of the 20th century *leading to his being called* the father of modern science fiction.

75. **(D)** As a federal employee you will *have to restrict* the expression of your political sympathies to the voting booth.

76. **(D)** Many people supported Ms. French *because* she was politically skillful.

77. **(B)** *Although she* became ill after eating at the restaurant, the ambassador did not sue the management.

78. **(E)** To stop inflation we *must have* both wage and price controls.

79. **(A)** Cesar Chavez has developed strong unions *to improve the conditions* under which migrant workers, who are currently paid extremely low wages, must live and work.

80. **(C)** The often expressed wish of the negotiators was that *the initiation of* a cultural exchange program would begin an era of increasingly cordial relations between the two countries.

81. **(A)** There are times when the medical profession appears more a mystical cabal *than a scientific field.*

82. **(C)** Living with our parents and *depending on them* for all our needs, we found life much simpler and our daily routine more circumscribed.

83. **(B)** My students approve *of the school principal's and my disagreeing* on an issue.

84. **(D)** Although it was very kind of you to arrange for the meeting to be *postponed, now* it will be impossible to reschedule his appearance.

85. **(E)** Following the agent's recommendation, the farmer *planted a stand* of alfalfa to restore nitrogen to his acreage.

86. **(D)** At least one language which is used *throughout life is learned* in childhood by every normal human being.

87. **(C)** The long-term aims of the three principal allies were very *different (a fact that was* abundantly clear to Sir Winston Churchill).

88. **(E)** Flying from London *to New York, a pilot will arrive* at the hour, by the clock, at which he departed.

89. **(C)** For five successive days *we were bombarded from* the air by the enemy.

90. **(E)** T. S. Eliot was not only a highly developed *scholar but also* a magnificent poet.

Part Three

THE ORAL ASSESSMENT DAY

OVERVIEW OF THE ORAL ASSESSMENT

The oral assessment is the centerpiece of the Foreign Service Officer examination process, and the score obtained will account for more than half of the weighted average final score of successful candidates. You might think of the written examination as a kind of elimination round designed to narrow the field for the main event. The great majority of those who succeed in the oral assessment will successfully complete the full examination process, although there will remain, after the oral assessment, a final screening procedure discussed later in this section.

The purpose of this section, quite simply, is to help you perform at a level that fully reflects your potential. If you read this chapter carefully and follow its advice and suggestions, you will improve your chances of being one of the fortunate few who are selected for the Foreign Service each year.

This introductory chapter will give you a brief overview of the day's events and will then offer a few general suggestions. The next chapter sets out the criteria for evaluating candidates and explains how they were derived. The third chapter, much longer than the first two, will take you through the various assessment exercises, one by one and step by step. Interspersed among the expository material you will find descriptions of possible pitfalls and some common-sense suggestions for avoiding those pitfalls and for approaching the exercises in ways that do justice to your talents. Sample questions, an example of a well-written candidate essay, and a sample summary are included. These descriptive passages and the accompanying comments will lead naturally to the last chapter of this part, which suggests how you can best prepare yourself in advance for the assessment day and explains why advance preparation can indeed make a difference in the results you obtain.

Why is it called the oral assessment day when several of the component exercises are written? Probably because, in terms of the scoring arithmetic, performance in the oral exercises weighs much more heavily in the day's overall results that performance in the written components. Much diplomatic and consular business is transacted in oral discourse, and the assessment day provides the opportunity to test candidates' proficiency in this crucial area.

A Word of Caution: This section describes the oral assessment day as it has been conducted during the last several years. However, nothing in government is immutable, and the Board of Examiners for the Foreign Service is currently revising its assessment day procedures. The specific exercises, questions, and timing will be different for your assessment. However, the goal of the assessment—to identify those candidates with the skills and characteristics that make for success in the Foreign Service—will remain the same. Careful attention to the criteria for evaluating candidates and to our advice for handling each stage of the oral assessment will stand you in excellent stead.

THE SCHEDULE FOR ASSESSMENT DAY

A few words on the mechanics of the process. You should arrive punctually, of course, at 8:15 on the appointed day. The receptionist will give you information on how the day is organized, pass out individual schedules, and so on. At 8:30 an assessor—the term used to describe a member of the examining panel—will welcome the candidates and brief them on the conduct of the various component examinations and exercises. Candidates begin their individual assigned exercises at 8:45.

There are three of these in the morning, each lasting 45 minutes and followed by a 15-minute break. These three exercises are (not necessarily in chronological order): an oral examination, composition of an essay, and preparation of a summary of written material provided to you. More about each of these exercises will follow.

After lunch your entire group will gather at 1:15 to prepare for and then carry out a collective oral exercise, called the group exercise, which usually ends at about 2:30. You will all gather again at 2:45 for the written in-basket exercise which lasts an hour and a half. Then an assessor will meet with all the candidates to explain the scoring process and what happens next. Questions and comments from the candidates are welcome during this session. The day will end with individual personal interviews.

A group normally consists of six candidates and must include at least four. Usually two groups are examined, simultaneously but separately, each by a team of four assessors.

HOW YOU WILL BE SCORED

After the group exercise, while you and your fellow candidates are working on the in-basket exercise, the assessors meet to score your performance under twelve so-called dimensions (see below). One of these dimensions—written communication— gets double weight because you will receive separate scores for your essay and your summary. If the assessors differ significantly on the appropriate score under any dimension, they will discuss your performance to reach a consensus score. All of your scores are added up and then divided by 13 (remember, your written work is scored twice) to derive your final result. If you pass, your in-basket results will also be graded.

The two assessors who conducted your oral examination in the morning will not evaluate your performance during the group exercise in the afternoon. Similarly, one pair of assessors will grade your essay, another your summary. This procedure gives each of the four assessors an equal role in scoring all candidates within a group. Bear in mind that you are in competition not with other members of your group during the assessment day but rather with all those who present themselves for the oral assessment during a given calendar year.

ASSESSMENT DAY SITES

The oral assessment is given in Washington, D.C. and also in several major cities around the U.S. (Atlanta, Boston, Chicago, Dallas, Honolulu, Kansas City, Los Angeles, San Francisco, and Seattle in 1987; the list changes somewhat from year to year). Outside Washington, the temporary assessment centers are typically lodged in vacant government office space, using whatever furniture can be borrowed for the purpose. These makeshift

arrangements usually produce a setting that varies from Spartan to dismal in appearance. Don't take this as an omen of your Foreign Service prospects. The assessment calendar depends upon the location. In Washington, it usually runs from March to September. In other locations, the opening and closing dates will differ from city to city. You will have to defray your own travel expenses.

HOW SHOULD YOU DRESS FOR YOUR ASSESSMENT?

Select clothes that approximate the dress code of the profession you wish to enter. You would not interview for a professional position with a corporation or law firm clad in sneakers, T-shirt, and blue jeans. Likewise, you should not present yourself for the Oral Assessment in such casual attire. Men need not feel obliged to wear a three-piece, pinstripe suit. A sport jacket, tie, and slacks will do nicely for those who prefer a less formal look. Women may ''dress for success'' if they wish, in a conservative tailored suit, but they shouldn't hesi-

tate to wear a less formal outfit—a dress or, say, a blazer and skirt combination—if they like it better. Candidates who like to dress in elegant clothes should by all means wear them for the assessment day, although this alone will not earn them a competitive advantage over their less elegant counterparts. Assessors know that most candidates are young and that few of them are rich. So just dress sensibly; beyond that, don't worry about your clothes.

Remember that one of the ground rules of the

assessment day is that the assessors know nothing and wish to know nothing about your personal background. This state of ignorance helps them to avoid bias in either direction. Candidates who use any pretext, during the oral examination or else- where, to insert some comments about their dis- tinguished educational, social or professional background are more likely to hurt than to help themselves.

HOW SHOULD YOU BEHAVE TOWARD THE ASSESSORS?

This question comes up mainly in relation to the oral examination, the only exercise which involves lengthy face-to-face interaction with the assessors. A manner of relaxed and pleasant courtesy will serve you best. The assessor is not your adversary. He has no trick questions to ask, no oral traps to set for you. Such tactics would be self-defeating; the assessor's purpose is to put you as much at ease as possible and to see how well you can perform free of crippling stage fright or similar emotional impediments. Assessors find good performances much more entertaining than bad ones. Granted, they will ask you some difficult questions; that is their role. But it is human nature to admire a deft response and to feel some discomfort at a clumsy one. You may find it hard to believe, but the asses- sors would rather see you pass than fail.

One or even both of the assessors who examine you may seem stiff and reserved. Does this mean that he is hostile toward you? Not at all. It would be a mistake to read malevolent intent into a per- sonal mannerism. No one wants to see you fail.

CAN YOU PREPARE FOR THE ORAL ASSESSMENT?

Emphatically, yes. Yet most candidates make little or no effort at advance preparation, according to experienced assessors. These assessors report sur- prise at how little most candidates know of the factual and theoretical material directly relevant to the profession for which they are being examined. Many of those blank spaces could have been filled with some effort, and many, many more of them with the kind of sustained effort that most success- ful students apply to their college semester finals.

Quite a number of candidates convey, in various ways, an impression of competence and lively in- telligence. Yet they somehow fail to demonstrate their potential convincingly by their actual per- formance during the assessment day. This, too, is attributed to lack of any organized preparatory effort. Some specific advice on how to prepare for the oral assessment day is offered later in this chapter.

CRITERIA FOR EVALUATING CANDIDATES

The term "dimension," in the argot of the assessment procedure, refers to the knowledge, skills, aptitudes, and personal characteristics that are considered most important to effective performance as a Foreign Service officer. These dimensions define the nature and scope of the testing and evaluation process. You should therefore be generally familiar with them and keep them in mind as you read the rest of this chapter.

The dimensions for evaluating candidates were carefully and systematically derived. First, several Foreign Service officers, from each of the Service's major functional specialty areas, were asked in personal interviews to describe in detail their daily work responsibilities and what was required to discharge those duties effectively. What, for example, do economic officers do exactly? What must they know, what skills must they possess to accomplish these tasks? The information drawn from the interviews was then used to prepare detailed written questionnaires which were sent in 1973 to most officers on active duty. From the responses to these questionnaires, officials of the Department of State's Board of Examiners (BEX), with the help of professional testing specialists, distilled 14 distinct dimensions that experienced practitioners had identified as most relevant to Foreign Service work. Candidates for admission to the Service are thus evaluated in terms of those dimensions. Questionnaires like those described above were sent out again in 1978 and 1981 to update the earlier information, and that process will be repeated in the near future.

There follows a list of the dimensions, together with a working definition of the first twelve drawn from BEX material. These twelve are the dimensions scored by the assessors. The definitions of the last two are summaries of somewhat lengthier BEX texts. Scoring of those two dimensions is based exclusively upon candidates' performance during the in-basket exercise.

ASSESSMENT DIMENSIONS AND DEFINITIONS

Communication Skills

Oral Communication Skills

Ability to speak clearly and concisely, with appropriate vocabulary and usage; articulateness, fluency.

Written Communication Skills

Mastery of spelling, vocabulary, structure, and syntax; logical written communication without distortion or confusion; good utilization of time.

Intellectual Skills

Analytical and Synthesizing Ability

Ability to process and organize a broad variety of information and synthesize relevant elements within limitations of time and resources.

Quality of Judgment

Ability to be practical and objective in the analysis of problems and in the evaluation of people. Reality-oriented, unbiased, able to sort out priorities and to act appropriately.

Perspective and Breadth of Knowledge

Perspective based on a broad range of interests and breadth of knowledge. Awareness of significance of political and economic issues, American cultural achievements, and American institutions.

Political Sensitivity

Understanding and perception of policy considerations and avenues of influence in larger context of political and economic issues and American institutions.

Cultural Awareness and Sensitivity

Understanding of American and foreign cultural values and motivations; empathy for and appreciation of cultural differences; understanding of cultural factors in foreign relations.

Leadership Skills

Ability to Negotiate, Lead, Mediate

Ability to take initiative, influence or persuade others by force of argument or leadership skills; ability to intervene and resolve difficult situations; ability to assume organizational leadership.

Adaptability/Flexibility

Openmindedness. Receptive to changing ideas and circumstances and ability to adjust to them.

Managerial/Problem-Solving Skills

Resourcefulness, Imagination, Innovation

Ability to combine divergent elements to arrive at viable, imaginative, and appropriate solutions or insights. Ability to show enterprise, ingenuity, inventiveness.

Interpersonal Skills

Interpersonal Awareness and Skills

Ability to sense reactions of others and respond appropriately, to work effectively with others, to interact easily. Able to be tactful, courteous, patient, empathetic, discreet; alert to environmental cues and events; personable and poised.

Stability and Adjustment

Ability to respond and act rationally and decisively under stressful conditions, keep control, think on feet, adapt planned behavior to unexpected interruptions or diversions. Is independent and self-confident.

Managerial Skills Tested by the In-Basket Exercise

Planning and Organizing Work

Organizing work for action; planning work, including grouping of related items and systematic use of available time; setting work priorities.

Management Skills

Supervising staff and delegating appropriately to staff to get work done; drawing upon staff resources in decision-making; resolving staff conflicts.

Some discerning spirits will detect areas of overlap and ambiguity among the dimensions, and others will smile at what may seem like an attempt to reduce the complexity of human behavior to neat little compartments that can be labeled and then measured. Yet no sensible person would contest the proposition that establishment of some explicit criteria against which candidates' performance can be observed, tested, and scored is essential to a fair and orderly examination process.

COMPONENTS OF THE ORAL ASSESSMENT DAY

We shall examine first the morning and then the afternoon sessions. There are three distinct sessions during the morning, and at any given time (breaks aside) two candidates will be having their oral examination, two will be writing their essays and the remaining pair will be doing their written summaries (assuming a normal group of six candidates). We will look at each of these sessions, beginning with the oral examination.

THE ORAL EXAMINATION

Two assessors will meet with a single candidate. The atmosphere will be as informal as possible. The assessors will alternate in asking questions. They will cover six topics within the allotted 45 minutes. They will ask four substantive questions, each one testing your knowledge and comprehension of a particular issue or topic within a broad knowledge area, and two "hypothetical" questions that are designed to test your ability to deal with practical problems of the sort that will arise in a Foreign Service setting. The opening amenities and explanations usually take up three or four minutes, leaving six or seven minutes to cover each question.

Assessors recognize an obligation to help a candidate feel comfortable and at ease during the examination, for the very good reason that it is pointless to examine the intellectual skills of a frightened or bewildered individual. It follows that the assessors will not deliberately confuse or intimidate you. Rather, they'll usually try to give you a hand if you seem to flounder. Assessors' styles will vary. Some will let you do almost all the talking, while others will ask frequent follow-up questions. Don't interpret either approach as a reflection on the quality of your answers.

The preceding paragraph deals only with the assessors' manner of conducting the examination. Don't misread it as a soothing description of examination content. Most candidates will find the questions challenging, and poorly prepared candidates will find some of them intimidating. Assessors may follow up your answer to ask you to justify it or to elaborate upon all or part of it. If there are inconsistencies in your response, you will probably be asked how you would reconcile them. If you take one side of a controversial issue, the assessor may ask you to say how you would deal with the more obvious counterarguments. This does not mean that the assessor thinks you put yourself on the "wrong" side of the issue; she simply wishes to test your command of the issue and your mental agility.

A few suggested "do's and don'ts."

- Do ask for clarification if you haven't understood the question, but don't ask for it so often that you have little time left for your answer.
- Do keep your composure even if you know you have botched an answer. You'll have plenty of chances to recoup. In fact, if you remain confident and unperturbed, the assessors will admire your poise under pressure and you may gain as many points under the stability and adjustment dimension as your poor answer cost you under perspective and breadth of knowledge.
- Don't hesitate, if you are completely stumped by a particular question, to acknowledge your ignorance and to ask for another question within the same general knowledge area (economics, politics, etc.).
- Don't fight the question; answer it. If you think it is a bad question, disguise your sentiments and get on with the answer.

You will get one substantive question on each of the following areas: the American scene (Americana, in the language of the Assessment Center); art and culture; economics, and politics. A good answer to these questions will include the facts, but it will also convey an understanding of their significance and of the interrelationships among them. It will show your ability to analyze information and to synthesize the important facts and arguments into a coherent response. Too many candidates answer with a sentence or two and then stop, forcing the assessor constantly to prompt and prod for more information. No matter how much factual material the candidate eventually produces, the response likely would not be considered acceptable because it has shown scant ability to analyze and synthesize. Scarcely better is a response which relates a string of facts but shows little sense of what is important and what is not, or of how one bit of information relates to the others. The flow and coherence of your answer will be just as important as the sheer quantity of factual material which you are able to adduce. Finally, you should be prepared to justify and defend your position. Your awareness of other viewpoints and your ability to make a persuasive case for your own will demonstrate perspective and breadth of knowledge, which is what the assessors are looking for.

As you answer the questions, be yourself and say what you think. There are no "canned" right answers. Don't try to guess what the assessors' biases may be and to cater to them, or to support administration policy unless you believe it is right.

The sample questions that follow the discussion of each substantive area are actual questions from past assessment cycles. These questions will not be used again but they indicate the kinds of questions you will face.

THE AMERICANA QUESTION

The *Americana question* likely will be very broad in scope. It may deal with a fairly recent period of American history, a current constitutional issue, present social, political or demographic trends, or a topical racial/gender issue. Or you could be asked to assess the effect of change in one broad aspect of American life—economic, demographic, technological, social—upon other aspects of the national scene. In all of this, you will need to show that you understand how one thing relates to another. You should be able to trace a reasonable chain of causality and to show how developments in one area have affected other areas of American life.

If asked to discuss a particular historical period, you should not be content merely to recite a list of the major events. Significant political developments have underlying social and economic causes, but the story won't stop there. Bank failures, for instance, had consequences disagreeable to many people, so Congress established the Federal Reserve Board. This political act later changed the country's economic life in many ways originally unforeseen by the Congress. There is a comparable interplay of cause and effect between domestic politics and foreign policy. You want to show that you understand such interconnections.

Sample Questions

List four or five domestic problems which the Carter administration must deal with over the next year or two. Pick one and explain what you feel would be the best plan of action for the government.

Some say that the 70s has been a decade of disillusionment, broken promises, and unexpected developments. What might justify such an observation? Can you suggest any historical parallels in our national experience?

THE ARTS AND CULTURE QUESTION

The arts and culture question will deal with American art and culture. What you may know of the Italian Renaissance, Elizabethan drama or classic Greek sculpture will not help you here. Some candidates try to wedge what they do know into their response to a question which asks for something else. This tactic will not work. If you really don't know anything about the question put to you, you will do better to say so candidly and to ask for another question in this field.

The question in this topic area might ask you, for example, to discuss a particular American art form (films, music, dance, painting, literature) or to name several major creative artists, discuss their works and assess their importance. Alternatively, you might be asked to discuss aspects of contemporary American culture outside the realm of creative arts.

The second of the sample questions that follow seems quite abstract. In practice, the assessors who asked it usually moved the discussion toward existing federal subsidy programs, an important aspect of our cultural life, by asking candidates to name and evaluate them.

Sample Questions

A professor at a university overseas is preparing a syllabus on contemporary literature in English. He asks for your recommendations for American authors. Who would you choose and why?

Some people say that the arts are no more deserving of government support than, say, the steel industry. What do you think?

THE ECONOMIC QUESTION

The typical economic question deals with a current domestic economic problem or trend or an international economic problem which significantly engages U.S. interests. A well-informed candidate who has no formal training in economics can give at least an adequate response. Unfortunately, many candidates cannot cope with the topic, and some appear panic stricken when the subject is raised.

Such candidates deserve little sympathy for their predicament. Economic issues of one kind or another have often dominated political discourse in recent years, and they have seldom been far from page one of the newspapers or the lead topic on the nightly TV news. During the 1980s, topics like inflation, high interest rates, the federal budget deficit, the relationship of tax rates to economic growth, tax reform, the decline of older manufacturing industries, protectionism versus free trade, and the exchange rate of the dollar have clogged the political agenda. The U.S. approach to some of these topics and to another series of related international economic problems has constituted a very considerable part of this country's foreign policy.

Without some understanding of the larger economic issues, an FSO could not explain adequately to a foreigner what is going on in the U.S. or set forth a credible rationale for about half of our foreign policy. Nor could this FSO ever attain more than a tenuous grasp of what is afoot in his country of assignment because so much of the political and social policy agenda there, as in all countries, is intertwined with underlying economic factors.

Any candidate who can pass the Foreign Service written exam and do well on other aspects of the oral assessment can become sufficiently conversant with economic issues to do well on the economic question, so long as he or she is willing to invest the time and effort to prepare for it.

Sample Questions

During the past year the U.S. dollar has been considerably stronger vis-a-vis other currencies than in the preceding several years. What are some of the advantages of this to the U.S. economy? What are some of the disadvantages?
Follow-up: The strengthening of the U.S. dollar has helped our major European trade partners and Japan to increase their exports to the United States. Yet, most of these countries have been complaining about the strength of the dollar. On what grounds?

Much has been said in recent years about an alleged decline in American productivity. Give evidence for or against this claim. What are the economic implications of your conclusion?

THE POLITICAL QUESTION

The political question will deal with foreign policy topics, or with an area of the world of significant interest to the United States. Domestic politics will enter the picture only to the extent that they impinge upon the conduct of foreign policy. (Domestic politics, you will recall, often come up in the Americana question). Like the other questions, this one is often quite broadly framed, but it will be concrete and not abstract in its thrust because it will relate directly or indirectly to the U.S. national interest. Some questions address current and topical issues. Others will take you into the recent history of international relations, for example by asking you to address U.S. interests in a given region or a particular problem and to describe how matters have evolved over the last few decades. The question is most unlikely to go back in time beyond World War II, but the assessors will expect candidates to be well versed in the history of U.S. foreign policy from World War II onward.

The questions prepared for use each year under this topic reflect an assumption that no one can have more than a superficial understanding of American foreign policy or make sensible judgments about it without a solid understanding of the history of the earlier period. If you do not already have such an understanding, you would do well to acquire it before the oral assessment day.

Balance of power considerations, regional or global, often directly affect foreign policy, and you should not be surprised if you are asked to deal with both the military and the political aspects of an issue. One could not, for example, intelligently discuss the major U.S.-Soviet arms control negotiations, past or present, without naming the major weapons systems involved and describing in general terms their capabilities. Nor is it possible to address NATO issues without reference to the regional balance of power and to the ways in which the regional military equation might, in the event of crisis, interact with perceptions of the balance between U.S. and Soviet central systems.

Do not be alarmed by the reference to military issues. The quality press and a number of readily available periodicals often have articles that explore military issues in some depth and in language comprehensible to nonspecialists. The issues are often complex and sometimes hard for the uninitiated to grasp, at first reading, but every

Foreign Service officer needs at least a basic understanding of this area of foreign affairs.

Sample Questions

You are political officer at an embassy in a Latin American country. One day, at the foreign ministry, you are asked, "Why did the United States support the United Kingdom against Argentina in the Falkland Island conflict?" How do you reply?

Follow-up: What should the United States do about the perception in Latin America that the United States assigns a secondary importance to Hemisphere concerns?

The relative strength of the United States and the Soviet Union has become a subject of heated public controversy, here and abroad. Which of the two countries do you think is stronger, and why?

Follow-up: What are some of the factors that make it hard to judge the balance?

We have now gone over all of the four knowledge-related questions. Let's look back at the dimensions and identify those that have been tested during your responses to these substantive questions.

Your score on the Perspective and Breadth of Knowledge dimension will be determined entirely by the quality of your answers to the four knowledge-related questions. Nothing else you do during the day will reveal anything very meaningful under that heading. You will also have given the assessors much of the basis for their evaluation of your Intellectual Skills—except judgment, which is defined in such a manner that this quality can seldom be observed during answers to the substantive questions. Further, the assessors will have some basis for rating you on both of the Interpersonal dimensions, and perhaps also under the dimensions of Adaptability and of Resourcefulness. And finally, you have had an excellent chance to demonstrate your Oral Communication Skills.

THE PROBLEM-SOLVING OR HYPOTHETICAL QUESTIONS

The two problem-solving or hypothetical questions will ask you to address administrative and consular problems similar to those that actually arise overseas. They will test a further range of skills and aptitudes. To do well on the substantive questions, candidates need a considerable body of formal knowledge and good conceptual skills. For

the problem-solving questions, they need a practical bent, common sense, and sound instincts about dealing with people. In terms of the dimensions, these two questions test particularly for Judgment, Adaptability and Flexibility, and Resourcefulness and Imagination. They also give the assessors another chance to gauge Interpersonal

Skills and Stability and Adjustment. Finally, certain of the administrative and consular questions require Sensitivity to local cultural patterns. These questions put you in a realistic Foreign Service situation, describe a problem you must deal with and ask you what you would say and do to solve it. You are not expected to know the applicable laws and regulations, but simply to make reasonable assumptions and base your response upon them. If you should take an action that is clearly beyond your authority, the assessor will likely interrupt and explain the situation, but you will not be penalized for making an incorrect assumption. When the question is initially posed, you may ask for clarification if you don't fully understand the situation, your role, the extent of your authority and so on. Just be careful not to take up so much time with your clarifying questions that little is left for your answer.

Some of the questions describe problems that will demand quick action. Others postulate types of problems where corrective action will necessarily take time. In either case, you are likely to do better if you ponder the situation briefly instead of plunging ahead with the first thoughts that come to mind. Do not waste time wondering what the predetermined "correct" solution is. None exists. There will be many bad "solutions" available but also several approaches which assessors will accept as valid.

Although these hypothetical questions put you in a realistic Foreign Service situation, you may well be asked to cope with a problem scenario that strikes you as quite far-fetched. That is because we have many Foreign Service posts in places that are themselves pretty far-fetched by American standards. In such places, odd things happen; sometimes they happen frequently.

Indeed, each of the problem questions has a basis in the actual work experience of Foreign Service officers. After each year's assessment cycle ends in the fall, assessors are formed into committees to draft questions for the next annual cycle. Officers with administrative experience will be asked to draft administrative problems, officers with consular experience will draft consular problems (the same process is followed, incidentally, for the substantive questions). The officers base their suggested questions on their own work experience or on experiences that colleagues have related to them. After these questions are drafted, the respective committees then meet several times to select the best ones and to hone and refine those

chosen. Then the committees show their work to BEX supervisory officials—also experienced Foreign Service officers—for a final review. Two of the criteria governing this selection process are the need for realism and for problems that pose some inherent difficulty.

As mentioned earlier, some problems, by their nature, require urgent action, while others could only be put right by a carefully thought out series of actions over a period of time.

The second type of problem may describe, for example, an untenable or difficult situation which has developed over time at the post and which you are expected to set right. Sometimes the problem will seem deceptively easy. Resist the temptation to offer a series of cliches and well-intentioned generalities. The assessors are looking for a focused and concrete approach.

You should respond with a plan of action in terms of specific steps at successive stages; say precisely what you would do at each one; point out likely difficulties and explain how you would cope with them; and make clear precisely who else is involved in each stage, how, and why.

A useful guideline is to refrain from answers which simply announce, "I will do A, then I will take care of B, and then I will do C," when neither A nor B nor C can be attained purely by incantation. The meat of a good answer will lie in a statement of exactly how you intend to get to A, then on to B and finally to C. Beware of the illusion, which afflicts some candidates, that simply saying it will make it so; you must also say how you will make it so.

Once you have embarked upon a course of action, the assessor will probably ask you to explain your choice. The follow-up questions may have a challenging ring to them. If you have thought through the problem carefully and believe you have made a sound choice, then stick to your guns. The assessor's line of questioning may be designed to test your mettle. The other possibility is that your first choice was injudicious and the assessor is trying to give you a chance to change direction. If, after reflection, you decide that your initial approach was indeed off target, don't be afraid to change your mind. Consistency in error is not a virtue. If you make the shift adroitly and offer sensible reasons for it, you should get good marks under the dimensions of Judgment and Adaptability and Flexibility, and your initial foray down the blind alley won't be held against you.

Sample Administrative Questions

You are the Administrative Officer in Country X. One morning a phone call awakens you at 1:00 a.m. On the line is a Marine guard on duty at the embassy. He tells you the embassy is on fire. How would you react?

Diplomatic relations have just been broken between the U.S. and your country of assignment. The embassy must be closed and the sixty official Americans must be out of the country within five days. As Administrative Officer you are in charge of overall logistics. How would you accomplish this task?

Sample Consular Questions

You are the consular officer charged with the protection and welfare of American citizens at your post. One day you get an excited call from a man identifying himself as a representative of the Associated Press. He asks, "Where are they taking the survivors of the Japan Airlines crash?" What do you do?

You are the consular officer responsible for the protection and welfare of American citizens. You receive a telephone call from the manager of a hotel telling you that a chambermaid has found a body of an American citizen dead in his bathtub. Both wrists were slit and he appears to have taken his own life. The hotel wants to know what to do with the body and the deceased's effects. What action do you take?

Follow-up: You learn the whereabouts of the deceased's parents and notify them. They do not believe their son's death to be suicide. What action do you take?

THE ESSAY

This is one of two exercises that will test written communication skills during the assessment day. It tests your ability to write, not your knowledge of the subject matter. Read the instructions carefully before you start and follow them to the letter. You will be allowed to pick one among several possible topics. As you write, bear in mind that grammar, spelling, and punctuation do matter. Assessors make allowances for the time pressure and will overlook one or two lapses. But a lot of errors will cost you points. Focus and organization also matter. Your stylistic elegance and cultivated vocabulary will count for little if the essay meanders aimlessly, loops back on itself, or is full of non sequiturs.

Use your time judiciously. After you have carefully read the instructions, take a few minutes to sketch out an outline for yourself. Many candidates who have obvious writing ability apparently prefer a stream-of-consciousness approach to that of following an outline. They think of an effective opening paragraph and then they write furiously until time is called. What often happens is that, without an outline to guide them, these essayists forget halfway through the piece the framework they had laid out for themselves in the opening paragraphs. As one intriguing idea succeeds another, part of the chosen topic may be forgotten, or the text may begin to deal with subject matter that is altogether outside the topic. The race to the finish finally ends with a spirited paragraph that leaves the reader nowhere, in that the end has scant logical connection to the middle and still less to the beginning.

While this may be somewhat overdrawn, it illustrates a problem common to many candidates' essays. Essays are graded on quality, not volume. You are not expected to exhaust the subject or to squeeze into your essay everything you know or can think to say about it. You will do yourself a favor if you take five minutes to prepare an outline. Then follow the outline as you write. The extra time involved will be well spent. Finally, try to save three or four minutes at the end for proofreading and for cleaning up the careless mistakes. It may improve your score.

Sample Essay

The text below is that of a candidate essay that received a very high score during the 1987 assessment cycle.

Topic: Discuss the Arguments for and Against "Protectionist Legislation" Dealing with Trade Competition.

The topic of "Protectionist Legislation" has been debaded (sic) long and hard this year, both at home and abroad. The pros and cons are myriad and would fill volumes. We have but three pages.

The proponents of protectionist legislation tend to favor domestic issues over foreign. "Free traders" tend to look more at global issues versus domestic. Yet both groups see their aim to be the strengthening of American industry.

Proponents of protectionist limits—tarrifs (sic), quotas, and non-tarrif (sic) barriers—see those limits as a tool whereby imbalances in world economics can be righted for the good of American industry. The subsidies foreign governments provide to fledgling industry, the low cost of labor overseas, a foreign government's "targeting" of certain U.S. industries are examples of the inequalities and unfair practices of the "free market." In fact, they sometimes claim the free market is a myth. Protectionist policies limit the damage a foreign competitor can do in the U.S. They "protect" American jobs and industries. They may be a means to limit trade deficits. They can allow the time U.S. firms need to reorganize to become more efficient and competitive. They also represent the "big stick" to those countries which limit their home markets to U.S. firms.

The opponents of protectionism are those who hold a basic belief in the "invisible hand" of free markets. They assert that protecting American firms from foreign competition fosters a sense of false security and thus complacency on the part of U.S. managers. Protectionist policies promote investment in industries whos (sic) competitive advantage has evaporated. More profitable investments can and should be made in other areas. Most immediate is protectionist limits drive consumer prices higher as foreign goods become scarce and domestic supplies follow the market price upwards. They contend that we should combat closed markets on all fronts, both domestic and international, to foster freer trade and stronger worldwide markets. The global economy's strength is what, in the final analysis, will determin (sic) the U.S. domestic economy's strength. And the surest way to assure that strength is to fight the barriers to free trade.

What is so good about this essay? It is clear. Each sentence says something worth saying about complex issues and makes its point simply, precisely, and with admirable economy; there is no superfluous language. Each sentence seems to be a necessary part of its paragraph, each paragraph necessary to the piece as a whole. No more and no less is said than need be said. The organization is excellent. The simplicity and economy of the style—remarkable when one considers the time constraints—give the essay a kind of classic elegance.

The piece does have a few shortcomings. For instance, the opening paragraph contains some hackneyed phrases: ". . . debated long and hard . . .," "the pros and cons are myriad and would fill volumes." In addition, there are four misspellings; three are evidently careless mistakes but proofreading should have caught them. Also, something is amiss in the fifth sentence of the last paragraph ("Most immediate is protectionist limits . . ."). Perhaps a couple of words were thoughtlessly omitted. Yet despite these weaknesses, this essay scored in the top 10 percent of all Foreign Service essays.

This should not be taken as a suggestion that all candidates should try to imitate the style of the sample essay. A freer style and livelier language can also be very pleasing and highly effective. But the sample essay does show the virtue of good organization; the writer had either drawn up an outline or had taken the time to sort out his thoughts thoroughly before he put pen to paper. It also illustrates the point that the quality of one's prose is more important than the quantity. Less can be better.

Please note that although this author apparently thinks he is limited to three pages (handwritten, double spaced), he is mistaken. The rules place no limit on the length of the essay.

THE SUMMARY

The summary tests writing ability of a different kind than the essay and it also tests your analytical powers. The exercise asks you to summarize for a senior official, in two hundred and fifty words or fewer, an official policy paper—perhaps a recent speech by the president or another high official. The subject could be an economic or political issue, arms control policy, nuclear deterrence or some other foreign policy topic. Be sure to read carefully the brief instructions you receive and to follow them scrupulously.

Begin by outlining the text you have been given to summarize. Sketch out the main points on a sheet of scratch paper or by underlining and marking up the text handed to you. Many candidates simply charge ahead; they compress the language of page one, then of page two, and so on. This "serial" approach to summary writing is usually a recipe for disaster. Only a thematic approach will work effectively.

The author of a speech or other public policy paper will usually make at least three but seldom more than five major points. Start your outline by noting or underlining these basic themes. Next, identify the subthemes or the arguments that support or elucidate each of the major themes you have identified. When this has been done, you will have reduced the piece to its logical skeleton and this logical skeleton will become your summary.

Of course you must convert the outline to standard prose, but keep the language lean, crisp and straightforward. Avoid bureaucratic circumlocutions even though the text you are working from may be full of them. Omit from your summary all the fluff which may be a ceremonial necessity but which is logically incidental to the core of the statement. Pare away ruthlessly the opening amenities, historical background, anecdotal material, ritual obeisances to the Constitution, the Declaration of Independence or other patriotic icons, and all the rhetorical flourishes. If you think a little of this "mood music" is necessary to convey the emotional flavor, devote a sentence or so to it but no more than that.

As with the essay, try to pace yourself so that a few minutes will remain after you have finished writing to allow for proofreading and patching up any rough spots.

The text that follows was among those given to candidates to summarize in the 1987 cycle.

NUCLEAR WEAPONS, ARMS CONTROL AND OUR NATIONAL SECURITY

Address by the Honorable George P. Shultz, Secretary of State, November 17, 1986

The United States and our allies will have to continue to rely upon nuclear weapons for deterrence far into the future. That fact, in turn, requires that we maintain credible and effective nuclear deterrent forces.

But a defense strategy that rests on the threat of escalation to a strategic nuclear conflict is, at best, an unwelcome solution to ensuring our national security. Nuclear weapons, when applied to the problem of preventing either a nuclear or conventional attack, present us with a major dilemma. They may appear a bargain—but a dangerous one. They make the outbreak of a Soviet-American war most unlikely; but they also ensure that should deterrence fail, the resulting conflict would be vastly more destructive—not just for our two countries, but for mankind as a whole.

Moreover, we cannot assume that the stability of the present nuclear balance will continue indefinitely. It can deteriorate and it has. We have come to realize that our adversary does not share all of our assumptions about strategic stability. Soviet military doctrine stresses warfighting and survival in a nuclear environment, the importance of numerical superiority, the contribution of active defense, and the advantages of preemption.

Over the past fifteen years, the growth of Soviet strategic forces has continued unabated—and far beyond any reasonable assessment of what might be required for rough equivalency with U.S. forces. As a result, the Soviet Union has acquired a capability to put at risk the fixed land-based missiles of the U.S. strategic triad—as well as portions of our bomber and in-port submarine force and control systems—with only a fraction of their force, leaving many warheads to deter any retaliation.

To date, arms control agreements along traditional lines—such as SALT I and II—have failed to halt these destabilizing trends. They have not brought about significant reductions in offensive forces, particularly those systems that are most threatening to stability. By the most important measure of destructive capability—ballistic missile warheads have grown by a factor of four since the SALT I Interim Agreement was signed. This problem has been exacerbated by a Soviet practice of stretching their implementation of such agreements to the edge of violation—and sometimes, beyond. The evidence of Soviet actions contrary to SALT II, the ABM Treaty, and various other arms control agreements is clear and unmistakable.

At the same time, technology has not stood still. Research and technological innovation of the past decade now raise questions about whether the primacy of strategic offense over defense will continue indefinitely. For their part, the Soviets have never neglected strategic defenses. They developed and deployed them even when offensive systems seemed to have overwhelming advantages over any defense. As permitted by the ABM Treaty of 1972, the Soviets constructed around Moscow the world's only operational system of ballistic missile defense. Soviet military planners apparently find that the modest benefits of this system justify its considerable cost, even thought it would provide only a marginal level of protection against our overall strategic force. It could clearly be a base for the future expansion of their defenses.

For well over a decade—long before the president announced three years ago the American Strategic Defense Initiative—the Soviet Union has been actively investigating much more advanced technologies, including directed energy systems. If the United States were to abandon this field of advanced defensive research to the Soviet Union, the results ten years hence could be disastrous for the West.

A SAMPLE SUMMARY

Summary of Address by Secretary Shultz on 11/17/86.

Shultz defended the president's Strategic Defense Initiative and said that its abandonment could bring disastrous results ten years hence. The U.S. and its allies must rely on nuclear deterrence far into the future, but Shultz urged simultaneous pursuit of advanced strategic defense research.

First, the present defensive strategy rests on the threat of escalation to strategic nuclear war. If it fails, Shultz said, the resulting conflict would be immensely destructive for all mankind.

Moreover, we cannot assume the stability of the nuclear balance. Soviet doctrine stresses nuclear war-fighting and survival. Their nuclear forces have grown beyond rough equivalency with U.S. forces. They can now put at risk our land-based missiles and some of our other systems with a fraction of their own forces, while holding others in reserve to deter retaliation.

Recent arms control agreements, such as SALT I and SALT II, have failed to bring significant reductions, particularly of the most destabilizing forces. Indeed, Shultz continued, the Soviets have stretched implementation of these agreements to the edge of violation, and sometimes beyond.

Finally, technological progress now casts doubt on the continued primacy of offensive nuclear forces. The Soviets have never neglected strategic defense, and for a decade they have actively investigated very advanced technologies, including directed energy systems. The U.S.S.R. has the world's only operational ballistic missile defense system. That system, permitted under the ABM Treaty, provides only marginal protection now but clearly could become a base for future expansion.

THE GROUP EXERCISE

Right after lunch, candidates begin preparing to play their parts in this exercise. Each group is assigned to a separate room for the purpose. The exercise deals with a mythical country. You are a member of an embassy task force charged with making recommendations to the ambassador. All candidates receive an envelope containing identical information on the country and on U.S. policy towards it. Each candidate will also receive a proposal which is given only to her and which she will present to the group. When the 45 minutes of preparation time is up, the assessors enter the room, the lead assessor gives brief instructions to the group, and the exercise proper begins.

Before moving on to a description of the exercise, it is important to note that among the written material given you are some instructions. You should read them with special care and follow them meticulously. Candidates who merely skim the instructions and do not really absorb them will pay for this in somewhat lower scores than they would otherwise have earned.

Why all this emphasis on following instructions? Just think about it. How useful is the young FSO, or for that matter the junior executive in any hierarchical organization, who charges off to accomplish his mission without knowing what exactly he is expected to do? Free spirits who have trouble taking instructions seriously would probably find other occupational pursuits more congenial than the Foreign Service.

Returning to the conduct of this exercise, the candidates now present their proposals in turn. Each candidate has eight minutes for his presentation. Two or three minutes of this time should be left for questions from other candidates. You have the uncontested right to center stage during these eight minutes.

Making the Most of Your Presentation

There are several things you can do to make the most of your oral presentation. First, use the most efficient method of preparing your oral presentation. No matter how thoughtful its content, poor delivery can spoil its effect. You will do best if you jot down some notes on all the important points you wish to make and refer to those notes from time to time while you are speaking.

Candidates who don't use this method run the risk of falling into one of the following traps. Those who decide to wing it, committing most of what they will say to memory and referring occasionally to the written material they were given when memory fails, will usually wind up with a statement that is jumbled in its content and jerky in its delivery. Some important points will be forgotten and others recalled only after much awkward shuffling of papers.

Those who write out the text of their statement and read it to the group when their turn comes tend to lose the interest of their audience. A presentation that uses the spoken style is always fresher, more direct, and more appealing to the listeners than one which is read.

Next, consider the manner of delivery. Speak in a lively voice which conveys the impression that you are interested in what you have to say. Find a happy medium between a timid murmur and a parade ground bellow. Get resonance in your voice by speaking from the chest instead of from the throat. Your voice should carry beyond the other group members seated across the table from you and to the assessors who are seated behind them—and behind you—and who will want to hear you clearly above the sound of the air conditioning or the outside noises that often get in the way. You will not have enough voice projection just from the larynx, so speak from the rib cage. Avoid a monotonous drone; vary the intonation and the pace to fit the content. Some of the things you will have to say are more important or more interesting than others. Modulate your voice accordingly. Pause for emphasis at significant points. Pause also, for a little longer than normal, whenever your audience seems to lose interest. This will awaken their curiosity (has she lost her notes, forgotten what she wants to say?), and you will have their undivided attention when you resume.

Avoid also the usual taboos of public speaking. For example, don't stare at the wall, or the ceiling, or the papers in front of you; look your listeners in the eye. Don't allow distracting speech or other mannerisms to mar your delivery; try not to interject "uh" after every ten words or so, and don't rock back and forth in your chair while speaking.

When you do not have the floor yourself, be sure to listen carefully to the other speakers and to take notes on the main points of their proposals. Ask questions at the end of their presentations if you feel the need for clarification or for more information. All of this will be helpful, indeed essential to full and effective participation in the negotiation and decision-making phase which follows the presentations. An absence of questions during the presentation round virtually guarantees dull, confused or uninformed discussion during the next phase of the proceedings, while lively questioning of speakers will predictably lead on to discussions of much better quality.

The Decision-Making Session

After all the candidates have made their presentations, the lead assessor will take over briefly to explain how the group should present its collective agreement on the various proposals and to state the time allowed for reaching and recording its decision. The assessor will not appoint a group leader or suggest the procedure which should govern the discussions. Those matters are left to the group to deal with as it chooses. The exercise is structured so that the group cannot simply endorse all proposals presented. The final consensus will require a process of discussion, compromise, and negotiation. Your effectiveness in this phase will determine your score under the dimension, Ability to Negotiate, Lead, and Mediate.

There is no single formula for success here. Candidates with various combinations of relative strengths and weaknesses can acquit themselves admirably in this part of the exercise. By the same token, if we leave aside the tiny minority of extraordinarily talented persons, no particular set of skills will guarantee a good performance.

Some candidates have a "take charge" inclination and all the personality traits that earn someone the label of "natural leader." Most or all of the group will begin to defer to such a candidate; he dominates the discussion and largely shapes the final outcome. These "natural leadership" traits are most helpful to the candidate fortunate enough to have them, but they will not, by themselves, necessarily impress the assessors. The natural leader may, from overconfidence or from lack of discernment, analytical ability, and other useful intellectual qualities, carry the group to a decision that is unsound or even thoroughly botched. The ability to lead in the wrong direction is not a useful talent.

Another recognizable type is the thoughtful, reflective person who is not as assertive or dominant as the "natural leader." She can get impressive results from incisive comments on the merits of the proposals, well thought out suggestions for compromises, and clever mediation between opposing viewpoints. Her downfall can come from a propensity to believe that once she has offered a perceptive analysis or brought order out of conceptual chaos, her duty is done. The group may be impressed for a moment but it soon forgets, and the brilliant intervention may leave no imprint on the final decision. The lesson here is that the intellectually gifted candidates must enter the fray more than once or twice to achieve anything worthwhile. They must assert themselves repeatedly and become fully involved in the give and take that leads to the final decision.

A third common type is the person who does not dominate by force of personality or lead by strength of intellect, but who possesses a warm and outgoing personality, a nice sense of humor, common sense, and good instincts for interpersonal relations. If she uses her talents wisely, she can diffuse conflicts with laughter, persuade stubborn antagonists to bend a little, point out the flaws in some arguments without wounding anyone's pride, lead the group painlessly to sensible compromises, and win high marks from the assessors. She can fall short, however, if she regards the creation of good feelings as an end in itself and does not use her talents to influence the group directly, or indirectly, to move toward sound decisions.

This does not exhaust the list of personality types, but it should be enough to illustrate the point. You should not hang back during the discussion-decision phase from fear that you lack one set of talents or another. Rather, you should play from your strengths, wherever these may lie. But you must play the game. Those who remain largely silent and withdrawn cannot hope to impress the assessors favorably.

Scoring the Group Exercise

At this point, we might consider for a moment how the group exercise fits into the total assessment process. First, it is the only element of the testing procedure which allows the assessors to judge how skillfully and effectively the candidate can handle himself in a group setting. All FSO's, after they move above entry level rank, will spend much of their working days in meetings. In most of these, their role will be some combination of forceful advocacy and gentle persuasion, of leadership and search for compromises that preserve what is essential in their own position while offering tolerable outcomes for other key players. An officer is called upon to assume some or all of these roles in meetings within his basic work unit (section of the embassy, division or office of the department) when that unit's position on a given matter is decided; in intradepartmental or interagency meetings that are part of a policy development or policy execution process; and in bilateral or multilateral negotiations with officials of other governments. If an officer can play his role with distinction in this arena, he should have a bright future in the Service.

The assessors of course know this and look upon the group exercise as an important test of candidates' potential. The exercise is set up, to the extent possible, to duplicate the real world of meetings among professionals. Assessors watch carefully the two candidates they are responsible for evaluating to pick up signs of the presence or absence of the talents they need to distinguish themselves in this environment.

The second point worth noting is that the group exercise puts on display a different side of the candidates' personality and talents than did either the knowledge-related or the problem questions of the morning's oral examination. And indeed it often happens that candidates who shone in the oral examination will do rather poorly in the group exercise, and conversely. Remember in this connection that the pair of assessors scoring you during the group exercise did not see you perform in the morning and have no prior impression, favorable or unfavorable, of your capacities.

The group exercise tests all of the dimensions except Written Communication, Knowledge, and the two dimensions tested solely by the in-basket exercise. The discussion-decision phase provides the assessors their only chance to judge your ability to negotiate, lead and mediate. Many of the proposals in the group exercise repertory bring political or cultural factors into play, giving the assessors who did not examine you in the morning an opportunity to evaluate your sensitivity to both. The relevance of the group exercise to the remaining dimensions is obvious.

THE IN-BASKET EXERCISE

This exercise, the last of the day, begins about 15 minutes after the end of the group exercise and lasts for an hour and a half. All candidates assemble in the same room. They each receive identical envelopes which contain a description of the scenario governing the exercise; reference material, including the names and titles of persons who figure in the scenario and important dates; the contents of the in-basket (memoranda, letters, and so on) which require action, and detailed written instructions. For those puzzled by the term "in-basket," the usual government desk top is graced by two wooden or plastic trays, one for in-coming written material which the occupant of the desk should read and take action upon—her in-basket—and a second in which she places material which she has processed in some fashion.

This exercise tests your capacities under the dimensions of Planning and Organizing Work and Managing Staff and is the only component of the assessment day which permits an evaluation of these two dimensions. Your results will also be graded under four additional headings, which parallel four of the remaining dimensions: Organizational Leadership, Analysis and Synthesis, Interpersonal Skills, and Judgment. You will recall that this test is scored only for those candidates who receive an overall passing score from the assessors on the twelve dimensions which they evaluated during earlier sessions of the assessment day.

Why is the in-basket exercise a component of the assessment day? Because FSO's spend much of their time behind a desk and should be able to use the paper flow efficiently as a tool for planning and organizing their work and drawing to best advantage upon the services of their subordinate personnel. Everyday experience of the workplace demonstrates that people who can function very effectively in an oral mode do not necessarily do as well in handling organizational paperwork. Everyone who has spent some time in office work settings has witnessed or heard about the occasional supervisor who becomes so ensnarled in paper that the output of his whole unit suffers. The in-basket test was added to the assessment process as a means of measuring significant skills and aptitudes not evaluated by other elements of the examination process. The Foreign Service is not alone in using this type of testing method; a number of large corporations also use an in-basket test to help evaluate potential entry level executive staff.

The in-basket test scenario will take you back to the mythical country you just visited during the group exercise. The scenario sets up a situation in which you are obliged, during a brief period, to handle all pending work in your in-basket by using the written word.

The general situation you face in this exercise and the individual problems you must cope with are as realistic as possible, consistent with the testing objectives. BEX renews the in-basket contents with each annual assessment cycle, using methods like those described for drafting the questions for the oral examination. Individual assessors, all experienced FSO's, draft suggested in-basket problems which are then winnowed and refined within BEX. In the final step, BEX officers meet with professionals from the Educational Testing Service to shape the material, if necessary, to fit the testing requirements.

When you do the exercise, you will find that it presents several intrinsic difficulties. In this, it resembles the written examination, which you have already passed, and the other components of the oral assessment. Like them, it presents identical difficulties to all the other candidates.

So, when you open that rather thick envelope in front of you, don't be frightened by its bulk. Remind yourself calmly of what you have learned from taking other demanding written tests, namely that you will probably face a choice between the length and quality of your responses to the individual problems and the number of problems you attempt to solve. You may need to make a rough judgment about where the optimum trade-off lies between quality and quantity, between the thoroughness with which you address each item and the number of items you process during the limited time available. When you have made that judgment, you will then be prepared to pace yourself to achieve the best results.

As you approach the deadline, you may have to go through the same process again. That is, you may discover that there seems to be more work to do than time to do it, and you must make another judgment about an optimum trade-off. Wherever that trade-off lies, a couple of things are obvious. First, panic will ensure the worst possible outcome. Second, if eight or ten problems remain, you will get better results from doing something sensible about half of them than from mangling all of them in a frantic rush to finish.

By the end of the day, you will probably feel somewhat drained. This is altogether natural. The oral assessment day is a tough and strenuous series of tests. You may occasionally have felt inadequate to the challenge. But remember that you were not competing against the examination itself but against hundreds of other candidates who felt much the same stress and emotional pressure.

HOW TO PREPARE FOR THE
ORAL ASSESSMENT DAY

A majority of those who come for the oral assessment seem to have made virtually no effort to prepare for it. Perhaps this is because they feel that the test measures such a range of skills that advanced preparation is futile.

This is a miscalculation, on two counts. First, a candidate can significantly improve his score, if he is willing to make the effort, on the four knowledge questions in the oral examination; on both tests of writing ability; and on the group exercise. These components, taken together, will account for roughly three-fourths of the final score.

Second, to borrow a saying of traders, "the action takes place at the margin." To explain: Within any group undergoing an examination, there will be one or two percent who are so gifted that they are certain to succeed. A larger number will fall so far short in certain crucial areas of knowledge and skill that they have very little chance of passing. The rest fall into the third group, where neither success nor failure is foreordained, and it is here that the real competition occurs. For candidates within this group, the gain of a few points here and there can make the dif-

ference between passing or failing, or the difference between a bare pass and a solidly competitive score. In other words, for a substantial number of candidates, marginal gains (or losses) can decisively affect the outcome.

The suggestions already offered, and those that follow, are intended to help you make the marginal improvements which can be crucial and which are within your reach if you are willing to work for them. There are no gimmicks and no magic formulas; you will not get useful results without sustained effort.

Begin by making an inventory of your areas of relative weakness in terms of the specific knowledge and skills that will be tested. Decide which are the most serious and the easiest to correct in the time available. Then draw up a work plan which promises the most return for the time and effort expended and hold to it.

Let us now consider in turn the three areas within the assessment process where advance preparation will bring results, beginning with the substantive questions in the oral examination.

PREPARING FOR THE KNOWLEDGE QUESTIONS

You may wonder why we suggest on broadening and deepening your knowledge in a variety of fields when knowledge is only one among 14 dimensions tested.

The answer is that ignorance of the subject matter of these four substantive questions will tend to lower your oral examination score under as many as five other dimensions as well:

- Political Sensitivity and Cultural Sensitivity (if you don't know the facts, how can you show sensitivity to their significance?)
- Analytical and Synthesizing Ability (without the facts, what can you analyze or synthesize?)

- Oral Communication (if, for want of knowledge, you struggle through your answers, how articulate will you appear?)
- Stability and Adjustment and Interpersonal Skills (how much poise and self-confidence will you show if you flub one answer after another?)

The dimensions aside, if you give knowledgeable well-structured answers to the four substantive questions, the assessors will be impressed. They will be inclined perhaps even to give you the benefit of the doubt when they evaluate you on some of the dimensions where you didn't make quite as strong a showing. On the other hand, mediocre to poor responses to the knowledge questions tend to cast a dismal pall over your entire performance in the oral examination.

Use this check list to guide your preparations for the oral examination. Ideally, you should arrive with a thorough grounding in:

- American history, at least from the end of the Civil War to the present
- American foreign policy, at least from World War II onward
- The Constitution of the United States (if you are not very familiar with it, read it; the Constitution is neither a long nor a forbidding document)
- The important current issues and trends in the national life including the country's most pressing economic problems, both domestic and international, and the general landscape of its artistic and cultural life.

Immerse Yourself in Current Issues

You will need, if you haven't already done so, to immerse yourself in the issues and controversies that dominate the news and public discussion. Unfortunately, neither TV network news nor most newspapers will provide the breadth and depth of coverage you require. You should make it your business to read a quality newspaper daily and to read it thoroughly. Some quality papers include: The *Christian Science Monitor, The New York Times, The Washington Post* and *The Wall Street Journal.* For those of you who are not acquainted with it, the *Journal* covers much more than the stock and bond markets. Its coverage and analysis of broad economic issues is excellent to superb, and its articles and commentary on political, social, and intellectual issues are usually of very high quality. If you don't or can't subscribe to one of these papers, read it in a library.

Some TV news programs can be very helpful too: the Sunday talk shows, ABC's *Nightline,* and public television's *Washington Week in Review* and *Frontline.*

Read regularly the better periodicals as well. *The Economist* (a British newsweekly which has an American edition) covers political, foreign affairs, and other issues quite extensively. Its treatment of economic topics is excellent. Because it does not target a mass readership, *The Economist* can delve more deeply into the issues than other weekly magazines, but the style is informal and straightforward. The library should have it.

Foreign Affairs and *Foreign Policy*, both quarterlies, are excellent on international problems, political, economic, strategic, and so on. Back issues of the former (much the older of the two) should be available in libraries and would make fine source material for brushing up on foreign policy issues of past decades.

As you read, do more than just absorb the material passively. Think through the issues, question critically the viewpoints expressed and look for flawed arguments. Develop your own ideas on the issues, test them against what you read, and try them out in discussions or arguments with friends, acquaintances and relatives. There is nothing better than a friendly argument to focus the issues sharply in your mind. Above all, acquaint yourself with a variety of viewpoints—conservative, liberal and centrist, pragmatic and ideological.

For the cultural scene, read the art and culture sections of the newspapers mentioned, the *New Yorker* and *The New York Review of Books.* Browse through the better book stores; most will have a good selection of works on American painting, films, music, dance and so on. If you can't afford to buy them, note the most interesting titles and get them from the library.

Shoring Up Your Economics Background

What to do if you know little or nothing about economics? The precise answer will depend on many things, but the general approach that follows can be adapted to suit your specific circumstances.

First, you are of course already reading the quality papers and periodicals. As you read, identify about six topics which seem to be the major current national and international economic problems. Add to these the general problem of the economic development of the poorer countries. Then look for good articles that deal with your selected topics and study those articles. Read them two or three times and try to puzzle out the flow of argument and analysis. Then mark for future reference the points you can't follow, or make notes on them. Be systematic about it; set up a file folder for each topic, put all relevant material in it, and go back and review the material periodically to make sure you are learning it.

Nothing guarantees that the economic question you get will fall within the topic areas you have identified. But if you know nothing about the first question asked, request another economic question, and even a third if you must. It is better to know something about one question out of two or three than nothing about anything.

Along with extensive reading about the important current issues, you will need some systematic study of economic theory. If you have time, take basic economic courses. Some of the standard college Economics I and Economics II won't be directly relevant to your purposes but much will be. If you cannot fit formal instruction into your schedule, then get a basic economic text and study it on your own. Among standard texts, an excellent one is *Economics* by Paul Samuelson. A Nobel laureate, he is often called the "dean" of American economists, he is not identified with any of the various contending sects, and his style is lucid and readable. Skim the microeconomic sections and concentrate on macroeconomic theory.

One thing you want to get from formal study is familiarity with standard terminology and basic concepts. For instance, what exactly is inflation? What is money and what is meant by the term money supply? What is capital? (You think you know, but perhaps you don't really understand the concept). What is the difference between the merchandise trade balance and the current account balance? How do the two fit into a country's balance of payments? Why do many economists say that one of the most important things a poor country can do to promote economic development is to set a realistic exchange rate for its currency? Why is the statement, "The U.S. does provide foreign aid but most of the money stays in the country" largely meaningless? As a further partial checklist, make sure you comprehend such basic concepts as marginal utility, comparative advantage (it relates to foreign trade issues), the productivity of labor and capital, why changes in productivity rates are different from changes in production rates, and the elasticity of supply and demand.

Of course no assessor will start with a question like, "Define elasticity of demand," or "What is money." But you might well be asked about inflation, and that can easily lead on to the money supply. If you seem a little shaky at that point, the assessor, wishing to know whether you really understand the vocabulary you are using, might well ask you, "What is money?"

If you have begun to panic at this point, remind yourself of a few simple truths. If you are smart enough to pass the written examination, you can certainly learn basic economic concepts and terminology. As Samuelson put it (in the preface to the tenth edition of *Economics*), "political economy is not . . . hammock reading for a lazy summer afternoon." But no good college course is simply hammock reading. You are a little like the character in Molière's comedy, who suddenly discovers that he has spoken prose most of his life; you have already mastered subjects of equal intrinsic complexity to those you will face in studying economics.

The second thing you want to get from your study of economics is answers to questions that stumped you in the articles you have read on your list of major current issues. Search your text for helpful material on those points; when you find it, make notes on it and drop them in the topic folder.

In addition to your topic-oriented reading and your formal study, you should do something almost too obvious to mention. Find someone, or several people, knowledgeable about economics with whom you can discuss the points you have trouble grasping on your own. If you don't have an instructor, try friends, relatives, friends of friends, and so on. A Foreign Service officer has to be ingenious and cannot afford timidity. Use this problem to practice the skills you will need in your chosen profession.

PREPARING FOR THE WRITTEN EXERCISES

Most candidates are fairly comfortable with the written word, but many fall short in technique. This doubtless reflects the current academic fashion in this country of encouraging "creative self-expression" at the expense of discipline in form, grammar and organization. Foreign Service written material—reports, memoranda, policy papers and so on—requires clarity and precision of exposition, coherence in argument, economy of style, correct grammar, and careful organization.

If you know you are relatively weak in these areas, the obvious remedy is to take one or more rigorous courses in English composition. If you are no longer in college, see what evening courses are available. Remember that written communication gets double weight in the scoring, so a poor performance here can lower your overall score enough to affect significantly your final standing.

PREPARING FOR THE ORAL PROPOSAL

American education largely neglects the traditional study of rhetoric, and many candidates show almost no awareness of standard public speaking technique. Poor delivery can spoil the effect of excellent substantive content, and indeed there is little positive correlation between candidates' intellectual capacity and their ability to speak effectively to a group. Many are simply not conscious of the most basic techniques of voice control, gesture, body posture, and so on that are useful in getting and holding audience attention.

If you have no formal training in public speaking, and not enough experience at it to be sure of your ability, then you should take a course in public speaking. The first reaction to this will probably be, "What a waste of time and money!" But

it will be neither. Whether you decide to enter the Foreign Service or not, the ability to speak in public is a most useful skill to have. Moreover, a good course of instruction in the subject will not limit itself to the formal public speech but will give you command of a range of techniques, including ways of coping with stage fright, that will be useful to you in a variety of less formal settings as well.

After you have had some training, make a point of joining clubs and associations where you will often have the opportunity to speak in public. Your efforts in this area will repay themselves many times over, whatever profession you ultimately choose.

AFTER THE ORAL ASSESSMENT

BACKGROUND INVESTIGATION

Those of you among the elect will receive some forms that must be filled in and returned to permit further processing of your candidacy. In particular, a background investigation will be conducted to determine candidates' suitability for the Foreign Service, and completion and return of certain of the forms will be necessary to get that process under way.

The background investigation is necessary because all Foreign Service officers must have top secret security clearance. A casual reading of the news over the past couple of years would provide evidence enough of the need for thorough background investigation of all U.S. government employees holding sensitive positions. The investigation usually takes 6 to 9 months to complete, depending upon such things as whether the candidate has lived abroad or at several different locations in the U.S. Past foreign residence is not held against you, of course, but it does add extra steps

to the investigative process. In any event, the sooner you fill in and return the required forms the sooner the procedure can begin.

After you have sent in the papers necessary for the background investigation, you will receive an authorization for a comprehensive medical examination for you and for your dependents. These examinations are conducted at government expense and at facilities as convenient as possible to your place of residence. The medical examination determines whether you and your dependents are physically fit to serve at any Foreign Service post. It is essential because many of our posts are located in remote, unhealthful areas and lack adequate facilities for medical care.

Finally, you will be asked to send in your university transcripts and a 1000-word autobiography. The latter is a highly personal document, to be framed as you wish so long as it is both candid and informative.

TRYING AGAIN

If you don't pass the oral assessment the first time, you may repeat the process as often as you like. However, you must begin at the beginning each time and take and pass the written examination again to be eligible to repeat the oral assessment. The assessors, of course, will not know that you failed to pass on a previous attempt.

By the same token, if you pass the first time but think you could do even better on a second try, you

may also repeat the process, but you must begin with the written examination. Apart from the time and effort involved, you have nothing to lose since you will be awarded the higher (or highest) of the scores you received. If, for example, the second score is higher than the first, your name goes on the appointment register with the later date (see below, The Appointment Process) and will remain on the register for 18 months from that date.

THE FINAL REVIEW

The last step in the examination process takes place at the Assessment Center in Washington and does not involve the candidates' presence. Four assessors, none of whom examined you during the

oral assessment day, will read your entire file, which will now contain your written examination scores; the results of the oral assessment day, including the scores of the in-basket test; the personal information forms you submitted, along with your autobiography and transcripts; and the results of the background investigation. Each of the final review assessors reads the file independently, writes out a score, places it in a sealed envelope and passes the file on to the next assessor. When all four have finished, the scores are opened and averaged to give you a final review score.

If the scores of any two among the final review assessors differ by more than a given number of points, all four will meet to discuss the file. A similar meeting will be held if one or two assessors fail the candidate. The discussion in either case insures that, to the extent possible, all assessors are seeing and evaluating the "same" person— i.e., that none of them has overlooked or failed to give proper weight to positive or negative information in the file. None of the assessors is obliged to change his score after listening to his colleagues but in most cases there are adjustments. The procedure adds a safeguard against unconscious bias or a misreading or mistaken evaluation of the file. If, after this meeting, an assessor continues to believe that a candidate should fail, his score is entered at one point below the passing mark to ensure that a single failing score does not unduly affect the average score.

You will remember that, during the oral assessment day, the four assessors rating your performance were kept in ignorance, by design, of everything about your personal background. But what you have accomplished in your life outside of the assessment process may be highly relevant to your potential as an FSO. This information is evaluated during the final review and integrated into the scoring. The final review assessors will give positive weight to advanced degrees; scholastic honors; graduate study programs that provide language and/or area expertise useful to the Service; job experience, particularly in positions of significant responsibility; leadership in community or other activities, or extensive experience with foreign cultures. The list is illustrative and could be extended.

This is how the weighted scoring system works. The oral assessment day score is weighted at 52% of the final score; the in-basket score is weighted at 15% of that 52%. The written exam and the final review scores are both given identical weights of 24%.

THE APPOINTMENT PROCESS

The names of successful candidates go on appointment registers in a rank order determined by their scores. There are six registers: administrative, consular, commercial (for the Department of Commerce's United States and Foreign Commercial Service), economics, information/cultural (for the United States Information Agency—USIA), and politics. Successful candidates go on those registers for which they have qualified in the functional field portions of the written examination. If a candidate qualified, say, only under the administrative functional field test, her name goes only on the administrative register. If she qualified under all six functional fields, her name goes on all six registers, and so on. A candidate remains on a register for eighteen months. Most but not necessarily all candidates are offered appointments within that time.

When the Departments of State or Commerce, or USIA, wish to appoint new officers, the appointments are offered first to candidates whose names are at the top of the rank order in the registers concerned. Each offer of appointment is limited to service within State, Commerce or USIA and, within State, to a particular functional specialty. The functional register from which a candidate accepts an appointment will ordinarily determine her specialty. If you strongly prefer the consular field, let us say, but the first appointment offer you receive is for the economics speciality, it would be risky to accept it on the assumption that, once in the Service, you will be able at some point to maneuver yourself out of economic work and into the consular specialty.

Refusal of an offered appointment will not of itself change your rank order on the register or otherwise prejudice your chances of a future appointment. However, there is no guarantee that you will receive another offer. Your relative position on each register for which you have qualified will vary somewhat over time as new names are added and others dropped. You are welcome to call the Registrar's Office in BEX (202-235-9246) to ask about your relative position on appointment registers.

And when you finally receive an appointment to the field of your choice, you will embark on a challenging career in a Service where the country needs dedicated men and women.

Part Four

REVIEW OF ENGLISH GRAMMAR AND USAGE

THE ESSENTIALS OF ENGLISH GRAMMAR

PARTS OF SPEECH

1. Nouns

   A noun is the name of a person, a place, a thing, or an idea.

   Examples: teacher, city, desk, democracy

   There are different kinds of nouns:

   Common nouns are general: house girl street city

   Proper nouns are specific: White House Jane Main Street New York

   Collective nouns name groups: team crowd organization Congress

   Nouns have *cases:*

   Nominative: the subject, noun of address, or predicate noun

   Objective: the direct object, indirect object, or object of the preposition

   Possessive: the form that shows possession

2. Pronouns

   Pronouns can substitute for nouns.

   Examples: he, they, ours, those

   The noun or noun phrase to which a pronoun refers is the **antecedent.** Every pronoun must have a clear antecedent to give it meaning. A pronoun must agree with its antecedent in gender, person, and number.

   Example: Each of the boys has *his* lunch.

   (Each is singular and therefore requires a singular pronoun.)

   There are several kinds of pronouns:

   Demonstrative pronoun: this, that, these, those

   Indefinite pronoun: all, any, anybody

   Interrogative pronoun: who, which, what

3. Adjectives

   An adjective describes or modifies a noun.

   Examples: warm, quick, tall, blue

   Adjectives answer the following questions about nouns:

   Which one? I'll take the *red* scarf.

   What kind? A *wool* scarf keeps me warm.

   How many? There are *two* keys on the counter.

   Whose? The *students'* lounge is on the second floor.

4. Adverbs

   An adverb modifies a verb, an adjective, or another adverb.

   Examples: fast, slowly, friendly, well

   An adverb will answer the following questions about verbs, adjectives or other adverbs:

   Where? The dog ran *away*.

   When? I woke *early* this morning.

   How? I slept *soundly* last night.

   To what extent? She was *absolutely* certain about the answer.

Personal pronoun:			Nominative Case	Objective Case	Possessive Case
	Singular	1st person	I	me	mine
		2nd person	you	you	yours
		3rd person	he, she, it	him, her, it	his, hers
	Plural	1st person	we	us	ours
		2nd person	you	you	your
		3rd person	they	them	theirs

5. Verbs

Verbs show action or state of being.

Examples: hit, run, study (action verbs)

be, seem, become (state of being verbs)

A verb changes time by the addition of certain endings and helping verbs.

Examples: I *walk* to school. (present tense)

I *walked* to school yesterday. (past tense)

I *will walk* to school tomorrow. (future tense)

I *have walked* to school every morning this week. (present perfect tense)

I *had walked* halfway to school when the bus arrived. (past perfect tense)

I *will have walked* six blocks before I pass your house. (future perfect tense)

SELECTED RULES OF GRAMMAR

1. The subject of a verb is in the nominative case even if the verb is understood and not expressed.

   Example: They are as old as *we*. (As we are)

2. The word *who* is in the nominative case. *Whom* is in the objective case.

   Example: The trapeze artist who ran away with the clown broke the lion tamer's heart. (*Who* is the subject of the verb *ran*.)

   Example: The trapeze artist whom he loved ran away with the circus clown. (*Whom* is the object of the verb *loved*.)

3. The word *whoever* is in the nominative case. *Whomever* is in the objective case.

   Example: Whoever comes to the door is welcome to join in the party. (*Whoever* is the subject of the verb *comes*.)

   Example: Invite whomever you wish to accompany you. (*Whomever* is the object of the verb *invite*.)

   Example: The process server may leave the summons with whoever answers the doorbell. (*Whoever* is the subject of the verb *answers*. The entire clause is the object of the preposition *with*.)

   Example: Whomever the citizens wish to have govern them, they must first elect. (The order of the sentence is inverted, but *whomever* is the object of the verb *wish*.)

4. Nouns or pronouns connected by a form of the verb *to be* should always be in the nominative case.

   Example: It is *I*. (Not *me*)

   Exception: The old man's sight had failed so badly that he thought his son to be *me*. (The infinitive *to be* is serving a linking function. Since *his son* is the object of *thought*, the pronoun linked by the infinitive *to be* must be in the objective case. You may test this type of sentence, by reversing the order of noun and pronoun. Thus: The old man's sight had failed so badly that he thought me to be his son.)

5. The object of a preposition or of a transitive verb should use a pronoun in the objective case.

   Example: It would be impossible for *me* to do that job alone. (*Me* is the object of the preposition *for*.)

   Example: The attendant gave *me* the keys to the locker. (*Me* is the indirect object of the verb *gave*.)

NOTE: When the first person pronoun is used in conjunction with one or more proper names, you may confirm the choice of *I or me* by eliminating the proper names and reading the sentence with the pronoun alone.

   Example: John, George, Marylou, and (me or I) went to the movies last night. (By eliminating the names you can readily choose that *I went to the movies* is correct.)

Example: It would be very difficult for Mae and (I or me) to attend the wedding. (Without *Mae* it is clear that it is *difficult for me* to attend.)

6. *Each, either, neither, anyone, anybody, somebody, someone, every, everyone, one, no one,* and *nobody* are singular pronouns. Each of these words takes a singular verb and a singular pronoun.

    Examples: *Neither likes* the pets of the other.
    Everyone must wait *his* turn.
    Each of the patients *carries* insurance.
    Neither of the women *has* completed *her* assignment.

7. When the correlative conjunctions *either/or* and *neither/nor* are used, the number of the verb agrees with the number of the last subject.

    Example: Neither John nor *Greg eats* meat.

    Example: Either the cat or the *mice take* charge in the barn.

8. A subject consisting of two or more nouns joined by a coordinating conjunction takes a plural verb.

    Example: Paul *and* Sue *were* the last to arrive.

9. The number of the verb is not affected by the addition to the subject of words introduced by *with, together with, no less than, as well as,* etc.

    Example: The *captain,* together with the rest of the team, *was delighted* by the victory celebration.

10. A verb agrees in number with its subject. A verb should not be made to agree with a noun that is part of a phrase following the subject.

    Example: *Mount Snow,* one of my favorite ski areas, *is* in Vermont.

    Example: The *mountains* of Colorado, like those of Switzerland, *offer* excellent skiing.

11. A verb should agree in number with the subject, not with the predicate noun or pronoun.

    Example: Poor study *habits are* the leading cause of unsatisfactory achievement in school.

Example: The leading *cause* of unsatisfactory achievement in school *is* poor study habits.

12. A pronoun agrees with its antecedent in person, number, and gender.

    Example: Since you were absent on Tuesday, you will have to ask Mary or Beth for her notes on the lecture. (Use *her,* not their, because two singular antecedents joined by *or* take a singular pronoun.)

13. *Hardly, scarcely, barely, only* and *but* (when it means *only*) are negative words. Do NOT use another negative in conjunction with any of these words.

    Example: He *didn't have but* one hat. (WRONG)
    He had *but* one hat. OR He had *only* one hat.

    Example: I *can't hardly* read the small print. (WRONG)
    I *can hardly* read the small print. OR I *can't* read the small print.

14. *As* is a conjunction introducing a subordinate clause, while *like* is a preposition. The object of a preposition is a noun or phrase.

    Example: The day was crisp and clear *as* October days often are. (*Days* is the subject of the clause; *are* is its verb.)

    Example: He behaves *like* a fool.

    Example: The gambler accepts only hard currency *like* gold coins.

15. When modifying the words *kind* and *sort,* the words *this* and *that* always remain in the singular.

    Example: *This kind* of apple makes the best pie.

    Example: *That sort* of behavior will result in severe punishment.

16. In sentences beginning with *there is* and *there are,* the verb should agree in number with the noun that follows it.

    Example: There isn't an unbroken bone in her body. (The singular subject *bone* takes the singular verb *is*.)

    Example: There are many choices to be made. (The plural subject *choices* takes the plural verb *are*.)

17. A noun or pronoun modifying a gerund should be in the possessive case.

> *Example:* Is there any criticism of Arthur's going? (*Going* is a gerund. It must be modified by Arthur's, not by Arthur.)

18. Do *not* use the possessive case when referring to an inanimate object.

> *Example:* He had difficulty with the *store's* management. (WRONG)
> He had difficulty with the management of the store.

19. When expressing a condition contrary to fact or a wish, use the subjunctive form *were*.

> *Example:* I wish I *were* a movie star.

20. Statements equally true in the past and in the present are usually expressed in the present tense. The contents of a book are also expressed in the present tense.

> *Example:* He said that Venus is a planet. (Even though he made the statement in the past, the fact remains that Venus *is* a planet.)
> *Example:* In the book *Peter Pan,* Wendy says, "I can fly." (Every time one reads the book, Wendy *says* it again.)

ANTECEDENTS AND MODIFIERS

1. *It*, when used as a relative pronoun, refers to the nearest noun. In your writing, you must be certain that the grammatical antecedent is indeed the intended antecedent.

> *Example:* Since the mouth of the cave was masked by underbrush, *it* provided an excellent hiding place. (Do you really mean that the underbrush is an excellent hiding place, or do you mean the cave?)

2. *Which* is another pronoun that is subject to errors of reference. In fact, whenever using pronouns, you must ask yourself whether or not the reference of the pronoun is clear.

> *Example:* The first chapter awakens your interest in cloning, which continues to the end of the book. (What continues, cloning or your interest?)
> *Example:* Jim told Bill that he was about to be fired. (Who is about to be fired? This sentence can be interpreted to mean that Jim was informing Bill about Bill's impending termination or about his, Jim's, own troubles.)

In your writing, you may find that the most effective way to clear up an ambiguity is to recast the sentence.

> *Example:* The first chapter awakens your interest in cloning. The following chapters build upon this interest and maintain it throughout the book.
> *Example:* Jim told Bill, "I am about to be fired." OR Jim told Bill, "You are about to be fired."

3. Adjectives modify only nouns and pronouns. Adverbs modify verbs, adjectives, and other adverbs.

> *Example:* One can swim in a lake as *easy* as in a pool. (WRONG)
> One can swim in a lake as *easily* as in a pool. (The adverb *easily* must modify the verb *can swim*.)
> *Example:* I was *real* happy. (WRONG)
> I was *really* happy. (The adverb *really* must be used to modify the adjective *happy*.)

Sometimes context determines the use of adjective or adverb.

> *Example:* The old man looked angry. (*Angry* is an adjective describing the old man [angry old man].)
> The old man looked *angrily* out the window. (*Angrily* is an adverb describing the man's manner of looking out the window.)

4. Phrases should be placed near the words they modify.

> *Example:* The author says that he intends to influence your life *in the first chapter.* (WRONG)

The author *in the first chapter* says . . . OR *In the first chapter,* the author says . . .

5. Adverbs should be placed near the words they modify.
   Example: The man was *only* willing to sell one horse. (WRONG)
   The man was willing to sell *only* one horse.

6. Clauses should be placed near the words they modify.
   Example: *He* will reap a good harvest *who sows early.* (WRONG)
   He who sows early will reap a good harvest.

7. A modifier must modify something.
   Example: Having forgotten to wind it, the clock stopped at midnight. (WRONG)

Having forgotten to wind the clock, I found that it had stopped at midnight. (*Having forgotten to wind the clock* modifies *I.*)

Example: While on vacation, the pipes burst. (WRONG) (The pipes were not away on vacation.)
While we were away on vacation, the pipes burst.

Example: To run efficiently, the serviceman should oil the lawnmower. (WRONG)
The serviceman should oil the lawnmower to make it run efficiently.

NOTE: The best test for the placement of modifiers is to read the sentence literally. If you read a sentence literally and it is literally ridiculous, it is WRONG. The meaning of a sentence must be clear to any reader. The words of the sentence *must make sense.*

CHOOSING THE RIGHT WORD

The term *diction* includes the use of the correct word and the avoidance of excess wordiness. The list that follows presents many of the most commonly misused or confused words in the English language. Read through the list now and put a check next to those words which have given you trouble in the past. You may even recognize some words you have been misusing for years without knowing that they were troublesome. Skim lightly over the words you have under control; memorize uses of the others. If you have time, try using each word in a sentence of your own.

accede—means *to agree with.*
concede—means *to yield,* but not necessarily in agreement.
exceed—means *to be more than.*
> We shall *accede* to your request for more evidence.
> To avoid delay, we shall *concede* that more evidence is necessary.
> Federal expenditures now *exceed* federal income.

access—means *availability.*
excess—means *too much.*
> The lawyer was given *access* to the grand jury records.
> The expenditures this month are far in *excess* of income.

accept—means *to take when offered.*
except—means *excluding.* (preposition)
except—means *to leave out.* (verb)
> The draft board will *accept* all seniors as volunteers before graduation.
> All eighteen-year-olds *except* seniors will be called.
> The draft board will *except* all seniors until after graduation.

adapt—means *to adjust to change.*
adopt—means *to take as one's own.*
adept—means *skillful.*
> Children can *adapt* to changing conditions very easily.
> The war orphan was *adopted* by the general and his wife.

Proper instruction makes children *adept* in various games.
NOTE: adapt *to,* adopt *by,* adept *in* or *at.*

adapted to—implies *original* or *natural suitability.*
adapted for—implies *created suitability.*
adapted from—implies *changes to be made suitable.*
> The gills of fish are *adapted to* underwater breathing.
> Atomic energy is constantly being *adapted for* new uses.
> Many of Richard Wagner's opera librettos were *adapted from* old Norse sagas.

addition—means *the act or process of adding.*
edition—means *a printing of a publication.*
> In *addition* to a dictionary, he always used a thesaurus.
> The first *edition* of Shakespeare's plays appeared in 1623.

advantage—means *a superior position.*
benefit—means *a favor conferred or earned (as a profit).*
> He had an *advantage* in experience over his opponent.
> The rules were changed for his *benefit.*
> NOTE: to *take* advantage *of,* to *have* an advantage *over.*

adverse—(pronounced AD-verse) means *unfavorable.*
averse—(pronounced a-VERSE) means *disliking.*
> He took the *adverse* decision in poor taste.
> Many students were *averse* to criticism by their classmates.

advise—means *to give advice. Advise* is losing favor as a synonym for *notify.*
> *Acceptable:* The teacher will *advise* the student in habits of study.
> *Unacceptable:* We are *advising* you of a delivery under separate cover. (SAY: *notifying*)

affect—means *to influence.* (verb)
effect—means *an influence.* (noun)
effect—means *to bring about.* (verb)
> Your education must *affect* your future.
> The *effect* of the last war is still being felt.

A diploma *effected* a tremendous change in his attitude.

NOTE: *Affect* also has the meaning of *pretend.* She had an *affected* manner.

after—is unnecessary with the past participle.

SAY: *After* checking the timetable, I left for the station.

DON'T SAY: *After having checked* (omit *after*) the timetable, I left for the station.

ain't—is an *unacceptable* contraction for *am not, are not,* or *is not.*

aisle—is *a passageway between seats.*
isle—is a *small island.*
(Both words rhyme with *pile.*)

all ready—means *completely ready* or *everyone ready.*
already—means *prior to some specific time.*

By the time I was *all ready* to go to the play, the tickets were *already* all sold.

They were *all ready* to begin when the teacher arrived.

alright—is *unacceptable.* It should always be written as two words: *all right.*

all together—means *in sum, collectively,* or *everybody together.*
altogether—means *completely.*

There are *altogether* too many people to seat in this room when we are *all together.*

all ways—means *in every possible way.*
always—means *at all times.*

He was in *all ways* acceptable to the voters.

His reputation has *always* been spotless.

allude—means *to make a reference to.*
elude—means *to escape from.*

Only incidentally does Coleridge *allude* to Shakespeare's puns.

It is almost impossible for one to *elude* tax collectors.

allusion—means *a reference.*
illusion—means *a deception of the eye or mind.*

The student made *allusions* to his teacher's habits.

Illusions of the mind, unlike those of the eye, cannot be corrected with glasses.

alongside of—means *side by side with.*
alongside—means *parallel to the side.*

Bill stood *alongside of* Henry.

Park the car *alongside* the curb.

alot—is *unacceptable.* It should always be written as two words: *a lot.*

among—always implies that there are *more than two people or things.*
between—commonly appears to *only two people or things.*

The knowledge is secure *among* the members of our club.

Let us keep this secret *between* you and me.

NOTE: *Between* may be used with more than two objects to show the relationship of each object to the others.

The teacher explained the difference *between* adjective, adverb, and noun clauses.

amount, much, less—apply to quantities of objects that *cannot be counted one by one.*
number, many, fewer—apply to quantities that *can be counted one by one.*

Many raindrops make *much* water.

If you have *fewer* dollars, you have *less* money.

The *amount* of property you own depends on the *number* of acres in your lot.

annual—means *yearly.*
biannual—means *twice a year.* (*Semiannual* means the same thing.)
biennial—means *once in two years* or *every two years.*

anywheres—is *unacceptable.*
anywhere—is *acceptable.*

SAY: We can't find it *anywhere.*

ALSO SAY: *nowhere* (NOT nowheres), *somewhere* (NOT somewheres)

aren't I—is *colloquial.* Its use is to be discouraged.

SAY: *Am I not* entitled to an explanation?

as—(used as a conjunction) is followed by a verb.
like—(used as a preposition) is NOT followed by a verb.

Do *as* I do, not *as* I say.

Try not to behave *like* a child.

Unacceptable: He acts *like* I do.

as far as—expresses *distance.*
so far as—indicates *a limitation.*

We hiked *as far as* the next guest house.

So far as we know, the barn was adequate for a night's stay.

as good as—should be used *for comparisons only.*

This motel is *as good as* the next one.

NOTE: *As good as* does NOT mean *practically.*

Unacceptable: They *as good as* promised us a place in the hall.

Acceptable: They *practically* promised us a place in the hall.

as if—is correctly used in the expression, "He talked *as if* his jaw hurt him."

Unacceptable: "He talked *like* his jaw hurt him."

ascared—no such word. It is *unacceptable for scared.*

SAY: The child was *scared* of ghosts.

ascent—is *the act of rising.*
assent—means *approval.*

The *ascent* to the top of the mountain was perilous.

Congress gave its *assent* to the President's emergency directive.

assay—means *to try* or *experiment.* (verb)
essay—means *an intellectual effort.* (noun)

We shall *assay* the ascent of the mountain tomorrow.

The candidate's views were expressed in a well-written *essay.*

attend to—means *to take care of.*
tend to—means *to be inclined to.*

One of the clerks will *attend to* the mail in my absence.

Lazy people *tend* to gain weight.

back—should NOT be used with such words as *refer* and *return* since the prefix *re-* means *back.*

Unacceptable: Refer *back* to the text, if you have difficulty recalling the facts.

backward ⎫ Both are *acceptable* and may be
backwards ⎭ used interchangeably as an adverb.

We tried to run *backward.* (or *backwards*)

Backwards as an adjective means *slow in learning.* (Do NOT say *backwards* in this case.)

A *backward* pupil should be given every encouragement.

berth—is *a resting place.*
birth—means *the beginning of life.*

The new liner was given a wide *berth* in the harbor.

He was a fortunate man from *birth.*

beside—is a preposition meaning *by the side of.*
besides—is an adverb meaning *in addition to.*

He sat *beside* his sick father.

Besides his father, his mother also was not well.

better—means *recovering.*
well—means *completely recovered.*

He is *better* now than he was a week ago.

In a few more weeks, he will be *well.*

both—means *two considered together.*
each—means *one or two or more.*

Both of the applicants qualified for the position.

Each applicant was given a generous reference.

NOTE: Avoid using such expressions as the following:

Both girls had a new typewriter. (Use *each girl* instead.)

Both girls tried to outdo the other. (Use *each girl* instead.)

They are *both* alike (Omit *both*.)

breath—means *an intake of air.*
breathe—means *to draw air in and give it out.*
breadth—means *width.*

Before you dive in, take a very deep *breath.*

It is difficult to *breathe* under water.

In a square, the *breadth* is equal to the length.

bring—means *to carry toward the person who is speaking.*
take—means *to carry away from the speaker.*

Bring the books here.

Take your raincoat with you when you go out.

broke—is the past tense of *break.*
broke—is *unacceptable* for *without money.*

He *broke* his arm.

"Go for broke" is a slang expression widely used in gambling circles.

bunch—refers to *things.*
group—refers to *persons* or *things.*

This looks like a delicious *bunch* of bananas.

What a well-behaved *group* of children!

NOTE: The colloquial use of bunch applied to *persons* is to be discouraged.

A *bunch* of the boys were whooping it up. (*Number* is preferable.)

certainly—(and *surely*) is an *adverb.*
sure—is an *adjective.*

He was *certainly* learning fast.

Unacceptable: He *sure* was learning fast.

cite—means to quote.
sight—means *seeing.*

site—means *a place for a building*.
> He was fond of *citing* from the Scriptures.
> The *sight* of the wreck was appalling.
> The Board of Education was seeking a *site* for the new school.

coarse—means *vulgar* or *harsh*.
course—means a *path* or a *study*.
> He was shunned because of his *coarse* behavior.
> The ship took its usual *course*.
> Which *course* in English are you taking?

come to be—should NOT be replaced with the expression *become to be*, since *become* means *come to be*.
> True freedom will *come to be* when all tyrants have been overthrown.

comic—means *intentionally funny*.
comical—means *unintentionally funny*.
> A clown is a *comic* figure.
> The peculiar hat she wore gave her a *comical* appearance.

conscience—means *sense of right*.
conscientious—means *faithful*.
conscious—means *aware of oneself*.
> Man's *conscience* prevents him from becoming completely selfish.
> We all depend on him because he is *conscientious*.
> The injured man was completely *conscious*.

considerable—is properly used *only as an adjective*, NOT as a noun.

cease—means *to end*.
seize—means *to take hold of*.
> Will you please *cease* making those sounds?
> *Seize* him by the collar as he comes around the corner.

cent—means *a coin*.
scent—means *an odor*.
sent—is the past tense of *send*.
> The one-*cent* postal card is a thing of the past.
> The *scent* of roses is pleasing.
> We were *sent* to the rear of the balcony.

calendar—is *a system of time*.
colander—is *a kind of sieve*.
> In this part of the world, most people prefer the twelve-month *calendar*.
> Fresh vegetables should be washed in a *colander* before cooking.

can—means *physically able*.

may—implies *permission*.
> I *can* lift this chair over my head.
> You *may* leave after you finish your work.

cannot help—must be followed by a gerund.
> We cannot help *feeling* (NOT *feel*) distressed about this.
> NOTE: *cannot help but* is *unacceptable*.

capital—is *the city*.
capitol—is *the building*.
> Paris is the *capital* of France.
> The *Capitol* in Washington is occupied by the Congress. (The Washington *Capitol* is always capitalized.)
> NOTE: *Capital* also means wealth.

compare to—means *to liken to something which has a different form*.
compare with—means *to compare persons or things with each other when they are of the same kind*.
contrast with—means *to show the difference between two things*.
> A minister is sometimes *compared to* a shepherd.
> Shakespeare's plays are often *compared with* those of Marlowe.
> The writer *contrasted* the sensitivity of the dancer *with* the grossness of the pugilist.

complement—means *a completing part*.
compliment—is *an expression of admiration*.
> His wit was a *complement* to her beauty.
> He *complimented* her attractive hairstyle.

consul—means *a government representative*.
council—means *an assembly that meets for deliberation*.
counsel—means *advice*.
> Americans abroad should keep in touch with their *consuls*.
> The City *Council* enacts local laws and regulations.
> The defendant heeded the *counsel* of his friends.

convenient to—should be followed by a *person*.
convenient for—should be followed by a *purpose*.
> Will these plans be *convenient to* you?
> You must agree that they are *convenient for* the occasion.

copy—is *an imitation of an original work*. (not necessarily an exact imitation)
facsimile—is *an exact imitation of an original work*.

The counterfeiters made a crude *copy* of the hundred-dollar bill.

The official government engraver, however, prepared a *facsimile* of the bill.

could of—is *unacceptable*. (*Should of* is also *unacceptable*.)

could have—is *acceptable*. (*Should have* is also *acceptable*.)

Acceptable: You *could have* done better with more care.

Unacceptable: could of won.

ALSO AVOID: *must of, would of.*

decent—means *suitable*.

descent—means *going down*.

dissent—means *disagreement*.

The *decent* thing to do is to admit your fault.

The *descent* into the cave was treacherous.

Two of the nine justices filed a *dissenting* opinion.

deduction—means *reasoning from the general (laws or principles) to the particular (facts)*.

induction—means *reasoning from the particular (facts) to the general (laws or principles)*.

All men are mortal. Since John is a man, he is mortal. (*deduction*)

There are 10,000 oranges in this truckload. I have examined 100 from various parts of the load and find that they are all of the same quality. I conclude that the 10,000 oranges are of this quality. (*induction*)

delusion—means *a wrong idea* that will probably influence action.

illusion—means *a wrong idea* that will probably *not* influence action.

People were under the *delusion* that the earth was flat.

It is just an *illusion* that the earth is flat.

desert—(pronounced DEZZ-ert) means *an arid area*.

desert—(pronounced di-ZERT) means *to abandon*; also *a reward or punishment*.

dessert—(pronounced di-ZERT) means *the final course of a meal*.

The Sahara is the world's most famous *desert*.

A parent must not *desert* a child.

Execution was a just *desert* for his crime.

We had plum pudding for *dessert*.

different from—is *acceptable*.

different than—is *unacceptable*.

Acceptable: Jack is *different from* his brother.

Unacceptable: Florida's climate is *different than* New York's climate.

doubt that—is *acceptable*.

doubt whether—is *unacceptable*.

Acceptable: I *doubt that* you will pass this term.

Unacceptable: We *doubt whether* you will succeed.

dual—means *relating to two*.

duel—means *a contest between two persons*.

Dr. Jekyl had a *dual* personality.

Alexander Hamilton was fatally injured in a *duel* with Aaron Burr.

due to—is *unacceptable* at the beginning of a sentence. Use *because of, on account of,* or some similar expression instead.

Unacceptable: Due to rain, the game was postponed.

Acceptable: Because of the rain, the game was postponed.

Acceptable: The postponement was *due to* the rain.

each other—refers to *two persons*.

one another—refers to *more than two persons*.

The two girls have known *each other* for many years.

Several of the girls have known *one another* for many years.

either . . . or—is used when referring to choices.

neither . . . nor—is the *negative form*.

Either you *or* I will win the election.

Neither Bill *nor* Henry is expected to have a chance.

eliminate—means *to get rid of*.

illuminate—means *to supply with light*.

Let us try to *eliminate* the unnecessary steps.

Several lamps were needed to *illuminate* the corridor.

emerge—means *to rise out of*.

immerge—means *to sink into* (also **immerse**).

The swimmer *emerged* from the pool.

The painter *immerged* his brushes in a jar of turpentine.

emigrate—means *to leave one's country for another*.

immigrate—means *to enter another country*.

Many Norwegians *emigrated* from their homeland to America in the mid-1860s.

Today government restrictions make it more difficult for foreigners to *immigrate* to this country.

everyone—is written as one word when it is a *pronoun*.

every one—(two words) is used when each individual is stressed.

Everyone present voted for the proposal.

Every one of the voters accepted the proposal.

NOTE: *Everybody* is written as one word.

everywheres—is *unacceptable*.

everywhere—is *acceptable*.

We searched *everywhere* for the missing book.

NOTE: *Everyplace* (one word) is *unacceptable*.

feel bad—means *to feel ill*.

feel badly—means *to have a poor sense of touch*.

I *feel bad* about the accident I saw.

The numbness in his limbs caused him to *feel badly*.

feel good—means *to be happy*.

feel well—means *to be in good health*.

I *feel* very *good* about my recent promotion.

Spring weather always made him *feel well*.

flout—means *to insult*.

flaunt—means *to make a display of*.

He *flouted* the authority of the principal.

Hester Prynne *flaunted* her scarlet "A."

formally—means *in a formal way*.

formerly—means *at an earlier time*.

The letter of reference was *formally* written.

He was *formerly* a delegate to the convention.

former—means *the first of two*.

latter—means *the second of two*.

The *former* half of the book was in prose.

The *latter* half of the book was in poetry.

forth—means *forward*.

fourth—comes *after third*.

They went *forth* like warriors of old.

The *Fourth* of July is our Independence Day.

NOTE: spelling of *forty* (40) and *fourteen* (14).

get—is a verb that strictly means *to obtain*.

Please *get* my bag.

There are many slang forms of *get* that should be avoided.

AVOID: Do you *get* me? (SAY: Do you *understand* me?)

AVOID: You can't *get* away with it. (SAY: You won't *avoid* punishment if you do it.)

AVOID: *Get* wise to yourself. (SAY: *Use* common sense.)

AVOID: We didn't *get* to go. (SAY: We didn't *manage* to go.)

got—means *obtained*.

He *got* the tickets yesterday.

AVOID: You've *got* to do it. (SAY: You *have* to do it.)

AVOID: We *have got* no sympathy for them. (SAY: We *have* no sympathy for them.)

AVOID: They have *got* a great deal of property. (SAY: They *have* a great deal of property.)

hanged—is used in reference to a *person*.

hung—is used in reference to a *thing*.

The prisoner was *hanged* at dawn.

The picture was *hung* above the fireplace.

however—means *nevertheless*.

how ever—means *in what possible way*.

We are certain, *however,* that you will like this class.

We are certain, *how ever* you decide to study, you will succeed.

if—introduces a *condition*.

whether—introduces a *choice*.

I shall go to Europe *if* I win the prize.

He asked me *whether* I intended to go to Europe. (not *if*)

if it was—implies that *something might have been true in the past*.

if it were—implies *doubt,* or indicates *something that is contrary to fact*.

If your book was there last night, it is there now.

If it were summer now, we would all go swimming.

in—usually refers to *a state of being*. (no motion)

into—is used for *motion from one place to another*.

The records are *in* that drawer.

I put the records *into* that drawer.

NOTE: "We were walking in the room" is correct even though there is no motion. The motion is *not* from one place to another.

irregardless—is *unacceptable*.

regardless—is *acceptable*.

Unacceptable: Irregardless of the weather, I am going to the game.

Acceptable: Regardless of his ability, he is not likely to win.

its—is the possessive of *it*.
it's—is the contraction for *it is*.
> *It's* I who put its stamp on the letter.
> The house lost *its* roof; *it's* an exposed house now.

kind of
sort of } are *unacceptable for rather.*
> SAY: We are *rather* disappointed in you.

last—refers to *the final member in a series*.
latest—refers to *the most recent in time*.
latter—refers to the *second of two*.
> This is the *last* bulletin. There won't be any other bulletins.
> This is the *latest* bulletin. There will be other bulletins.
> Of the two most recent bulletins, the *latter* is more encouraging.

lay—means *to place*.
lie—means *to recline*.
> You may *lay* the books upon the table.
> Let sleeping dogs *lie*.
> NOTE: The verb *to lay,* except when referring to hens, may be used ONLY if you could replace it with the verb *to put*. At all other times use a form of the verb to lie.
> Note the forms of each verb:

Tense	Lie (Recline)
Present	I *lie* on the grass.
Past	I *lay* on the grass.
Pres. Perf.	I *have lain* on the grass.

Tense	Lay (Place)
Present	I *lay* the book on the desk.
Past	I *laid* the book on the desk.
Pres. Perf.	I *have laid* the book on the desk.

learn—means to *acquire knowledge*.
teach—means to *impart knowledge*.
> My *mother taught me* all that *I have learned*.

lightening—is the present participle of *to lighten*.
lightning—means *the flashes of light accompanied by thunder*.
> Leaving the extra food behind resulted in *lightening* the pack.
> Summer thunderstorms produce startling *lightning* bolts.

may—is used in the *present tense*.
might—is used in the *past tense*.
> We are hoping that he *may* come today.
> He *might* have done it if you had encouraged him.

it's I—is always *acceptable*.
it's me—is *acceptable* only in colloquial speech or writing.
> *Always unacceptable:* It's him
> This is her
> It was them
> *Always acceptable:* It's he
> This is she
> It was they

noplace—as one word, is *unacceptable* for *no place* or *nowhere*.
> *Acceptable:* You now have *nowhere* to go.

number—is singular *when the total is intended*.
> The *number* (of pages in the book) is 500.
number—is plural *when the individual units are referred to*.
> A *number of pages* (in the book) were printed in italic type.

of any—(and *of anyone*) is *unacceptable* for *of all*.
> SAY: His was the highest mark *of all*. (NOT *of any* or *of anyone*)

off of—is *unacceptable*.
> SAY: He took the book *off* the table.

out loud—is *unacceptable* for *aloud*.
> SAY: He read *aloud* to his family every evening.

outdoor—(and *out-of-door*) is an adjective.
outdoors—is an adverb.
> We spent most of the summer at an *outdoor* music camp.
> Most of the time we played string quartets *outdoors*.
> NOTE: *Out-of-doors* is *acceptable* in either case.

people—comprise *a united or collective group of individuals*.
persons—are *individuals that are separated and unrelated*.
> The *people* of New York City have enthusiastically accepted "Shakespeare-in-the-Park" productions.
> Only five *persons* remained in the theater after the first act.

persecute—means *to make life miserable for some-one.* (Persecution is illegal.)

prosecute—means *to conduct a criminal investigation.* (Prosecution is legal.)

Some racial groups insist upon *persecuting* other groups.

The District Attorney is *prosecuting* the rack-eteers.

precede—means *to come before.*

proceed—means *to go ahead.* (*Procedure* is the noun.)

supersede—means to *replace.*

What were the circumstances that *preceded* the attack?

We can then *proceed* with our plan for resisting a second attack.

It is then possible that Plan B will *supersede* Plan A.

principal—means *chief* or *main* (as an adjective); *a leader* (as a noun).

principle—means *a fundamental truth or belief.*

His *principal* supporters came from among the peasants.

The *principal* of the school asked for cooperation from the staff.

Humility was the guiding *principle* of Buddha's life.

NOTE: *Principal* may also mean *a sum placed at interest.*

Part of his monthly payment was applied as interest on the *principal.*

sit—means *take a seat.* (intransitive verb)

set—means *place.* (transitive verb)

Note the forms of each verb:

Tense	Sit (Take a Seat)
Present	He *sits* on a chair.
Past	He *sat* on the chair.
Pres. Perf.	He *has sat* on the chair.

Tense	Set (Place)
Present	He *sets* the lamp on the table.
Past	He *set* the lamp on the table.
Pres. Perf.	He *has set* the lamp on the table.

some time—means *a portion of time.*

sometime—means *at an indefinite time in the future.*

sometimes—means *occasionally.*

I'll need *some time* to make a decision.

Let us meet *sometime* after twelve noon.

Sometimes it is better to hesitate before signing a contract.

somewheres—is *unacceptable.*

somewhere—is *acceptable.*

stationary—means *standing still.*

stationery—means *writing materials.*

In ancient times people thought the earth was *stationary.*

We bought writing paper at the *stationery* store.

stayed—means *remained.*

stood—means *remained upright or erect.*

The army *stayed* in the trenches for five days.

The soldiers *stood* at attention for one hour.

sure—for *surely* is unacceptable.

SAY: You *surely* (NOT *sure*) are not going to write that!

take in—is *unacceptable* in the same sense of *deceive* or *attend.*

SAY: We were *deceived* (NOT *taken in*) by his manner.

We should like to *attend* (NOT *take in*) a few plays during our vacation.

their—means *belonging to them.*

there—means *in that place.*

they're—means *they are.*

We took *their* books home with us.

You will find your books over *there* on the desk.

They're going to the ballpark with us.

theirselves—is *unacceptable* for *themselves.*

SAY: Most children of school age are able to care for *themselves* in many ways.

these kind—is *unacceptable.*

this kind—is *acceptable.*

I am fond of this kind of apples.

NOTE: *These kinds* would also be *acceptable.*

through—meaning *finished* or *completed* is unacceptable.

SAY: We'll finish (NOT *be through with*) the work by five o'clock.

try to—is *acceptable.*

try and—is *unacceptable.*

Try to come (NOT *try and* come).

NOTE: *plan on going* is unacceptable; *plan to go* is acceptable.

two—is the *numeral 2*.
to—means *in the direction of*.
too—means *more than* or *also*.
    There are *two* sides to every story.
    Three *two's* (or 2's) equal six.
    We shall go *to* school.
    We shall go, *too*.
    The weather is *too* hot for school.

unique—means *unequaled*. Since only one object can be unique, the word does not allow for comparative or superlative forms. *Uniquer* and *uniquest,* or *more unique* and *most unique,* are logical impossibilities. Some other words which fall into this same category are: *round, square, perfect, equal,* and *entirely.*

was ⎱ If something is *contrary to fact* (not a
were ⎰ fact), use *were* in every instance.
    I wish I *were* in Bermuda.
    Unacceptable: If he *was* sensible, he wouldn't act like that.
    (SAY: If he *were* . . .)

ways—is *unacceptable* for *way.*
    SAY: We climbed a little way (NOT *ways*) up the hill.

went and took—(*went and stole,* etc.) is *unacceptable.*
    SAY: They *stole* (NOT *went and stole*) our tools.

when—(and *where*) should NOT be used to introduce a definition of a noun.
    SAY: A tornado *is a* twisting, high wind on land (NOT *is when a* twisting, high wind is on land).
    A pool *is a place for swimming* (NOT *is where people swim*).

whereabouts—is *unacceptable* for *where.*
    SAY: *Where* (NOT *whereabouts*) do you live?

NOTE: *Whereabouts* as a noun meaning a place is *acceptable.*
    Do you know his *whereabouts*?

whether—should NOT be preceded by *of* or *as to.*
    SAY: The president will consider the question *whether* (NOT *of whether*) it is better to ask for or demand higher taxes now.
    He inquired *whether* (NOT *as to whether*) we were going or not.

which—as a relative pronoun refers only to *objects.*
who, whom—refer only to *people.*
that—as a relative pronoun may refer to *either objects or people.*
    This is the vase *which* the cat knocked over.
    This is the vase *that* the cat knocked over.
    The boy *who* won the prize is over there.
    The boy *that* won the prize is over there.

while—is *unacceptable* for *and* or *though.*
    SAY: The library is situated on the south side; (OMIT *while*) the laboratory is on the north side.
    Though (NOT *while*) I am in your office every day, you do not attempt to see me.

whose—is the possessive of *who.*
who's—is the contraction for *who is.*
    Whose car is in the street?
    Do you know *who's* ringing the doorbell?

who is ⎱
who am ⎰ Note these constructions.
    It is I *who am* the most experienced.
    It is he *who is* . . .
    It is he or I *who am* . . .
    It is I or he *who is* . . .
    It is he and I *who are* . . .

your—is the possessive of *you.*
you're—is the contraction for *you are.*
    I hope *you're* planning to leave *your* muddy boots outside.

SENTENCE STRUCTURE

1. Every sentence must contain a verb. A group of words without a verb is a sentence fragment, not a sentence. A verb may consist of one, two, three, or four words.

    Examples: The boy *studies* hard.
    The boy *will study* hard.
    The boy *has been studying* hard.
    The boy *should have been studying* hard.

    The words that make up a single verb may be separated.

    Examples: It *is* not *snowing*.
    It will almost certainly *snow* tomorrow.

2. Every sentence must have a subject. The subject may be a noun, a pronoun, or a word or group of words functioning as a noun.

    Examples: Fish swim. (noun)
    She is young. (pronoun)
    Running is good exercise. (gerund)
    To argue is pointless. (infinitive)
    That he was tired was evident. (noun clause)

    In commands, the subject is usually not expressed but is understood to be *you*.

    Example: Mind your own business.

3. A phrase cannot stand by itself as a sentence. A phrase is any group of related words which has no subject or predicate and which is used as a single part of speech. Phrases may be built around prepositions, participles, gerunds, or infinitives.

    Example: The boy *with curly hair* is my brother. (Prepositional phrase used as an adjective modifying *boy*)

    Example: My favorite cousin lives *on a farm*. (Prepositional phrase used as an adverb modifying *lives*)

    Example: Beyond the double white line is out of bounds. (Prepositional phrase used as a noun, the subject of the sentence)

    Example: A thunderstorm *preceding a cold front* is often welcome. (Participial phrase used as an adjective modifying *thunderstorm*)

    Example: We eagerly awaited the pay envelopes *brought by the messenger*. (Participial phrase used as an adjective modifying *envelopes*)

    Example: Running a day camp is an exhausting job. (Gerund phrase used as a noun, subject of the sentence)

    Example: The director is paid well for *running the day camp*. (Gerund phrase used as a noun, the object of the preposition *for*)

    Example: To breathe unpolluted air should be every person's birthright. (Infinitive phrase used as a noun, the subject of the sentence)

    Example: The child began *to unwrap his gift*. (Infinitive phrase used as a noun, the object of the verb *began*)

    Example: The boy ran away from home *to become a marine*. (Infinitive phrase used as an adverb modifying *ran away*)

4. A *main, independent,* or *principal* clause can stand alone as a complete sentence. A main clause has a subject and a verb. It may stand by itself or be introduced by a coordinating conjunction.

    Example: The sky darkened ominously and rain began to fall. (Two independent clauses joined by a coordinating conjunction)

    A *subordinate* or *dependent* clause must never stand alone. It is not a complete sentence, only a sentence fragment, despite the fact that it has a subject and a verb. A subordinate clause usually is introduced by a subordinating conjunction. Subordinate clauses may act as adverbs, adjectives, or nouns. Subordinate adverbial clauses are generally introduced by the subordinating conjunctions *when, while, because, as soon as, if, after, although, as before, since, than, though, until,* and *unless.*

Example: *While we were waiting for the local,* the express roared past.

Example: The woman applied for a new job *because she wanted to earn more money.*

Example: *Although a subordinate clause contains both subject and verb,* it cannot stand alone *because it is introduced by a subordinating word.*

Subordinating adjective clauses may be introduced by the pronouns *who, which,* and *that.*

Example: The play *which he liked best* was a mystery.

Example: I have a neighbor *who served in the Peace Corps.*

Subordinate noun clauses may be introduced by *who, what,* or *that.*

Example: The stationmaster says *that the train will be late.*

Example: I asked the waiter *what the stew contained.*

Example: I wish I knew *who backed into my car.*

5. Two independent clauses cannot share one sentence without some form of connective. If they do, they form a run-on sentence. Two principle clauses may be joined by a coordinating conjunction, by a comma followed by a coordinating conjunction, or by a semicolon. They may also form two distinct sentences. Two main clauses may NEVER be joined by a comma without a coordinating conjunction. This error is called a comma splice.

Example: • A college education has never been more important than it is today it has never cost more. (WRONG—run-on sentence)

• A college education has never been more important than it is today, it has never cost more. (WRONG—comma splice)

• A college education has never been more important than it is today and it has never cost more. (WRONG—The two independent clauses are not equally short, so a comma is required before the coordinating conjunction.)

• A college education has never been more important than it is today, and it has never cost more. (correct form)

• A college education has never been more important than it is today; and it has never cost more. (WRONG—Do not use a semicolon with a coordinating conjunction.)

• A college education has never been more important than it is today; it has never cost more. (correct form)

• A college education has never been more important than it is today. It has never cost more. (correct form)

• A college education has never been more important than it is today. And it has never cost more. (correct form)

• While a college education has never been more important than it is today, it has never cost more. (correct form—Introductory subordinate clause is separated from the main clause by a comma.)

6. Direct quotations follow all the rules of sentence formation. Beware of comma splices in divided quotations.

Example: "Your total is wrong," he said, "add the column again." (WRONG)
"Your total is wrong," he said. "Add the column again." (The two independent clauses form two separate sentences.)

Example: "Are you lost?" she asked, "may I help you?" (WRONG)
"Are you lost?" she asked. "May I help you?" (Two main clauses; two separate sentences)

7. Comparisons must be logical and complete.

Example: Wilmington is larger than any city in Delaware. (WRONG)
Wilmington is larger than any *other* city in Delaware.

Example: He is fat, if not fatter, than his uncle. (WRONG)

He is as fat *as*, if not fatter than, his uncle.

Example: I hope to find a summer job other than a lifeguard. (WRONG)

I hope to find a summer job other than *that* of lifeguard.

Example: Law is a better profession than an accountant. (WRONG)

Law is a better profession than accounting. (Parallel)

8. Avoid the "is when" and "is where" construction.

Example: A limerick is when a short poem has a catchy rhyme. (WRONG)

A limerick is a short poem with a catchy rhyme.

Example: To exile is where a person must live in another place. (WRONG)

To exile a person is to force him to live in another place.

9. Errors in parallelism are often quite subtle, but you should learn to recognize and avoid them. The Foreign Service Officer Exam relies upon difficult questions to differentiate highly qualified candidates from adequate candidates.

Example: Skiing and to skate are both winter sports. (WRONG)

Skiing and *skating* are both winter sports.

Example: She spends all her time eating, asleep, and on her studies. (WRONG)

She spends all her time *eating, sleeping,* and *studying.*

Example: The work is neither difficult nor do I find it interesting. (WRONG)

The work is neither difficult nor interesting.

Example: His heavy drinking and the fact that he gambles makes him a poor role model. (WRONG)

His heavy *drinking* and *gambling make* him a poor role model.

10. Avoid needless shifts in point of view. A shift in point of view is a change within the sentence from one tense or mood to another, from one subject or voice to another, or from one person or number to another. Shifts in point of view destroy parallelism within the sentence.

Example: After he *rescued* the kitten, he *rushes* down the ladder to find its owner. (Shift from past tense to present tense) CHANGE TO: After he rescued the kitten, he rushed down the ladder to find its owner.

Example: First *stand* at attention and then you *should salute* the flag. (Shift from imperative to indicative mood) CHANGE TO: First *stand* at attention and then *salute* the flag.

Example: Mary especially likes math, but history is also enjoyed by her. (The subject shifts from *Mary* to *history;* the mood shifts from active to passive.) CHANGE TO: Mary especially likes math, but she also enjoys history.

Example: George rowed around the island and soon the mainland came in sight. (The subject changes from *George* to *the mainland.*) CHANGE TO: George rowed around the island and soon came in sight of the mainland.

Example: The captain welcomed *us* aboard, and the crew enjoyed showing *one* around the boat. (The object shifts from first to third person.) CHANGE TO: The captain welcomed us aboard, and the crew enjoyed showing us around the boat.

Example: *One* should listen to the weather forecast so that *they* may anticipate a hurricane. (The subject shifts from singular to plural.) CHANGE TO: *One* should listen to the weather forecast so that *he* may anticipate a hurricane.

CIVIL SERVICE BOOKS

TEST PREPARATION

Accountant / Auditor
ACWA: Administrative Careers With America
Air Traffic Controller Qualifying Test
Air Traffic Controller Training Program
American Foreign Service Officer
Beginning Clerical Worker
Bookkeeper / Account Clerk
Building Custodian / Building Superintendent /
    Custodian Engineer
Bus Operator / Conductor
Case Worker
Computer Specialist GS 5-9
The Corey Guide to Postal Exams
Correction Officer
Correction Officer Promotion Tests
Court Officer / Senior Court Officer / Court Clerk
Distribution Clerk, Machine
Drug Enforcement Agent
Electrician / Electrician's Helper
Emergency Dispatcher / 911 Operator
Federal Clerk / Steno / Typist
File Clerk / General Clerk
Fire Department Lieutenant / Captain /
    Battalion Chief
Firefighter
Gardener / Grounds Maintenance Worker
Investigator / Claim Examiner
Law Enforcement Exams Handbook
Machinist / Machinist's Helper
Mail Handler / Mail Processor
Maintenance Worker / Mechanical Maintainer
Mark-up Clerk / Clerk Typist /
    Clerk Stenographer—U.S. Postal Service
Plumber / Steam Fitter
Police Administrative Aide
Police Officer
Police Sergeant / Lieutenant / Captain

Postal Exams Handbook
Post Office Clerk / Carrier
Preparación para el examen de cartero
Probation Officer / Parole Officer
Rural Carrier
Sanitation Worker
Senior Clerical Series
Special Agent
Special Officer / Senior Special Officer /
    Bridge and Tunnel Officer
State Trooper / Highway Patrol Officer /
    State Traffic Officer
Track Worker
Traffic Enforcement Agent
Train Operator / Tower Operator / Assistant
    Train Dispatcher

CAREERS / STUDY GUIDES

Civil Service Administrative Tests
Civil Service Arithmetic and Vocabulary
Civil Service Clerical Promotion Tests
Civil Service Handbook
Civil Service Psychological and Psychiatric
    Tests
Civil Service Reading Comprehension Tests
Civil Service Tests for Basic Skills Jobs
Complete Guide to U.S. Civil Service Jobs
Federal Jobs for College Graduates
Federal Jobs in Law Enforcement
General Test Practice for 101 U.S. Jobs
How to Get a Clerical Job in Government
Practice for Clerical, Typing and
    Stenographic Tests
SF 171: The Federal Employment
    Application Form
Supervision

AVAILABLE AT BOOKSTORES EVERYWHERE

MACMILLAN
U.S.A

BOOKS FOR JOB HUNTERS

CAREERS / STUDY GUIDES

Airline Pilot
Allied Health Professions
Automobile Technician Certification Tests
Federal Jobs for College Graduates
Federal Jobs in Law Enforcement
Getting Started in Film
How to Pass Clerical Employment Tests
How You Really Get Hired
Law Enforcement Exams Handbook
Make Your Job Interview a Success
Mechanical Aptitude and Spatial Relations Tests
Mid-Career Job Hunting
100 Best Careers for the Year 2000
Passport to Overseas Employment
Postal Exams Handbook
Real Estate License Examinations
Refrigeration License Examinations
Travel Agent

RESUME GUIDES

The Complete Resume Guide
Resumes for Better Jobs
Resumes That Get Jobs
Your Resume: Key to a Better Job

AVAILABLE AT BOOKSTORES EVERYWHERE

MACMILLAN